Downhome
Gospel

✳

Downhome Gospel

African American Spiritual Activism in Wiregrass Country

Jerrilyn McGregory

UNIVERSITY PRESS OF MISSISSIPPI · JACKSON

www.upress.state.ms.us

The University Press of Mississippi is a member of the Association of American
University Presses.

First printing 2010
∞
Library of Congress Cataloging-in-Publication Data

McGregory, Jerrilyn.
   Downhome gospel : African American spiritual activism in Wiregrass Country /
Jerrilyn McGregory.
      p. cm.
   Includes bibliographical references and index.
   ISBN 978-1-60473-782-0 (cloth : alk. paper) — ISBN 978-1-60473-783-7 (ebook)
   1. Gospel music—Wiregrass Country (U.S.)—History and criticism. 2. African
Americans—Music—Wiregrass Country (U.S.)—History and criticism. I. Title.
   ML3187.M45 2010
   782.25'08996073075—dc22   2010015128

British Library Cataloging-in-Publication Data available

To the future,
Syrus, Kalli, and Elijah

Contents

PROLOGUE   ix

INTRODUCTION   xv

1. "Come Go with Me"   3
   Liberation Songs

2. "Ev'ry Day'll Be Sunday"   26
   Burial Sodalities

3. "There's a Meeting Here Tonight"   51
   Baptist Modalities

4. "On the Way to Glory"   74
   The Shape-Note Tradition

5. "God Has Smiled on Me"   100
   Traditional Gospel

6. "The Gospel Train Is Coming"   126
   Wiregrass Contemporary Gospel

7. "I Feel No Ways Tired"   154
   Sarah's Daughters

EPILOGUE   177

NOTES   183

BIBLIOGRAPHY   199

ACKNOWLEDGMENTS   209

INDEX   212

Prologue

Although African American, I am no Zora Neale Hurston. Even this esteemed folklorist candidly expressed disappointment about her initial excursion to conduct fieldwork in Eatonville, Florida, where she grew up. She fell short due to her failure to code switch: "But, I went about asking, in carefully accented Barnardese, 'Pardon me, but do you know any folk-tales or folk-songs?' The men and women who had whole treasuries of material just seeping through their pores looked at me and shook their heads." In *Mules and Men*, Hurston elected self-reflexively to dramatize her research experience. However, this ethnographic project is not that of an insider studying her own native culture. While not a full-fledged autoethnography, I engage in a kind of transpersonal ethnography. To clarify, instead of professing neutrality, occasionally I proffer my own subjectivity so that readers might experience my journey into Wiregrass Country. Therefore, I elect not totally to delete my voice. My intent is not to idealize, realizing how folklife can stagnate as well.

I entered Wiregrass Country *tabula rasa*. I presented a clean slate. I was a neophyte in the South, a neophyte in Wiregrass Country, and a neophyte studying rural culture. Ironically, my urban fieldwork in Philadelphia was my first introduction to southern African American folk culture. There, for the first time, I witnessed folk cultural traditions (even baptism by immersion), instead of "sprinkling" as relates to my own Methodist upbringing. These migrants did not forsake their cultural awareness, as my working-class family had. My first true exposure to southern African American culture came in 1987, employed by the Philadelphia Folklore Project. While conducting fieldwork in this urban context, African American residents often expressed to me that Philadelphia was "nothing but a small country town," expressing a strong sense of continuity with their southern heritage. Afterward, I consciously elected to move to the South in search of the core cultural experience that had eluded me. I soon alighted in a historic region called Wiregrass Country.

I first entered Wiregrass Country about fifteen years ago. The region's northernmost boundary was a five-hour drive from where I then lived in Georgia's Plantation Belt. From the highway, as I entered Tift County, of course, nothing immediately cataclysmic happened. I scheduled the first fieldwork visit as a day trip to acquaint myself with Wiregrass Georgia. Initially, as I drove through this rural landscape, I mainly detected the lack of large, cavernous barns with missile-shaped silos. Being from the Midwest, I pondered this difference—a bona fide mystery. To me, penned animals, irrigation machines, and neat rows of corn spoke rural America. Only later did I learn what sets this region apart. Wiregrass farmers freely ranged their animals in the nearby piney woods until about the 1950s, only fencing them in when obligated to do so by law.

I have seen shotgun houses all my life. Born in Gary, Indiana, I even lived in a modified one for my first five years. But I never espied them in pastel colors such as these: lilac, goldenrod, rose, and so on. I thought I had disembarked in the Caribbean. Compared to the brown- and gray-shingled variants of my youth, this color scheme pleases the eye and induces a strengthening sense of anticipation about the lives of the people dwelling inside. Their yards, too, are not intended to be strictly ornamental, lacking the finely edged sod and extraneous detailed lawns. Instead of trimmed lawns, swept yards and clearings serve as signs of occupancy. While not always manicured, the yards are without wild undergrowth due to the real threat of rattlesnakes and other poisonous snakes possibly lurking nearby. The very landscape speaks to diversity, a place without housing covenants. Democratized, an affluent home might nest meticulously beside a man-made pond, while the next nearest neighbor inhabits a dilapidated trailer.

Moreover, unlike my first home, porches are not only ubiquitous but of everyday use. By then, my southern experience had been limited to northern Georgia. There, I noted porches more of the rocking-chair variety—seldom with the presence of a soul. A novelty to me, seeing African Americans ensconced on their porches, putting them to some functional use, I would stop to chat and take photographs. One time, in Thomasville, Georgia, I photographed two small African American girls simply lying topsy-turvy in lawn chairs against the turquoise backdrop of their house. In Calhoun, Georgia, I photographed not the archetypal hair-braiding ritual so often captured in African American photographs and art, but one of a hairdresser inserting a neat column of blue rollers to permed hair. Then, while in Cairo, Georgia, I photographed two African American sisters chitchatting amicably while shucking peas, not from their own garden but from a local U-Pick farm. They engaged in a mythopoeic porch culture long presaged in

Porch life in Wiregrass Country: girls topsy-turvy

my reading of Zora Neale Hurston, but still a novelty to me. In Philadelphia I noted similarly that people occupied their outdoor stoops, but, with the advent of air conditioning, seldom during the heat of the day.

On my initial excursion, Columbus McGriff was the first Wiregrass resident I informally interviewed. Out of curiosity, I halted my car for the first time that day. The outside veneer of his home compelled me to stop. A homemade sign announced: "Old Dude Shop." McGriff was actually in the process of constructing a housefly out of wire hangers. Nicknamed Old Dude, McGriff sat on the porch of his home, which also housed a shoeshine shop and a penny candy store. Affixed to a V-shaped base of wood on the eaves of his little emporium reigned an eagle made of wire coat hangers. It sat atop a platform embedded with shoe-polish lids and crushed aluminum soda cans. Multicolored panels added a circus tent façade to the roofing. The walls of the building displayed more decoratively painted shoe-polish tins. He told me about once living in New York City, where he performed buck dances at the Apollo Theater and appeared, in a bit part, in the film *Stiletto*. After a while I accompanied him inside, and on the wall hung a framed feature page from a newspaper with the headline: "Whimsical Wire:

Scrap-wire folk artist Columbus "Old
Dude" McGriff in his candy shop

Imagination Fuels Struggling Cairo Artist's Creations." I viewed many other
items he'd made: a flock of eagles, airplanes with fully operational propel-
lers, a green tractor with a steering wheel that turned, and a full-bodied,
human-sized green dinosaur. Then I accompanied him a couple blocks to
meet his brother, Boysie McGriff, whose front yard exhibited a dinosaur of
his own creation. The brothers informed me how, stimulated by creativity
and poverty, they began as children to make toys out of coat hangers for
their younger siblings. Boysie admitted that his brother was the more accomplished artist.

I left intending to return that summer and begin my fieldwork in earnest. In three months, upon returning, I was horrified to see the outside
veneer of McGriff's place stripped bare and padlocked. Gone were all the
items that had incited my first visit. I managed to remember the direction
to his brother's house, where he confirmed my fears. Columbus McGriff
was deceased. While I had waited for funding to sustain my summer research, he had died. Following closely on the heels of his demise, an art
dealer purchased his entire stock of artistic pieces from McGriff's heirs.

Over time, site visits and chance meetings like these pointed me to a
better awareness of the region and its people. I stood to enlighten myself
as well as others about a region that practically fell off the map of history. I
now view my first book on the region's folklife, *Wiregrass Country*, as commencing my spiritual journey. I could not have arrived in the South at a better time. Luckily, its folklife endures, and African Americans there expend
much time, energy, and economic resources singing sacred music for the

benefit of all who hearken to their sound. Many of the African American traditions sustained in this obscure region escape public notice. I hope to close the gap by shining a spotlight on the downhome gospel in Wiregrass Country. I examine how African Americans fashion intricate networks to sing sacred music, with cultural continuity and a communitarian outlook.

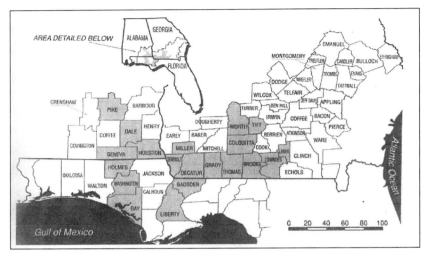

Map of Wiregrass Country

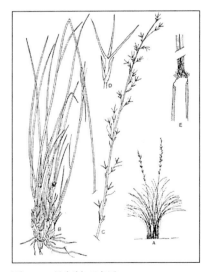

Wiregrass (*Aristida stricta*)

Introduction

In 1990, as a follow-up to my urban ethnographic research, I elected to move to the South to study African American folklife. My timing was perfect. I learned that the University Press of Mississippi had begun a "Folklife in the South Series." Of the unclaimed regions, I selected to document Wiregrass Country. At the time, I had no idea that the region defied public recognition throughout most of its historic existence. This region is variously referred to as the piney woods, pine barren, or, for tourism, Plantation Trace. Although wiregrass (*Aristida stricta*) grows from the Chesapeake Bay to the rim of Texas, only one geographical area acquired this vernacular name. The tri-state area that I refer to as Wiregrass Country includes the rolling meadows of southwestern Georgia, sweeps westward across the Alabama border, and veers southward into the Florida Panhandle (see Figure 3). Ignoring geopolitical boundaries, the region encompasses a tri-state area that includes nearly a third of the counties in Georgia and at least nine each in southeastern Alabama and the Florida Panhandle. Of course, the boundaries blur.

Wiregrass does not flourish once the land is cultivated, and the plant depends on fire to germinate. Associated with the longleaf pine forest, it is part of a fire ecosystem. With this locale experiencing possibly more lightening strikes than any place else on Earth, the region's flora and fauna both adapted to this fire-driven community. With Smoky the Bear's emergence as a national icon to prevent forest fires came the demise or near extinction of several native species, including the ivory-billed woodpecker (which depends on fire-maintained, old-growth pine savannas), the red cockaded woodpecker, and wiregrass. As a result, few present-day inhabitants have ever seen tufts of this plant, with its tallish, wiry blades. Only controlled burns are now allowed.

Wiregrass Country represents a marginalized space within the South. It is less well known than Appalachia, Cajun Country, or the Black Belt.

A newspaper column from August 2, 1889, delineated how the area was "greatly misunderstood": "To the traveler who passes hurriedly through the pine region of Southern Georgia the land looks poor and uninviting. Its only value seems to be the magnificent timber which it bears. The stately pine has its admirers everywhere, but the soil that produces it with its gray, sandy appearance, is looked upon with disfavor. The 'wire grass region' has been applied as a term of reproach to the southern counties of our state, which were regarded as only favorable to the production of gophers, scrub cattle, and razor back hogs." Much of its history, unfortunately, is subsumed by a regional history that homogenizes the South. For instance, a plantation system did not typify Wiregrass Country. Instead, poor yeoman farmers settled into this relatively vast area. Due to the infertility of its soil, cotton never was quite king. Also, historically, the region was sparsely populated and remains so today. No cities of more than 70,000 people lie within this vast region. Larger metropolises such as Savannah, Macon, Montgomery, and Tallahassee encircle it.

Therefore, those with any knowledge of this cultural area portray it as being historically underpopulated, economically poor, and predominantly white. Because of the poor soil quality and the threat of malaria, white people did not flock there, although a number did deliberately settle there. Its newcomers hailed from the Carolinas and depended on ranging their animals. As revealed by historian Robert Preston Brooks, "After the manner of the frontier, these people lived on the products of their herds, on game, and cornbread." Wiregrass Country attracted a hardy, independent brand of yeomen farmers and domestic animals. The razorback hogs and scrub cattle found the early growth of wiregrass equally succulent and delicious. Because there was no fence law, farmers signaled ownership by branding their livestock and by permitting them to range freely. Fencing materialized only in the 1950s. Theirs were low-maintenance livestock that scrounged to obtain their own vittles. Yet the animals were also relatively tame due to having some human contact and care. By the time officials had outlawed free-ranging livestock, an exclusively agrarian way of life was already waning, though farmers tended to hold on to their homeplaces, their family domiciles.

In 1991, I began a widespread documentary folklife project, which culminated in the publication of my book, *Wiregrass Country*. The region deserved a general folklife study, and I needed to acclimate myself. By 1994, I knew fully that my follow-up monograph would have to focus on the region's African Americans and their sacred music preferences. As part of a collective, the African Americans of Wiregrass Country continue to preserve one of the oldest forms (Sacred Harp) to the newest (contemporary gospel). As part of my research, I have conducted about 150 site visits, including formal interviews. Although sacred music informs my present study, the main objective is to illustrate how the music is almost secondary within this particularized social and economic milieu. By sticking to my ethnographic fieldwork agenda, I simultaneously achieved the southern folk cultural experience that once eluded me.

The overall aim of this book is to introduce Wiregrass Country's African Americans and to examine their sacred music performed outside of Sunday church-related activities. As in many regions, sacred music performances are a trademark of life in Wiregrass Country. In general, sacred music plays a magnanimous, stimulating, and scintillating role within people's everyday lives. Singing conventions and all-night gospel sings fortify the spiritual as well as the social life of many who reside there. In this region, African Americans maintain a social world of their own creation. Their cultural performances embrace some of the most pervasive forms of African American sacred music: spirituals, common meter, Sacred Harp, shape-note, and traditional and contemporary gospel. As an outgrowth of the old Sacred Harp singing conventions, African Americans maintain stringent reciprocal support networks and are constantly traveling, giving voice to their blessed joy via song. They privilege the role of spiritual activists, willing to live their lives fully in accord with a divine purpose.

In Wiregrass Country, the people often say, "You don't have to sing like an angel." For them, praising the glory of God in song does not require trained voices, but only the desire to display one's God-given talent, without reproach. (Monotone myself, I could only wonder what it means to sing publicly and not be silenced. Growing up, I learned early in both church and school that I need not bother to sing.) African American Wiregrass sacred performance communities speak in song not just to God but to one another. Their performances engage an aesthetic that privileges a range of musical notations and possibilities. Folklorist Ray Allen recognized that "most authors approach the discussion in terms of western categories of melody, harmony, rhythm, vocal timbre, group organization, and other stylistic traits." To explore this propensity, musicologist Jeff Titon wrote of an Appalachian community for which "good" singing implied "a smooth blend of sweet voices on pitch and in correct time, the qualities of school-trained singers." There, participants deem singing without harmony as "old-fashioned." In practice, they display "authentic singing," but in theory, they privilege a more conventional Western aesthetics. These aesthetic values, then, tend to represent the ideal. African American Wiregrass sacred performance communities, however, often disrupt this binary. Membership in these reciprocal support networks depends on a genuine commitment to a democratized meritocracy. This stance is in keeping with Zora Neale Hurston's explicit assessment that "each singing of the piece is a new creation. Members are bound by no rules. No two times singing is alike, so that we must consider the rendition of a song not as a final thing, but as a mood. It won't be the same thing next Sunday."

I do not mean to imply that this aesthetic is only indigenous to the Wiregrass or African Americans. Of course, many congregations cross-culturally center a distinct canon of taste. This study, however, seeks to go beyond Archie Green's idea of "the contrast between normative church style and folk style." What is perhaps unique to Wiregrass sacred performance communities is that democratization extends beyond Sunday ritual practices into everyday cultural performance. Whereas folklorist Lynwood Montell noted that some white participants attending sacred music conventions in Kentucky resent those "lacking in vocal quality," I have yet to hear any similar expression. The aesthetic style of African American singing is well documented as quite distinctive. As noted by musicologist Eileen Southern, it is "distinctive for its shrill, hard, full-throated, strained, raspy, and/or nasal tone, with frequent exploitation of falsetto, growling, and moaning."

Therefore, "good" music is God's music regardless of the manner delivered. When there is censure, generally it is imposed textually. Aesthetically speaking, one Wiregrass aficionado explained it thus: "Each song ought to be able to tell a story within itself. If it doesn't have any meaning, then it isn't worth singing." Sacred music must carry the weight of veracity as well: "Too many of them have lied . . . some in group don't speak to one another." This text explores the importance of words, not just the sounds. Based on an aesthetic set by an African root heritage and reinterpreted in light of a basic southern inheritance, it is not the emotional weight of a good vocal performance but the lyrical content that counts most. In addition, according to musicologist Christopher Small, "From the start the key to the singer's power in the church was not the possession of a beautiful voice, though many have in fact been endowed with remarkable vocal qualities, but authority, the authority of one who has lived what he or she sings about, and the ability to communicate the sense of the experience. If you haven't lived it, they say you can't sing it." The lyrics must indicate verisimilitude. On a deep structural level, critics of Wiregrass scared music find actual phrases within certain songs problematic, pejoratively calling them lies. For instance, a contemporary gospel song, "Falling in Love with Jesus," is problematic because one literally should already love your Savior.

The title, *Downhome Gospel*, is not intended as a misnomer. This study engages a variety of African American sacred music traditions, beyond just gospel music. Not to be doctrinaire, I consider gospel music as being more than a transcendent sound. Some view the musical term "Negro spirituals" to be an oxymoron because, within a traditional West African worldview, all music fulfills an everyday spirituality. Similarly, in the context of this study, all traditional forms of African American sacred music are sanctifying. Those who sing them are proselytizing through song, preaching "the Gospel Truth." In a strictly biblical sense, their goal is to help all grow closer to God, Jesus Christ, and personal salvation. Gospel means joy, hope, expectation, and news that makes glad. Foremost, then, my emphasis is on sacred performance communities that encourage gospel-centered living.

I locate the Wiregrass as being downhome, in line with Jeff Titon's blues-oriented formulation. As he defined it, *downhome* does not reference a place but "a spirit, a sense of place evoked in singer and listener by a style of music." The style the singers most privilege is informed by gospel originator Thomas Dorsey's gospel blues. Although living outside of any significant metropolitan area, Wiregrass residents do not exist in isolation. As an actual manifestation of the push and pull factors central to the urban migration process, their existence is not stagnant. Although their forms of sacred music are also dynamic, they still lend themselves to charges of "being country" because they embrace the older traditional and earlier contemporary gospel forms. Although they cling to styles of singing evocative of a particular southern musical landscape, locals interact with a broad spectrum of family and friends, near and far. They share a sense of locality and identity, which signifies Wiregrass Country as their homeplace. Their sensibilities create a spiritual space for engaging sacred musical traditions, a Wiregrass ethos entrenched within a southern domain.

The field data upon which this study is based comes from several types of sources: participant observation, archival research, and interviews with participants. The methodology relies on both synchronic and diachronic approaches. Participant observation involved my total immersion, not only gaining access within each reciprocal support network, but expanding my personal understanding related to spirituality. In addition to a systematic analysis of the constituent media that make up sacred music performances throughout Wiregrass Country, I also collected historical material. The vast majority of interviews were with those who could provide a historical perspective and special knowledge concerning their particular performance community and its networks. Interviews were not fixed. A list of topics specific to the individual served as a framework, but these were modified in situ, allowing unprompted responses to unfold in accordance with topical areas of special interest to each interviewee. In this manner, I benefited from their articulation of personal experience narratives to shed vivid light on all that they believed spiritually.

Ultimately, I found their pedagogy transformative. I owe a great debt of gratitude to my Wiregrass teachers. The sacred music that they maintain begs for greater exposure and recognition. In this study, I do not mask their names, affiliations, or voices. Indeed, I seek endogenous meaning(s) from an insider's perspective. Ethnography is an approach that demands a full portrayal of a subject. Participant observation means my immersion within their cultural and social milieus—not as a pretense to learn repertoires myself. I sung along with the masses as so moved. I write more in keeping with the field of sociomusicology. The emphasis is not so much on the music's technique, form, or content but on the extratextual, the social context and use. Therefore, this book studies sacred music from the framework of the social organization and social structure of its makers.

My methodology conforms to anthropologist Steven Feld's stipulation "to study [musical representations] on the ground, in the field, up close, over long periods of time, where sound structures are observably and undeniably socially structured." This sociomusicological approach intends to capture vividly the music and its creators. Each sacred performance community is comprised of networks. To my way of thinking, a sacred performance community is an organized, spiritually aligned auxiliary formed on the basis of a shared view of the social gospel that translates into devout cultural productions. When individuals accept membership into a sacred performance community, they enter not on the basis of denomination but formulate a network, an expansive community with a similar aesthetic and scriptural orientation. The community also possesses shared expectations regarding their social and ritual interaction. These expectations may be (re) negotiated from time to time.

Belonging is a pervasive part of everyday life for members associated with African America's core culture. As Houston Baker eloquently stated, "Black people share their history to a much greater extent than do other Americans, and a part of that history is the folklore that has helped it survive." Most belong to social groups, clubs, churches, lodges, unions, or athletic teams. The social organizations also provide a natural context for the performance of various genres of folklore, especially music. These social units satisfy an individual's need for routine social interaction and are usually based, to a certain degree, on collective economics. My study explores the range of African American sacred music forms emblematic of their religious folklife. In order to provide a holistic look at African American sacred performance communities, I focus on the social organizations that furnish the contexts for sacred musical expression, sustaining a range of reciprocal support networks. By no means do I claim African Americans to be monolithic. However, based on my urban and rural research of African Americans, there could be no tradition bearers without a core cultural base from which to function.

Many folklorists tend to fetishize the most popularly known folklore genres, such as urban legends, blues, and quilting. We often create gaps by failing to explore social patterns in relation to what folks actually do. Through a disregard of the social contexts of performance and celebration, this orientation toward genre negates a fundamental aspect of African American culture, which, I contend, is a nonverbal element: a communitarian worldview. My preferred methodology is to downplay a strict genre approach. I seek to give voice to individuals and their collectives without objectifying them by having only a genre-specific focus. Unless spontaneous, during the interviewing process I did not create field recordings of repertoires.

In this study I attempt to uphold a theoretical position that I first advanced in my urban fieldwork. The approach, then and now, is to explore how African American artistic expressions are maintained and advanced via social-group interaction. For example, spirituals flourished as the music of enslaved Africans who collectively composed and sang them, bringing a meaningful dialogue to both their spiritual and social lives. Blues was the first major African American musical style created by individual musicians; yet country blues singers were not songwriters off alone in their garrets writing lyrics. Instead, blues flourished spontaneously, composed within a multitude of natural contexts. Jazz improvisation, too, was born in the lively interaction of jam sessions, with individual artists driven to new heights of expressivity. In African American culture, such social interactions were celebratory and served as a medium for the formation and retention of some of the most stylistic genres of American verbal and musical art.

My basic goals in writing this book are to furnish the full cultural and historical contexts for the perpetuation of sacred music in the Wiregrass, to examine the formation and operation of numerous sacred performance communities, to compare these reciprocal support networks as essential to the development of their spirituality and communitarian outlook, and to provide an integrated view of the unique spiritual roles afforded women. In essence, I document the spiritual and social functions of sacred music in the daily lives of Wiregrass African Americans. While engaged in my fieldwork, I often felt like the townspeople in Hurston's novel, *Their Eyes Were Watching God*, discovering spittoons: "Maybe more things in the world besides spitting pots had been hid from them."

In chapter 1, I present Wiregrass Country as a southern region like others, yet with its own ambiance. It is part of a fire ecosystem, contributing to a noteworthy pattern of social interaction. I briefly describe the role that African Americans played during the American Indian Wars. Also, I explore how the region's African American presence disrupts certain stereotypes regarding southern history. To achieve their chief goal of becoming landowners, after emancipation, many once enslaved migrated to a region not noted for a plantation economy. The Wiregrass, then, holds the distinction of becoming a southern locale with prosperous African American landowners. This history is translated musically on the Twentieth of May, when African Americans celebrate their emancipation at sites throughout Wiregrass Country. The Twentieth of May furnishes a primary context in which they traditionally gather to sing and pass down local history in the spirit of celebration.

Chapter 2 explores the perpetuation of burial societies. These sodalities integrate ritual movements and drama with sacred music. Many scholars equate burial leagues such as Sunday Morning Band with the past. With historical continuity, however, the region sustains a host of these benevolent associations, its cultural retention of a system of collective economics. A predominance of African Methodist Episcopal (AME) churches, particularly in Wiregrass Florida, represent the cultural center for the continuation of what locals call Turnouts, lodge anniversary programs. Some of these are secret societies and date back to 1868, without a break. As with the Masons and other secret societies, initiation and mutual aid are of great significance to these organizations. For members, anniversary weekends also operate as homecomings and reunions as family and friends reunite for these celebrations.

In chapter 3, I examine how, for African Americans, the repetition of cultural performances complies with a cyclical time orientation. Known for their protracted meetings, historically Baptists have utilized Fifth Sundays to convene for district meetings. Because churches still worship on alternate Sundays, I introduce Fifth Sundays as significant dates to assemble for an array of cultural productions, although the focus is on Baptist union meetings within the tri-state region. I present a range of these modalities to demonstrate their subtle heterogeneity. On these Sundays, all memberships converge at one site, departing significantly from their regular Sunday worship experience. These meetings also function as occasions for social-izing youth into adulthood as well as becoming maestros themselves.

Chapter 4 explores the shape-note tradition, which is perhaps one of the most obscure forms of sacred music still practiced by African Americans. I document a full complement of conventions that typify the region. I de-scribe how Sacred Harp music entered into the African American lexicon of songs. The Wiregrass Singers of Ozark, Alabama, represent the last tradi-tion bearers to sing fa-so-la, the four-shape notation system. Both the four-note and seven-note democratic systems continue to coexist. Although the scholarship about this tradition is extensive, via my ethnography, I substan-tially update this literature. It, too, speaks to the African American com-munitarian outlook. Commemorative sings and singing conventions also rely on reciprocity. Because most Sacred Harp singers are aged, even more than in the past this tradition now welcomes racial integration. On the other hand, the seven-shape dorayme tradition remains a relative mainstay within many southern communities. In Greenville, Alabama, locals con-structed an edifice strictly dedicated to singing sacred music, unhampered by church politics and logistical concerns.

In chapter 5, I focus on the evolution of shape-note singing conventions. In Wiregrass Georgia, singing conventions brought about their own trans-formation with the introduction of traditional gospel music and a choral response. The Father of Gospel, Thomas Dorsey, influenced a major shift in sacred music performances. Neoteric bodies such as the Thomas-Grady Counties Singing Convention answered his call early. Despite the longev-ity of these choral singing conventions, they have yet to gain scholarly at-tention. Thomasville, Georgia, is unique. It supports no fewer than four full-fledged unions or conventions. While most musicologists create a false dichotomy, centering the North as the site for the early spread of the gospel blues, members of the Thomas-Grady Counties Singing Convention's for-mation of gospel choirs indicates otherwise.

Contemporary gospel music, too, garners much scholarly attention but rarely within a southern, rural context. Chapter 6 introduces singing unions and anniversaries common to contemporary gospel music devotees. Mem-bers of these networks are not without their critics. The criticism centers on the propensity to sing for financial gain and generally without a ministe-rial presence. The main context for these gospel musical performances is in celebration of a group's anniversary. These performances depend on reci-procity, and over the course of a weekend singers travel great distances to support one another's endeavors. Along with the differing locales, concerts to raise money are a mainstay of these performance communities. The tri-state region contains a host of amateur performers. However, the glitzier contemporary gospel musicians tend to thrive in proximity to the hubs, near the state capitals of Tallahassee and Montgomery.

Chapter 7 offers a survey of local African American women who act as the bulwark of their networks. Because the affiliations they serve operate apart from the formal institution of their churches, women members achieve greater autonomy. They illustrate the traditional ways in which women disrupt patriarchal structures. Their aggrandized status affords an opportunity to trace the division of labor that grants a culturalized vision of gender. I introduce a bevy of women who defy restrictive portrayals of churchgoers. These women are the ones who gain honorific titles such as Ma, Mother, and Aunt. The chapter concludes with a delineation of women-centered programs that speaks to the complexity of gender within church-related organizations.

The Wiregrass boasts a relatively unique concentration of African American history. Before I even knew about the region's sacred music, I studied its historical past. Principally, African American history tends to promote a liturgy of tears, depicting a host of betrayed tenant farmers, all-consuming poverty, and bouts with rabid oppressors. Yet the history of many African Americans in Wiregrass Country defies this single portrayal. I do not mean to suggest that there were no such hardships. Instead, this remark stands to illustrate the extent to which African American rural existence is not a summation of their oppression. Unlike those in the Black Belt, many residents of Wiregrass Country acquired their own land. They were land poor but enriched via their sacred music networks. They sing persistently with much adulation, which makes their spiritual lives concrete. For further appraisal, I ask you to come go with me into Wiregrass Country.

Downhome
Gospel

✴

CHAPTER 1

"Come Go with Me"
Liberation Songs

The South contains more regions than anywhere else in the nation. Yet, Wiregrass Country managed to fall through the cracks of southern geography. The specificity of the region's history is seldom taught, even in its local schools. For instance, some of the most meaningful battles in the South between U.S. forces and Native peoples occurred within Wiregrass Country. With the settlement of whites, battle lines became equally drawn around the issues of slavery. The region offered a haven for runaway slaves, who often joined forces with the American Indians, becoming their translators and chiefs. Fugitives also developed maroon societies within its hostile, natural environment. Local farmers grew increasingly fearful of these developments, and warfare with the Creeks and Seminoles continued for decades. Paradoxically, the institution of slavery never was a salient economic system in the Wiregrass. Yeomen farmers migrated there due to the prospect of acquiring cheap homestead property. Eventually, upon emancipation, African Americans consciously elected to populate the region for the same reason: to become landowners themselves. Wiregrass history challenges long-standing assumptions about African American life, history, and culture. Its inhabitants owe much of their love of sacred music to a dynamic historical past.

Before being called Wiregrass Country, the region was American Indian Country. Southeastern Indians such as the Hitchiti, Yuchi, and Alabama were descendents of the earliest peoples to occupy this region. Nomadic and seldom remaining long in one location, the ancient peoples left little material evidence of their occupancy. Huge burial and ceremonial mounds alone generally confirm their indigenous existence. Wiregrass Country affords some archaeological evidence of the Gulf Culture. For instance, they founded towns built around spectacular mounds, which served as ceremonial grounds for religious temples. Blakely, Georgia, is the historic site of the Kolomoki Mounds, built between 250 and 950 A.D. Native peoples located their towns near rivers and streams, until the nearby land grew infertile. Then they abandoned them and developed new agricultural settlements. They trusted nature to produce wiregrass, which is succulent in the spring, to attract wild game for hunting.

Numerous flags have flown over Florida. For the most part, its Native inhabitants experienced the political force behind them all. Upon contact with Spanish conquistadors, Native peoples faced extermination by disease, annihilation, and enslavement. During the mission era, considered one of the Spaniards' successes, the Apalachee Indians abounded in northern Florida. They survived the mission system and had evolved agrarian societies, differing significantly from the hunter-gatherers who preceded them. Eventually, however, British attacks forced them into an alliance with the French. Consequently, the Apalachee departed the region, seeking protection in a French outpost in Mobile. The Creeks entered the historic region thereafter. Incoming Europeans, settling in Georgia and Alabama, pushed Creek Indians into nearby Wiregrass Florida, which they already knew through trade and other shared cultural traditions.

Inevitably, the lives of fugitive enslaved Africans and the local Native peoples intertwined. People of African descent resided with American Indians for about three centuries before the Native peoples' forced removal. As noted by Daniel Littlefield, by the late eighteenth century, "'Blacks' or 'Negroes' or 'Africans,' whether slave or free, resided in the Indian country in talwas, on plantations, and sometimes in separate black communities." The history of the Negro Fort illuminates the complexity of the African American presence within the area. The Negro Fort on the St. Marks River in Wiregrass Florida was one of the most formidable bastions remaining after British forces pulled out of the region. It served as a supply station, fueling the war between the Creeks and American settlers. General Andrew Jackson led the American battalions that converged on this site by land and sea. As *Wiregrass Country* relates, "In 1816, gunboats attacked the fort, setting off an ammunition room and killing several hundred fugitive slaves. Those who did not escape to other villages and were not massacred were reenslaved."

Eventually, forced removal of Native peoples along the treacherous Trail of Tears, to what is now Oklahoma and Arkansas, became a catalyst for more prolonged fighting. Emerging independent of the Creeks, the Seminoles of Florida engaged the United States in its longest war prior to Vietnam (1818–1858). General Thomas Jesup viewed the later Seminole War as "a Negro, not an Indian war; and if it be not speedily put down, the South

Negro Abraham.

This proud African warrior, "Negro Abraham," joined the Seminole Nation from its beginning and survived the attack that destroyed Negro Fort. Courtesy of the Florida State Archive, Tallahassee

will feel the effects of it on their slave population before the end of the next season [1837]." Fighting for their liberation, escaped African fugitives united with the Seminoles and assumed leadership positions as interpreters and advisors. They became known as Black Seminoles and were invaluable because they possessed a greater knowledge of white Americans. According to historian William Katz, "Africans proved far more familiar with Florida's tropical terrain." The Seminoles welcomed fugitives to increase their population, and those fleeing bondage sought protection.

In some regards, the vast Wiregrass region offered somewhat of a buffer zone, because it was not commonly a part of the southern plantation system and aristocracy. Along with infertile soil, the general lack of waterways also contributed to why a plantation economy failed to typify this region. For instance, in 1839 Appling County, Georgia, reported 205 slaves. As Wiregrass historian Mark Wetherington confirmed, "Well into the 1870s, continuity still characterized the manner in which farmers perceived their role in society, and the three fundamental pillars of the yeoman's economic independence—farming for home use, livestock raising, and timber cutting—seemed to have changed little." On the other hand, Thomas County, Georgia, boasted more slaveholders than most Wiregrass counties put together, yet it opposed secession. Wiregrass Country is a bit of an anomaly: across time, the land and its people escaped much external notice in relation to the Civil War, Reconstruction, and the civil rights movement.

Relatively speaking, the social impact of these historical moments tended only to trickle down.

Yeomen farmers were usually poor landowners. Antebellum Wiregrass land frequently sold, at best, for a dollar per acre as compared to one hundred dollars elsewhere. Much of the land without economic development was disposed of by a lottery system. As a result, geographer Roland Harper explained, "The largest farms were in the wire-grass [sic] country, but land there was then worth only a few cents an acre, and only about one-twentieth of the farm land was improved." Relatively few African Americans resided there until post-emancipation. Because land was so cheap, the prospects of becoming landowners were tantalizing. Historian Anne Patton Malone indicated that "Freedmen often became part of Yeomanry in the 1870s and 1880s, and a few reached the middle class." In Margaret Walker's novel *Jubilee*, the journey of the protagonist mirrors that of many emancipated African Americans. With much anticipation Vyry and her new husband trek from a cotton plantation to "Wiregrass Country in the Alabama Bottoms." The Wiregrass came to hold the distinction of being a southern locale with some of the richest African American landowners.

When sharecropping was the norm in other regions of the South, Wiregrass African American landownership amounted to an aberration. Moreover, to produce any crops on its land took arduous work. Walker's novel illustrates: "Throughout the whole wiregrass section it required very hard work to make the soil produce. In some places it was rocky and hilly, in others it resembled the sandy loam of the nearby coastal plains." The region's soil quality, however, improved with the development of commercial fertilizers. In Wiregrass Georgia, by 1910 African Americans represented thirty-eight percent of the population. The family of a local resident, Mandy Butler, substantiates local possibilities for African Americans. At the turn of the century, her grandfather owned five hundred acres of land in Mitchell County. After allocating fifty acres each to three offspring, he rented out four more parcels of land for half shares. Ultimately, though, his success is not measured strictly by material acquisition. Butler attested that "He was successful materially, but he wasn't so successful otherwise." According to family history, his misdeeds were legendary, including killing a man for calling him a liar during a Baptist conference meeting.

Similarly, Milton Young of Graceville, Florida, affirmed a heightened economic progress, atypical elsewhere in the South. He shared this kernel of family history: "My wife's granddaddy, he always told us that he homestead this land, in 1862, a hundred twenty acres. That's my wife's family. They had a little above the average at that time because most of us didn't have anything. And he said that he came here to this place and started cutting pine trees and built a two-room house. That's what he had for twenty or thirty years, he said. When he got in a little better shape, he began to raise some peas and corn and selling butter. And started them a wooden house." In formal interviews, many descendants speak to family landownership with great pride. Much of this land has since been sold or leased to white neighbors as subsequent generations migrated away from the land. Today, the Florida Panhandle community of Brownville consists of landowners who evince a triple heritage, being descendants of African Americans, American Indians, and whites. They are known as Dominickers, a term derived from the black-and-white speckled barnyard fowl with a pronounced, bright rose comb. The hens lay brown eggs. These mixed heritage families are close-knit; and, during the segregation period, they maintained their own separate schools.

Beginning with the post-Reconstruction era, the region experienced greater human diversity. According to Malone, "The traditional racial composition of the region was significantly altered by the influx of industrial Blacks and black tenants." When the era known as the New South arrived belatedly in the Wiregrass, the lumber and turpentine industries were the major enterprises. African Americans increasingly entered the region as wage earners and were employed as haulers, dippers, and chippers. Malone indicated, additionally, that by the 1890s African American industrial workers from the Carolinas, Virginia, and elsewhere in Georgia constituted "the landless poor." Taking advantage of rent-free land offers, a later wave of white tenant farmers emigrated there, too. This influx led to the displacement of many African American tenant farmers.

Another recurrent motif hinges on the troubles and travails of African Americans, which inform their collective memories. Oral histories reveal that those with a family history of sharecropping also construct anecdotes infused with pride and heroism. For instance, Louise Sapp of Thomasville, Georgia, recounted a certain incident involving a family member: "We moved on there one month and moved off the next month. And [the landowner] had told my granddaddy that when he moved don't take none of the furniture that he moved on his place, because he had been taking everybody's furniture and my granddaddy, worried with God, you stand there and wait. And he went and got Mr. John Travelino's wagon. And he put his jacket across his lap and rode right pass that man's house and he was sitting right on the porch rocking and we moved. He had been taking other people's furniture but he didn't take our furniture, and then they became the best friends. He come and haul him and take him places." Countless

An old-fashioned stiller; African American turpentiners predominated in Wiregrass Country. Courtesy of Georgia Agrirama, Tifton

oral histories preserve similar accounts of African American forebears who stood their ground, earning the respect of their would-be oppressors.

Similarly, former schoolteacher Gladys Westbrook grew up in Hazelcrest, Georgia. She divulged a precarious situation involving her father and southern race relations: "He bought gas and he gave a hundred dollar bill to the man, who put it in his safe, and that man kept that hundred dollar bill. [My father] went back for it and [the white man] told him: 'No, it wasn't a hundred dollar bill.' [My father] knew it was because he didn't have but one in his pocket. And something bad happened to that man later on. It certainly did. Something bad happened to him, and he suffered a long time. My daddy said, 'You see what will happen if you don't do the right thing. That man took my hundred dollar bill and made out like he didn't.' (You see churches were taking up money for my daddy and mamma.)" Such cautionary tales inform listeners about how and how not to act. Also, they instill and impart the importance of communalism. However, for the most part, because of the scarcity of African Americans in Wiregrass Country and a reduced general population, the races managed to coexist.

Equally significant, by the 1900s several plantation sites in Wiregrass Country came under the control of northern industrialists. They discovered that the piney woods in this location offered certain health benefits and would vacation there for "the cure." For example, "Near Thomasville are great pioneer estates created by wealthy northerners with family background, the first to explore this winter-resort section, before Florida had become widely known as a playground." These hunting plantations improved the quality of life for African Americans reared on them. Ironically, on these former southern plantations, African Americans proved to be true beneficiaries. As I document in *Wiregrass Country*, "These so-called northern plantations are held in special regard by the African Americans who were reared on them and whose parents made up the plantation workforce." Even during the Depression years, workers experienced economic security. Moreover, they received encouragement to send their offspring to college, and the landowners assisted by erecting churches and providing health care. Many of their descendents are professionals today.

Others, not as financially secure, routinely testify to not knowing want or hunger, even without a nickel among them. Alice Stennett stated it best: "We cooked and we ate and we worked." She is not the only one to reminisce fondly about being the child who delivered freshly butchered meat to neighbors nearby: "We shared everything; if the other neighbors down the street wasn't killing hogs, they had chickens with a lot of eggs and young broilers to cook. You bring me some of this, and I'll give you some of that." A barter system was in effect. The African Americans of Wiregrass Country maintained a communitarian outlook that prevailed during good times as well as bad. This collective impulse was a sustaining force that promoted their survival from slavery to freedom. Then they created many occasions to sing their much-loved sacred music.

Beyond their workaday existence, locals relied on holidays for relief from their daily routines. Emancipation Day celebrations supplied an early context in which they gathered annually. In the Wiregrass, African Americans enjoy the Twentieth of May, not the popularized Juneteenth. May 20 is the date the General Order arrived in Wiregrass Georgia and Florida. In Wiregrass Alabama, celebrations fell on May 28. After the Union army won the Battle of Antietam, one of the bloodiest scrimmages, as a strategy President Abraham Lincoln thought this was probably the best time to issue his Emancipation Proclamation. Lincoln signed the actual Emancipation Proclamation on January 1, 1863, but it could not be enforced until the end of the Civil War, and those enslaved in states not engaged in the war of secession could not be freed under the original decree. After the war's end,

The reading of the Emancipation Proclamation reenacted from the steps of the Knott House on May 20, 2009

the date the Union army delivered the freedom decree differed throughout the South. In Texas, Juneteenth celebrations originated to commemorate the date of June 19, 1865, when enslaved Africans there received official notice of their freedom via General Order Number 3 from Union General Gordon Granger. The news traveled very slowly.

In Texas, Juneteenth is now a recognized state holiday, sanctioning its schools to close and state workers to take off with pay on June 19. According to Historian Elizabeth Hayes Turner, "Wrought with allegorical hope, Juneteenth reminded Texans that freedom in any era is worth celebrating." In Galveston, Texas, "By 1919, Juneteenth Day had become so important that white employers gave their workers the day off." To celebrate their emancipation proved tantamount to an act of subversion, a day of absence away from doing the work of the dominant society. Due to the longevity of this celebration in Texas, other African American communities have since appropriated it. Today, Juneteenth is celebrated throughout the United States. Some northern cities currently celebrating this holiday include Milwaukee, Minneapolis, and Washington, D.C. The holiday dates back substantially in the West; with a close proximity to Texas and its migrants, places such as Denver, Omaha, Oakland, and Los Angeles have long honored the date. A campaign is afoot to nationalize the celebration. In 2008, Vermont became the twenty-ninth state to recognize the end of slavery with a state holiday. Also that year, Harlem celebrants embraced the holiday with their first festival marking the occasion.

As a revivalist movement, many communities single out Juneteenth as the oldest surviving emancipation celebration. Yet, it is erroneous to negate historical fact. A month earlier, on May 20, 1865, Union General McCook read the Emancipation Proclamation in Tallahassee, Florida. Due to this capital city's strong antebellum economy, its strong association with its aristocracy, and its hardwood forests, I do not situate Tallahassee as being historically and culturally linked to the Wiregrass. Nonetheless, African American Tallahasseans still celebrate with equal flair, offering insight into the original first taste of freedom. Celebrants reclaim public spaces such as the historic Knott House, where McCook delivered the news, and the proclamation is still read annually. Also, descendants of Henry Hill Sr., Sarah Johnson Hill, and Gertrude Hill Williams—to name a few ancestral figures—continue to assemble on their family's compound. To celebrate, their very own Henry Hill Park comes alive to educate young people and to ensure that no one forgets the past infamy slavery represents or the jubilation its abolition ignited.

In Tallahassee, celebrants still arrive in droves to picnic, play games, recite, and dance to a live band. In keeping with tradition, most attend to sample the homemade lemonade made in fifty-gallon steel drums. At many large African American social events in the Panhandle, the lemonade is like an elixir. Many bring their own containers because it is important to carry some of this tonic home. Customarily, there is a division of labor that places the making of the lemonade, cooking of meats, and frying of fish within the male domain, with women supplying main dishes and desserts. There are no local vendors. The Hill family absorbs all expenses, as is also the custom. Throngs of people line up to eat the soul food appropriate for such an auspicious occasion. Guests cannot partake, however, until after the traditional program of soloists and speeches, along with an occasional youth fashion show or a Christian male mime company.

African Americans in northern Florida embrace all versions of their heritage. Unabashedly, they appropriate elements with long established roots in European cultures. Hybridity speaks to innovations within a tradition, a flexible and fluid way of being, which recognizes that the ground on which they celebrate is a product of transculturation. It acknowledges the ability of those under oppression to utilize, uncritically, everything available as a part of their survival imperative. Holidays transmogrify within this region's own postcolonial history, allowing cultural homogenization and heterogenization to both gain sway. For example, as traditionalized, Twentieth of

Otis and Hunter Hill beat bass and snare drums at an Emancipation Day celebration in Tallahassee

May celebrations syncretize well with May Day. As is customary, celebrants incorporate maypole plaiting. In addition, African Americans proudly appropriate this European-based custom, jauntily accompanied by the rhythmic beating of bass and snare drums. As a hybrid of fife-and-drum music, this form of drumming possesses great longevity in Leon County. At the Civil War's end, reputedly, Union soldiers conferred these percussion instruments upon the freedmen. Locals enjoy this style of musical entertainment during the celebration of other holidays as well, including Martin Luther King's Birthday.

In conformity to past teachings, no detail is generally overlooked, except for the greasy pole, another tradition with a European strain. Local residents relished attempting it with their own twist. They would cut down a sweet gum tree and then take a knife and draw the bark off the tree. The tree would secrete resin that was very slippery and slimy. If you could climb to the top of the pole, you were the winner. According to family history, however, the man who brought the ham placed on top of the pole always took it back home. Generally, no one could accomplish the deed. This spectacular, ludic custom no longer exists, except in narrative form.

Education remains the focused theme of every Freedom Day. It is customary for children to recite age-appropriate poetry written by Langston Hughes and other famous African Americans. To foster an interest in intellectual pursuit, for about three weeks before the celebration, all of the Hill children used to go to Mama Sarah's house to obtain a speech. Family historian Otis Hill stressed how as a child he had "to practice, practice, practice."

For the most part, Emancipation Day celebrations traditionally took place in the safe space of churches and school yards. As Georgia resident Bertha Wrice recalled, "The only thing that I remember: when I was coming up as a child, we remembered that during those days the sharecroppers— we had sharecroppers and whatnot—but during that time, the Twentieth of May, they would never work. They wouldn't let them work on that day. They would let them go to the churches. They used to go to church and have sermons and they would sing and after they finished with all of that, then they would come back and get spreads, what they call a picnic." While not as well known, Twentieth of May observances also occurred on the actual date, no matter on which day of the week it fell. In the Wiregrass, ironically, the holiday they called Freedom Day continued until the passing of civil rights legislation. Some attribute school integration as the reason emancipation events now occur on the weekend closest to the exact date. By 1994, I discovered hubs of Emancipation Day activities in the Wiregrass in Quincy, Florida; Thomasville, Georgia; and Quitman, Georgia. Perhaps, the Twentieth of May holiday thrived due to Wiregrass Georgia's and Florida's proximity to Tallahassee. Those celebrations that continue chiefly function as the brainchild of civic-minded citizens or religious groups to impart knowledge of local history to youth in the spirit of celebration. The Hill family's printed statement seemingly affirms this: "We wish to thank **all** program participants, especially the children, for making this Emancipation Day a success. **They are the future.**"

I learned that community organizers in Crestview, Florida, revitalize a virtual cornucopia of Emancipation Day activities, including a parade. The late Caroline Allen, local historian and founder of the town's Carver Hill Museum, spearheaded the movement to revive this celebration in 1975. Being a Texan, herself, when approached to mount a Juneteenth celebration, she balked, insisting the celebration honor local May traditions. Residents observe the Twentieth of May with a formal program, which includes May Day festivities. On the first weekend after May 20, the community gathers to crown a May Day queen, host a neighborhood parade, and hold cookouts. Allen attested, "A lot of the cooking and things that people used to do on May 20th, they do on the day of the festival." The parade is no longer as extensive nor does it caravan through the downtown area. Instead, the museum is the focal point where the ceremonies end with instructing youth how to plait the traditional maypole. I concur with folklorist John Roberts, who wrote, "While these performances would be attributed to the obvious European origins of May Day celebrations, they also revealed the belief of many African American teachers that learning European social dancing was important for the social well-being of the African American student." The maypole also ties in as mainstay of past May Day celebrations so popular globally. Due to the proximity of the holidays, the maypole syncretizes well into the fiber of the Twentieth of May. Maypole plaiting is an ancient rite of spring as well as a political pirouette for independence and freedom movements. Therefore, it should come as little surprise that African Americans in the Wiregrass recenter it.

Just across the Florida state line in Thomasville, Georgia, those who grew up on hunting plantations recall the Twentieth of May as holding great significance as well. They customized their holiday to suit their leisure. Besides a big baseball game, there was the prerequisite barrel of lemonade and the men barbecuing the meat as a nocturnal pastime. Many recollect this scene best: "They probably got their biggest kick out of it the night before, because they never had an opportunity to be away from the smaller kids, and their wives and younger boys, younger men, and, you know, we had an opportunity to come out and hear some of the good old tales that they were telling. All the fellows that done the cooking . . . boy you could hear some strange things." With several hunting plantations clustered nearby, the Twentieth of May was among the cycle of holidays (including Christmas and Easter) in which workers would gather at one site. In this way, for decades Freedom Day marked an important transition for African Americans that could not be denied them.

However, it is the Quitman, Georgia, observance that provides the most heightened performance of sacred music within this historical context. Quitman, located in Brooks County, is listed on the National Register of Historic Places. Unlike most Wiregrass towns, it offers a wide variation of architectural structures attesting to it being a regional anomaly with a past plantation aristocracy. In 1994, I first traveled there to witness their Emancipation Day activities. From Tallahassee, none of the two-lane roads are direct, unless you elect to travel out of the way along the interstate before heading north. Taking the back roads, it is sobering to think about how landowners cleared all this space, relying on mules as well as this locale's anomalous slave labor. Quitman's revival of Emancipation Day was in its fifth year. Deacon Owen Wrice was the celebration's organizer. Wrice is a retired railroad worker and farmer with lasting memories of the importance of this occasion while growing up. Commencing on a Friday, the scheduled events would culminate with a Monday night finale. I arrived at Bethany Missionary Baptist Church tardy yet gratified to witness a spirit-filled standing-room-only crowd. I entered *in medias res* but with certainty that the program conformed to most Sunday morning services, meaning at most I had missed the devotional period.

At many African American sacred and secular events, Devotion remains a ubiquitous presence, as at the Hills' celebration. Anthropologist Walter Pitts noted a pattern of binary frames that transculturally encompass rituals within African American Baptist worship and African-derived religions in the Caribbean. The first frame is staid, subdued, and derived from singing European hymns, whereas the second privileges more Afrocentric ritual acts. As acknowledged by Pitts, "The only rituals that do not exhibit this binary structure are rites of passage such as baptisms, weddings, and funerals, which have their own distinctive structures." It is a format that I first witnessed documenting folklife in Philadelphia. I grew to accept Devotion as partial proof of the retention of a cyclical orientation, functionally granting additional minutes so that one might arrive "in time, not on time." Its structure is relatively interchangeable no matter what the full context. The devotional leaders, normally male deacons, are in charge of this frame. Lined hymns along with standard European hymns generally key this frame, alternating with exuberant, oratorical prayers.

Although the structure is predictable, devotional leaders such as Deacon Wrice can refreshingly line a Charles Wesley–style hymn such as "Father, I Stretch My Hands to Thee" by rote memory with an invigorating vocal edge. Few African American deacons and other devotional leaders do not own an Isaac Watts hymnal, although they are selective in their preferences. Lining out the hymns conforms to what musicologist Samuel Floyd referred to as the African American "musical trope of tropes": call-and-response. In lining out a hymn, the song leader sings one line at a time with the congregation in pursuit antiphonally singing it back. Folklorist Alan Lomax aptly depicted this framing device: "Many observers described black lining hymns as a mysterious African music. In the first place, they so prolonged and quavered the texts of the hymns that only a recording angel could make out what was being sung. Instead of performing in an individualized sort of unison or heterophony, however, they blended their voices in great unified streams of tone." African Americans ultimately stamped it as being part of their common identity.

The second frame allows for greater fervor. In Quitman, the second frame featured local church choirs. The host choir commenced by singing two selections, and each choir thereafter also sang what they call A and B selections. Moreover, they scavenged from an array of sacred music genres, reinterpreting them into downhome gospel blues. For instance, typically repertoires embrace revamped variants of a well-liked Charles Wesley lined hymn, "A Charge to Keep I Have," as well as a retooled standard hymn, "Near the Cross." Within the common meter music tradition, "A Charge to Keep" usually involves a lead singer drawing out syllabically each word in a singsong fashion. Instead, it is choral groups that, as singer Gwendolin Sims Warren related, "breath[es] new life into it and adapt[s] it to their history, culture, and situation." Historically, common meter music served as a transitional form that unified African Americans into sacred performance communities from slavery to freedom.

As musicologist John Storm Roberts noted in *Black Music of Two Worlds*, Black music's "many styles may perhaps be arranged chronologically according to which began first, but all are still sung today and are widely popular." For example, "Near the Cross" is regularly gospelized, rearranged with an up-tempo beat. A collaboration with words by Fanny Crosby and music by William H. Doane, this composition appears in most standard hymnals. During the devotional, meter music and standard European-based hymns establish a prefatory tone—the calm before the storm of heightened emotions. Outside of the first binary frame, however, these hymns are candidates for exuberant gospelization, with its up-tempo "wandering refrains," that is, a reliance on incremental repetition. Reverend Wyatt Tee Walker referred to such texts as "hymns of improvisation."

Setting it apart from a regular church service or program, this Emancipation Day event's historical raison d'être embraced a liberation theme. As singer and scholar Bernice Johnson Reagon expressed, "One word, 'freedom,' documents the time period. One would not have been able to sing freedom during the time when slavery was an integral part of this country." Thus, as a reminder, Owen Wrice eloquently admonished and cajoled the audience:

> *You ought to be glad you're free!*
> *Every time you hear the word freedom,*
> *or anything that sounds like freedom,*
> *you ought to say: "Hallelujah."*
> *Every time you hear the word, free,*
> *you ought to say "Hallelujah!"*
> *You can be able to sing the old spirituals*
> *of long years ago:*
> *"Free at last.*
> *Free at last.*
> *Thank God, Almighty,*
> *I'm free at last."*

On these occasions, the spoken word approaches a poetics of expressiveness. Thus, I attempt to capture the stylistic, oral component by transcribing and accentuating his actual spoken words. Of course, Wrice was riffing off Martin Luther King's historic speech. Moreover, the lines connect and blur one hundred years of the struggle for equality. In conjunction, as Jon Michael Spencer indicated, "The spirituals lyricized an inward liberation." A mental freedom heralded a physical one. The freedom to overcome oppression begins within. In keeping with the spiritual activism of their ancestors, they convene.

The celebration operates as a day of remembrance and reclamation. Within the region, Quitman is one of the historical sites where African Americans more commonly are descendents of enslaved Africans. Given this context, the celebration means something more than a sheer revitalization movement. The experience of enslavement is not just a remote, displaced recollection. They celebrate in recognition of those who endured, locally, ancestral forces whom the African Americans of Quitman continue to know by name. They honor their past with a loving ferocity, whereas other African Americans might be ashamed. These Wiregrass residents' lives may be humble, according to some standards, but not for those for whom freedom is not just an abstraction. They know from whence they came and pledge never to forget. Being devout Christians, however, they are by no means embittered.

As part of their historical discourse, the past is referred to as "yesteryears." The Twentieth of May is a time set aside to let "your mind go back—go way, way, *way* back." As anthropologist Charles Briggs situated this kind of discourse among Mexican orators, "These discussions consist, in general, of the statement of some fact about the past, its comparison with a feature of life nowadays, and then the assertion of an underlying principle that relates the two." For example, Wrice further reflected:

We,
   as Black people,
have a conversation
   that we could sit all night
     and talk about it.
Because I could let my mind go back,
   on this night,
     we could look up and see the stars.
When it rained,
   we had pails all throughout the house.
We had to move furniture all around the house.
We have so much to be so grateful for.
We didn't go to the grocery store to buy everything

we need.
We went in the pantry
    and got it,
    or we went in the woods
        and got it.
That's why we,
    as a race of people,
        we have that survival know how.
We didn't have to have everything out of the store;
    that's why God just gave us:
        this commonsense and that mother wit.
Just believe in Him,
    and trust in him,
    and he will make a way.

Always, a survival imperative enters into the big-picture talk, as a living testimony of not only "the good ol' days" but how, like the trickster, they survive against tremendous odds.

Subsequently, I note yet a final tertiary frame. The final frame is devoted exclusively to the genre known as Negro spirituals. Certain spiritual songs possess the power to transcend the ages. Often it is those spirituals most associated with subversive hidden messages that have great longevity. "Swing Low, Sweet Chariot" is one of the mainstays. Warren also wrote of its appeal: "The chorus and verses of 'Swing Low, Sweet Chariot' are sung in the call-and-response style. That, combined with their multiple repetitions of 'Coming for to carry me home,' bring the song's multiple meanings and multi-layered messages to an emotional pitch that was a comfort to singers and listeners alike." The earlier frames, featuring the devotion and choir selections, do not center the overarching purpose for the gathering. For the most part, the Negro spirituals provide the climax of the night's activities when several local ministers form an impromptu, harmonizing quartet. The opening formula begins with a spontaneous narrative, calling upon their ancestors:

We had people,
    of this community,
        who lived 107 years.
[For instance] Her name was Etta Mae Scott.
We had members
    of this community
        who lived ninety-odd years.

And during their lifetime,
they were out in the cotton fields,
picking cotton for the other man.
Every now and then,
their burdens would get heavy;
and they needed a place that they could steal away.
They needed somewhere where they could go and talk.
And I hear old lady, Hannah Scott;
old man, William Wright;
old lady, Etta Mae Scott;
old man, Lawyer Scott;
Every now and then,
I hear Sarah Thompson.
And they go on down by the riverside.
And when old slaves were out in the fields,
and they wanted to talk with one another,
they tell each other:
"I'm going to lay down my burdens
down by the riverside."

Annually, during this frame devoted to remembrance of yesteryears, "Down by the Riverside" speaks volumes to this economically beleaguered community. Today, its message seeks to reinforce the old faith in laying one's burden down so that the Lord can fight your battles. Also known as "Study War No More," this song crossed over popularly during the social protest era of the 1960s. As musicologist John Lovell's research uncovered, it "started out as a song of the struggle for freedom; after the Civil War, it was translated into a peace song for people fed up with fighting." For Wiggins, spirituals speak to the political struggle to end racial oppression via its use of metaphors: "some having to do with difficult movement through space, some with the threat of adverse physical conditions, some with endurance and the passage of time." Within this context, this song acknowledges ancestral strength and longevity in times of strife. Spirituals were songs created as leverage, as salve, as voice, as social commentary, and as a bridge across troubled times.

Traditionally, African Americans called their fairly fast-paced, syncopated songs (performed in a call-and-response pattern) jubilee spirituals. Accordingly, in these songs, "the story of situation is unveiled in the verse and celebrated in the chorus." In addition, Reagon highlighted the degree to which the African American oral tradition sustains narratives about the function of spirituals: "These stories tell of how the songs and the singing serve the survival of the community." If the dialectic between individualism and community spawned the creation of spiritual songs, then today African Americans rely on them more commemoratively to invoke that same sense of solidarity.

In essence, participants are recalling their historical and cultural past through song. The spirituals function as a means of preserving communal values and maintaining unity. In this manner, the collective recovers minute, esoteric details about everyday life without idealizing its suffering. Many of the between-song narratives expressively thread some arcane memories. For example, one member of the impromptu quartet related:

> *But when I was a little boy,*
> > *Deacon Tony Cephus*
> > > *would be standing out in the yard there.*
> *I'd see him walk out to the signpost*
> > *and he would get that line*
> > *and he would begin to tone*
> > > *that old bell.*
> *(You young persons don't know what I'm talking 'bout.)*
> > *But it had a different tone*
> > > *than the white man's bell.*
> *So, when that bell tone,*
> > *you'd know church was on*
> > > *somewhere in the area.*
> *Momma would tell us, say:*
> > *"Ya'll better go to the church*
> > *and see what's happening out there."*
> *We didn't have no ride.*
> *We was on feet;*
> > *but we went,*
> > > *and we rushed right back.*
> *And in those days,*
> > *there wasn't no undertakers.*
> *If you die tonight,*
> > *they bury you tomorrow.*
> *We rush back*
> > *and tell mother.*
> *She send us in the field to tell Papa.*
> *Sometimes,*

> *they be already done laid out,*
> > *and they was on their way to the church with it.*
> *Papa would have to come out the field,*
> > *get ready,*
> > > *and then go to the church.*

This narrative led to the inspired singing of "I Wonder Can You Hear the Church Bell Toning Way over Yonder." Its theme speaks to bygone days when a death knell was a functional part of community life. Folklorist Martha Emmons recounted the meaning behind a similar hymn, "Tone the Bell Easy." She noted, "'Dying easy' is the theme of much talk—and more singing—by these life-loving people."

Past Freedom Day celebrations are commemorated on Saturdays via an old-fashioned picnic. Structurally, activities commence at the same church. However, the schematic plans engage not a full-blown service but a sermonette. As the term suggests, a sermonette keys the audience to expect a brief biblical message. Some of what transpires on the night before also approaches the eloquence of a sermonette:

> *I can imagine Jehosophat asking the question:*
> > *"What do we do when we know not what to do*
> > > *but our eyes are on you."*
> *And I can imagine Jehosophat asking the question:*
> > *"What do we do when we know not what to do?"*
> *You see,*
> *you see,*
> *when our forefathers and our foremothers*
> > *were out in the cotton patch,*
> > > *they probably asked the question:*
> *"What do we do when we know not what to do?"*
> *And when one of the slaves heard the question*
> > *across the field,*
> > > *I imagine one of them said,*
> > > *"Swing Low [begins to sing]*
> *When we have trouble in our mind*
> > *and we don't know what to do.*
> *Our children won't do right*
> > *and our husbands won't do right*
> > *and our wives won't do right.*
> *And I have trouble in mind,*

and we don't know where to turn.
But you remember what Jehosophat said:
"We do not know what to do,
*   but our eyes stay on you [the Lord]."*
Every time one of those slaves were out there
*   picking cotton*
*   or cropping tobacco*
*   or even filling boxes*
And they got trouble in mind
And they didn't know what to do
I imagine one of them said:
*   "I gonna lay down my burden*
*   down by the riverside" [sings couple stanza]*
When you got trouble on your mind [singing over words]
*   but my mind staying on you [the Lord].*

Also on Saturday, illustrating the importance granted to passing down heritage, groups form, each with an elder "to tell you what it was back yonder." At fifteen-minute intervals, the elders remain seated in place while everyone else rotates so that all might benefit from their wisdom: "just like Christ when he got ready to feed the multitude." Much of the spoken discourse also reifies the pervasive phrase used: "the old patriarchs." The mention of patriarchs is not to reinforce notions of male domination at the expense of the women folk. Instead, its usage invokes the archaic past, re-inscribing the historic roles both men and women played as co-laborers.

Actually, Emancipation Day picnics conform the most to earlier celebrations. Tommie Gabriel, from Pebble Hills Plantation, recalled: "They gave us the day off to celebrate and in the last years they put on picnics for the people out there. They had baseball or horseshoe or whatever they would like to do on that day." For the most part, gone are the parades, the baseball games, and group excursions. According to Historian William Rogers, "If anything blacks held more excursions than whites, and May 20th seemed to be a natural day to celebrate." In the past, the celebration amounted to a feast day and offered a far greater range of food than any other holiday in the year. In the present context, because younger generations seldom experienced the tradition while growing up, it is the offering of a feast that probably lures many of them to take part in the spirit of celebration.

In spite of the home folks' best effort, Emancipation Day remains a hard sell for those for whom it is just another day. In Wiregrass Country, the circle has been broken, unlike celebrations in Texas and the institution of

Juneteenth celebrations elsewhere, which attract celebrities and evolve into spectacles. Wrice admitted that he himself did not understand the full significance when younger:

> To have the Twentieth of May celebration,
>   and we would have the picnic part
>   and that's all I remember about it.
> I would be so happy
>   when that Twentieth of May date come along;
>   and we would get that soda water and eat ice cream.
>   All the stands around and everything cost a nickel.
> What can you get for a nickel today?

As folklorist Wiggins attested, "A primary function of freedom celebrations is to keep the Afro-American saga alive in the minds of celebrants." Being close-knit, small Wiregrass towns like Quitman feel the encroachment of senseless violence and illicit drugs perhaps more intensely than those in a metropolis.

One year the funeral of a local youth coincided with the Emancipation Day celebration. Everyone personally knew this young man and the family members he left behind. For Emancipation Day organizers, scheduled events offer a panacea. The impetus is to save their children from today's trials and tribulations by promoting self-knowledge:

> We have come through hard times.
> We were in bondage
>   just like the Children of Israel were in bondage
>   and God delivered us.
> And we ought to tell the story
>   because God has told us to tell the story
>   so that every generation will know
>   where we come from.
> If we don't tell the story,
>   our jails are going to be filled up
>   and we are not concerned.
> But we've got to be concerned;
>   we got to get involved.

It is not just enough to remember bygone days. Participants must also awaken the secular community from its apathy, relying on old spiritual songs to reference present-day struggles. In this manner, they invest themselves with the need to communicate past shared values.

In 2005, I was invited to judge an Emancipation Day gospel music contest in Quincy, Florida. The impetus is always the same. Quincy is one of the few towns in the Wiregrass with a predominantly African American population. Over the years, I have attended several attempts by local organizers to revitalize Twentieth of May celebrations there. To avoid conflict with other probable Emancipation Day programs, these organizers elected to blend its celebration with the Memorial Day weekend. As another innovation, the contest was scheduled to take place during a breakfast kickoff to precede a roster of upcoming weekend events. Scheduled for 9:00 a.m. on a Saturday morning, the advertised first prize was three hundred dollars. There also were prizes for three age groups of younger gospel singers. To my understanding, there was a lot of fanfare leading up to this occasion. Contemporary gospel music, in particular, thrives in this small town. Yet the advertised sum was not enough to attract a large constituency to a novel festivity held early in the morning.

As a matter of fact, judging was delayed two hours because a premier anticipated group, The Butler Family, had yet to appear. The five adult contestants lobbied to compete before the youngster category. Only after we began our deliberation for all the categories, the Butler family arrived fashionably dressed and with full musical accompaniment. Everyone else wore sports attire, because a community picnic was to follow. With all the decisions already completed, we had no choice but to disqualify them. As it turned out, the early birds, a duet, Helen Jackson and Pastor Jahazel Dawkins of Bostick Temple Christian Center, won. One of their contenders, Peewee, good-naturedly accused them of merely hollering. When I asked Jackson about their selections, "Soon We'll Be Done" and "If I Had Wings I'd Fly Away," she stated, "Don't sing it if it don't mean something." Such Freedom Day programs bear witness to a microcosm. Even in competition, everyone remains grounded in keeping with Christian experience. Within this predominately African American city, the prize money was substantial to the winners. But I observed how in Christian fellowship individuals regularly compete with spontaneity and without vituperation.

Operating with cultural specificity, these marginalized people maintain a number of communitarian obligations. Attempts to revive Emancipation Day sometimes fail, not strictly due to complacency. Forging new cultural productions are difficult for those already overly extended, keeping a host of distinct social obligations alive and vibrant. Regardless, in performance, it is often the songs of old that continue to supply the balm needed to grant their nowadays lives meaning. They rejuvenate these songs so as not to tone the bell and to announce their cultural cohesion. Musicologist Spencer certified that within the civil rights movement, "Singing was not only a source of courage, it was a means of responding to events and audaciously 'talking back' to the establishment." Now these liberation songs speak to their willingness to maintain communities by privileging the survival imperative first imprinted by their ancestors. I am still astounded by the time and energy invested in the name of family, community, and ultimately belonging. Freedom, then, signifies a spiritual peace, conferring a way of being in the Wiregrass. Their freedom to overcome begins within and issues forth, often in song.

It was within this historical context that African Americans in Wiregrass Country first assembled to sing. The rigorous singing rarely occurred exclusively during formal church activities. As Jeff Titon acknowledged, "In church and at home people sang hymns and religious songs that bore little relation to the Europeanized product of the Fisk Jubilee Singers." Because churches met on an irregular basis, as a testament to their spiritual reality families sang together while shelling peanuts or performing other chores. Expressly, they sang to fulfill recreational and spiritual needs. A commonly heard expression is "I love God; and I love His music." Through their singing, Wiregrass African Americans enact a musical view of the universe. This worldview engages music as a mediating force that takes on a life of its own. When individuals sing to the Supreme Being, psychic benefits accrue. However, when an entire sacred performance community sings, the intended benefits increase exponentially. The communitarian power infusing their music speaks to their desire to fill their world with divine melodies. For them, their spirituality is an everyday reality, a necessity, to be lived as well as communicated and verbalized via song.

CHAPTER 2

"Ev'ry Day'll Be Sunday"

Burial Sodalities

In the Wiregrass, the hymn "Ev'ry Day'll Be Sunday" speaks multitudes. It alludes to how local residents seek a sense of sacredness in daily living the gospel, with an eye toward eternity. This chapter explores the centrality of burial societies as one of the social vehicles used during this life's journey. While the remembrance of bondage still infused the thoughts of recently freed men and women, they organized burial leagues. For example, memberships in Sunday Morning Band dates back to August 8, 1868. It all started in Columbia County, Florida, at Bethel Church and grew into a statewide phenomenon. Traditionally, burial societies ensure a decent, respectful interment in anticipation of a hereafter of endless Sundays. Out of slavery, as scholar Karla Holloway attested: "Thus, a black community would anticipate the financial burden that would greet its members, given the frequency of unforeseen illness, death, and associated costs of burials. In response, these benevolent secret societies, with their contributions to a common till, provided a consistent source of financial relief for their community's persistent experiences with death and dying." Burial societies fostered anniversary programs, called Turnouts, offering a sacred–secular context in which to initiate and recruit new members. Numerous societies arose, possessing a cornucopia of names, which often speak for themselves or can be quite enigmatic, such as Independent Bands I and II, the International Benevolent Society, Inc., the Loyal Americans, and the Ninth of Moses.

Their legacy bespeaks an African survival. This retention should not come as a surprise given the provenience of belief in respecting elders, ghosts or haints, and ancestral forces. Historian Edward Ball positioned burial leagues to be West African survivals in which "many cultures had developed special cliques to take care of grieving relatives and carry out burials. When a person in the clique died, all other members were required to attend the funeral (ensuring a good Turnout) and to contribute to the deceased's family (donations that acted as a kind of life insurance)." Therefore, American fraternal mutual aid societies syncretize well with West African–based customs. According to historian David Beito, historically, "More Americans belonged to fraternal societies than any other kind of voluntary association, with the possible exceptions of churches." Moreover, he documented organizations such as The Odd Fellows that required its membership "to consider applications for aid on a case-by-case basis." In comparison, African American burial leagues possibly owe their longevity to a systematic and consistent practice of reciprocity. They represent spiritual activism in full effect.

Even the spread of life insurance did not thwart the perpetuation of African American burial societies in Wiregrass Country (especially Florida). Beito emphasized how educating their membership about self-reliance and thrift was another paramount function of the typical American lodges. Customarily, African American burial societies and other fraternal societies, no doubt, ascribed to some of the same values. Then again, the bylaws of the Independent Pallbearers Union of South Alabama and Northwest Florida indicate succinctly as its first goal: "to help bury the dead." The life passage rite is the most important of all African-based ceremonies. In addition, whereas women often faced segregation into women's auxiliaries within most American voluntary organizations, the African American mutual aid groups do not discriminate among members.

Furthermore, they also reconstitute secret societies. As famed sociologist, historian, and political essayist W. E. B. Du Bois stated: "Secret societies have always played an important part in West Africa. They include a large variety of associations of which the majority is mutual benefit clubs. Membership confers social distinction and one method of bestowing charity." In the United States, the foremost function of African American lodges, beyond ensuring a respectful funeral, is to promote morality and religion. The Independent Pallbearers' second tenet expresses that members "be of good moral character and qualifications. This Union will not tolerate anything that is unjust." Similarly, Sunday Morning Bands' pronounced principles are: "Religion, morality, the diffusion of knowledge, and benevolence." Although nondenominational in practice, these are, in the main, Christian organizations. To become a member of these secret societies, one must be at least twelve years old, must ask, and must be Christian. Similarly, asking is always the first step to belonging to Masonic Lodges. Lodges such as Sunday Morning Band represent secular–sacred performance communities because, beyond seeking the sheer divine, they actively answer their members' everyday physical needs.

Such societies also constitute sodalities. These associations are formed for charitable purposes. Burial societies function primarily as bounded communities, committed to achieve a desired outcome. By definition, Bayliss Camp and Orit Kent's study configure the term *burial society* to describe organizations that use both hazing along with the deployment of ritual enactments. As centered in *Lay Down Body: Living History in African American Cemeteries*, "Burial societies and lodges served as the precursors to modern-day insurance companies, filling important gaps in security and peace of mind created by racial discrimination. In exchange for a monthly, or in some cases weekly, premium or dues, these organizations guaranteed their members health care in the event of sickness or accident. . . . But perhaps most importantly, they contracted to guarantee a proper funeral and burial for their dues-paying members." Interestingly, Beito identified a golden age of fraternalism in the United States, with such organizations generally tapering off by the 1930s. Yet, among African Americans, the Depression era was the point of heightened fraternal activities, with the formation of several independent bands. This indicates how the political economy influences the development, growth, and survival of such African American voluntary associations.

Through the maintenance of organizations such as mutual aid societies, African Americans have ritualized social relationships into a repetitious cycle. These societies historically exist(ed) to administer to the distressed and to help bury the dead. A small monthly fee is paid to a common treasury that provides upon death benefits in a set amount toward one's funeral. Among people of African descent, collective economics is the driving force. Akin to similar sodalities in West Africa, where *esusu* is the popular terminology deployed to identify these reciprocal support networks. As a form of collective economics, such leagues offer assurance of a fitting interment and, during one's lifetime, personal sustenance. The most widely known association with burial societies recognizes those of the Sea Islands. Speaking of their function, folklorist Mary Twining noted: "the underlying reason for their existence is to maintain social order, offer ethical direction, and provide economic succor and some measure of emotional security."

For African Americans, mutual aid societies are still popular due to the spiritual, social, and cultural practices they maintain. For instance, the International Benevolent Society, Inc., founded in 1906, has a membership of more than 150 lodges in six states and includes military branch units, making it international. It is set up based on a Masonic Grand Lodge structure and celebrates established annual events such as Founder's Day on the fourth Sunday in May and a Youth Day, to encourage camps for young members, on the fourth Sunday in July. Having broadened its focus beyond "simpler services," it stresses scholarships, social welfare, and economic development programs. Still a benefit of membership includes assistance in financing funerals and a proscribed interment service in which officers and fellow mourners engage in specific ritual acts at the gravesite. After a prayer by the chaplain, these instructions follow. The instructions state: "Then place the left hand over the heart and take a sprig of evergreen [a symbol of eternity] in the right hand and raise it straight above the head three times (1. faith, 2. hope, 3. charity), and as it comes down the third time, drop the evergreen in the grave." All respond: "Our link has been broken."

For me, the dominance of AME churches came as a surprise. AME churches truly thrive in Wiregrass Florida. Within the rest of the region, I perceived a balance between the two largest denominations: Missionary Baptists and the African Methodist Episcopalians. With a history dating back more than two hundred years in Philadelphia, the AME church grew out of a protest by disgruntled enslaved and formerly enslaved Africans angered by St. George Church's move to segregate them during a worship service. They founded the first independent denomination to be formed by African Americans, Mother Bethel AME Church, under the leadership of Richard Allen. In 1852, Daniel Payne became an AME bishop. Along with many of his appointments, he is credited with the denomination's infusion into, especially, the Florida Panhandle. As reported by historian Clarence Walker, after the Civil War, "the white church was giving up its plans to minister to freedmen, thereby leaving the rich crop of black souls to be harvested by the AME Church."

Often spoken of in the past tense by contemporary scholars, burial societies such as Sunday Morning Band continue to support their core communities in times of crises. Such bands combine an interesting display of time-honored ritual acts, along with other symbolic elements. People of African descent often share an intricate relationship with their recently deceased members. Although they may interact with other denominations, most who know about these bands assert "That's an AME thing." In Jackson County, Florida, AME churches emerged as the center of a flurry of these sodalities, organizations requiring a special commitment. Nineteenth-century AME Bishop Daniel Payne "denounced 'Fist and Heel' worship, drumming, 'Voudoo' dancing, and all the other 'strange delusions' he witnessed among the freedmen." Similarly, AME church leaders also opposed Masonry. Ironically, today these secret societies share many commonalities as well as members. Perhaps they share commonalities due to an early gesture to subvert this denomination's intolerance of Masonic Temples.

Bethlehem AME Church in Cottondale, Florida, which was founded during slavery by Henry Call

Laborers in the Vineyard of the Lord: The Beginnings of the AME Church in Florida, 1865–1885, by historians Larry Rivers and Canter Brown, clarified that over this period "the AME Church had proved itself the single most effective organizational force for Florida's black residents." The book also documented Marianna's Bethlehem AME's founding by Henry W. Call on a Thursday night in 1863 with a general handshaking, "while the white overseer looked on unaware of anything more than a prayer meeting." In Jackson County, during Reconstruction, Henry Call and Jacob Livingston became presiding elders, playing a major role in the many newly established AME churches and becoming a testament to this denomination's aspirations in the region. The Rivers and Brown text illuminated that by June 1876, including Bethlehem, Springfield, and Antioch, the Marianna District of Jackson County contained ten separate churches. Not even the larger Jacksonville, Florida, had more.

Wiregrass Country may also be unique in its great acceptance of women clergy. The expectation is for these southerners to be more doctrinaire in opposition to women in the pulpit. In keeping with the custom of acknowledging fellow clergy, it is not uncommon for presiding officers to query: Are "there any ministers in the house, male or female, that would like to come, sit with us?" However, it is the AME church that is in the forefront of ordaining women. While researching gravesites in Liberty County, Florida, where stands of wiregrass still grow freely, I encountered Alex McGlockton. Previously, I had photographed his wife's burial plot in a nearby churchyard. Its headstone contains her photograph. McGlockton lived in Tallahassee, and I interviewed him there in his home. He informed me about his wife, Sara Virginia Lee McGlockton, an AME minister. She was born in Liberty County, Florida, in the Rock Bluff community, and along with her husband grew up a member of the local Bethel AME Church. The name of the founding mother church is widespread.

As relates to women ministers, McGlockton expressed the kind of religious views typical within the region. He explained certain intricacies:

> *I still kept my membership. As I said already, I never changed my membership since I've been a member in Rock Bluff. I thought of changing following her once or so, but I never did. She was strong; she went without me. If I wanted to say it, spiritually wise and God-like wise, I think that's what God had plans for—me to keep going doing my thing and her to keep doing her thing—because she went pastoring one church and then she went pastoring two churches and she died pastoring both churches. If I wanted to phrase that back in my thinking, if you read in the scripture, God always sent his people out to do whatever he told them to do. He didn't tell them to carry nobody with them. He just told them to go. In one instance, it looks like I remember he was supposed to take his family with him. Several instances, they just went. My wife's thing—she just went and did what she had to do or did what she was supposed to do or did what she was told to do. Something about me, I respect ministers. I accept them because I don't know; and who am I to say: who are they and where they are and what they was supposed to be?*

I discovered that he shares the viewpoints of many Wiregrass African Americans. During formal interviews, they enlightened me by qualifying and classifying their worldview as relates to interdenominational marriages.

Moreover, in my estimation, the western Panhandle has the greatest depth when it comes to burial sodalities. In the early fall each year, members associated with Henshaw Chapel AME, Bethlehem AME, Springhill AME, and so on host their anniversary programs called Turnouts. One independent band chairman, Raymond Dickens, described the Turnout season as "two months in the year—September to October—when lodges owned, operated, and spent by Black folks." Each burial society stakes out a Sunday within about a six-week period. As part of the ritual process, devotees attach a special meaning to the time at which they enact their rituals. Although Sunday Morning Band has *mourning* as a closely associated homonym (according to contemporary members), the name only alludes to the ritual time, regarding the day of the week and the portion of the day when the Turnouts traditionally occur. They constitute a band not only in the lexical sense of being a musical group, but as a unified body pledged to share its resources.

Mourning is a universal experience, yet diverse cultures view death and dying differently. Distinctions often center on differences in duration, frequency, function, and intensity. In terms of duration, it is traditional for African Americans to "hold the body out" for seven to ten days and to host elaborate wakes to assure that life passage rites are carried out in a proper fashion. Regarding frequency, literally, we die only once (that's a given), but habitually certain African Americans are known to attend funerals of nonacquaintances and distant relatives regularly to pay final respect. Functionally, funerary customs for people of African descent speak to connectedness with a broader community, the ancestors. African Americans are as concerned about their comfort as that of the living. Intensity applies to numerous well-established burial customs that are meant to honor and amuse the deceased.

Bands usually hold meetings in lodge buildings, independent older structures located in proximity to a church ground. As part of the ritual act, on the designated Sunday morning of their Turnout at approximately 11:00 a.m., members "step off" two abreast from their lodge to the church, where they host their anniversary program. As an eyewitness, Sharoresier White described the unfolding event: "Upon seeing them, everyone listens to the familiar theme, listen[s] to the timed shuffle of feet, the systematic clapping of hands, and watch[es] the 'jazzy' dipping of the uniformed train of band members. Yes, the day has begun." Turnouts supply another context in which traditional spirituals dominate. Holloway confirmed this: "Although the main function of these societies was to cover the costs of burial, they also guaranteed their deceased members the pomp and ceremony critical to the occasion. Badges, gloves, special collars, and aprons—often at the wake and again at the gravesite were necessary displays."

En route, the marchers ritualistically sing the spiritual "When the Saints Come Marching In." "Low Down the Chariot" is another spiritual with an otherworldly theme sung perennially. In addition, as Reverend Christa Dixon pointed out in her book of reflection on the spiritual "Swing Low, Sweet Chariot," the song "helps transform our fears of death into an expectant hope born of faith." While marching in, the band claims the outdoors as part of their ritual space. Along the way, they make a distinct tramping sound with their feet and, with pomp, cross underneath a gauntlet of decorated wooden staffs. Members wear specialized colors: women dress in all white (sometimes with capes) and the men wear white shirts and dark slacks or suits (sometimes with draped ribbons for sashes). Also, they wear ornate tasseled ribbons as badges. The purpose of the Turnout is not to evangelize but to recruit new members and to raise funds for the society.

Once in the churchyard, the signature theme song unfolds. The bands issue the following lyrics forth in a call-and-response pattern:

Oh, what Band is this?
Sunday Morning.

Oh, what Band is this?
Sunday Morning.
Oh, what Band is this?
Sunday Morning,
Sunday Morning Band.

There's one,
There's two,
There's three little angels.

There's four,
There's five,
There's six little angels

There's seven,
There's eight,
There's nine little angels
Ten little angels in the band.
Oh, I'm tramping, tramping
Heaven must be my home.

Oh, I'm tramping, tramping
Heaven must be my home.

This signature song conforms to the antiphonal, syncopated, polyrhythmic style of spiritual songs. Being part of the marching in, it is sung a cappella. According to communicant Sharoresier White, "This is the refrain that the members use to strut and parade when performing." The ceremony overall demonstrates the degree to which African Americans utilize a musical system that does not isolate song, dance, and drama. This insight draws upon what ethnomusicologist John Miller Chernoff identified as the "functional integration" of music and culture. Therefore, it is the totality of such ritual experiences—dance, music, costumes, and so on—that key such ceremonies as rituals of revitalization.

The ritual superstructure of these Turnouts also offers some interesting layers of ritualization, decorum, ceremony, liturgy, and celebration. Folklorist Roger Abrahams indicated expressly that the festive events of enslaved Africans were "animated by the style, spirit, and social and aesthetic organization of sub-Sahara Africa." For example, processions fulfill a canonical purpose throughout West Africa and the African Diaspora. They represent a documented part of the social life of masquerades in Sierra Leone, Carnival in the Caribbean, and Mardi Gras in this country. Although tame in comparison, *tramping* is the endogenous term used for the ceremonial shuffling of the feet to produce a scraping sound. In British-speaking America, the drum may have been outlawed but not the art of drumming. The feet become a percussive instrument. Additionally, Sunday Morning Band's tramping of feet denotes that their movements intend to represent more than merely "marching in." Of significance to this tradition, anthropologist Drewal stipulated that in Nigeria such rituals are conceived of "as journeys—sometimes actual and sometimes virtual." Tramping, then, signifies undergoing a virtual ontological journey.

Instead of going directly into the sanctuary, once in the churchyard, bands traditionally perform what I can best describe as a reel, using intricate hand gestures and foot movements. Processions move in marching formation two by two. Because of the prevalence of women, the few men are paired with women until only women remain, who then pair off. Facing one another in a double line, they interact as partners. Although each band replicates certain motions such as moving forward to touch outstretched hands, some bands elaborate more by incorporating simple foot gestures, involving extending outward a leg in unison. I discern that their movements must have other esoteric meanings. They manifest in total silence. The gestures are performed in a staccato fashion, but not as sharp and brisk as that of a military unit. The patterns incorporate or, perhaps, once influenced the kinetic movements performed by African American Masons, sororities, fraternities, and drill teams.

Consideration should be given to some of the ritual objects as well. For example, the wooden staffs serve as one of the primary material devices imbued with meaning. In Masonry such staffs are called Deacon Rods. Historically, by crossing sticks, enslaved Africans demonstrated a commitment to one another. As part of an initiation rite, they now crossed staffs to honor and bless the symbolic new life that was about to begin. The staffs embodied the strength and vitality of trees. The rules of decorum dictate that only band members are qualified to march underneath them. Upon death, however, small twigs are placed upon the deceased's crossed hands.

Rather than signifying the end of life, the twigs symbolize entry into yet a new life passage rite: ancestry.

Sunday Morning Band processions move in a linear formation. According to historian Sterling Stuckey, however, "The Circle is linked to the most important of all African ceremonies, the burial ceremony." Yet, the opening frame of Sunday Morning Band's ritual privileges the line. On one hand, the ritual act suggests hybridity, but could it also be inversive? In traditional West African societies the circle furnishes the principle metaphor for the life process. Knowledge of the line, however, was not foreign. In the context of Sunday Morning Band's funerary customs, in African cosmology the horizontal axis of the cross "signifies the sea or river that divides the world of the living and dead, the heavens above and the earth below, this world and the next." The allusion is too perfect to ignore. No doubt, African Americans fostered public display events that privileged the line to satisfy a Western linear orientation, to blend in, and to circumvent larger scrutiny. For as Stuckey proposed, "By operating under the cover of Christianity, vital aspects of Africanity, which some considered eccentric in movement, sound, and symbolism, could more easily be practiced openly."

Color symbolism also requires some explication. White regalia constitute the primary ritual color of all the bands. In some traditional West African traditions, "white cloth is used for protection against [evil spirits]." With cultural specificity, being associated with death, in ritual practice white intends to appease malevolent forces. The color also symbolizes the ontological journey connecting humans with the spirit world. Its ubiquitous presence in African American sacred performances syncretizes well with Christian beliefs about the color white, especially as it relates to purity and rebirth. In Yoruba culture, the cloth of ritual novices is white. The Turnout amounts to an initiation ritual where this color predominates. Anthropologist Elisha Renne specified how the Yoruba use cloth to bring structure to their lives in a world in which humans, nature spirits (*ebora*), and the ancestors are in delicate balance with one another. Within this context, white cloth provides the path through which humans and spirits can travel between each other's world as needed.

Initiation is a requirement. Usually, the day before the Turnout new members are "made," which probably engages elements of hazing. E. Michael Mendelson accentuated how rituals of secret societies, both ancient and modern, promote "tests of patience and fortitude, deliberately inflicted sufferings, disciplines of silence and heroism, followed by gradual revelation of mysteries concerned with the presence of dying in all living, which take away the sting of death and are followed by the candidate's return to the world as a resurrected being, an initiate." Accordingly, burial societies engage members' very sense of mortality. In addition, each lodge has a password, but (I understand) members of other lodges may discern it using a certain avenue of questioning. Lodges also have secret knocks, handshakes, signs, and their own walk. For instance, as relates to secret knocks: "It is an old custom to give three distinct knocks at the door in order for candidates to gain admission into Freemasonry." If the confidentiality is broken, according to the endogenous belief, the culprit's tongue will be cut out.

Yet, like most secret societies, these bands consider themselves secret organizations, but they have nothing to hide. Part of the rationale for secrecy is perhaps, as performance theorist Margaret Drewal suggested for the Yoruba, "to preserve the intensity and impact of experiencing [the ritual] for the first time." Secrecy takes on a more charged meaning, given the past directives during enslavement. Within this historical context, secret meetings involved a clandestine congregation engaged in a subversive act. Such reciprocity implies that they are involved in an economy of mutual interest that has both immaterial (such as mutual respect and solidarity) and material (monetary sacrifices and other gifts) as aspects. Moreover, from all appearances, band initiation rituals are more private than secret. In Jackson County, Florida, such initiations confer membership unto a collective, not determined by life stage, but to bind individuals regardless of age and gender. Therefore, secrecy becomes the touchstone for reinforcing group values. Moreover, as Jules-Rosette indicated: "Attitudes toward death are often highly secretive, and they may be among the last cultural expressions to change when a group is uprooted."

Like Masonry, the process of initiation is referred to as "riding the goat," vernacularly speaking: "If you want to join, you got to ride the goat." Among Masons, it is reported that initiates literally ride a "vehicular saddle in the shape of a stuffed goat." As a root metaphor, the goat is a universal, celebratory symbol. From the perspective of the bands, for initiates the goat translates into tribulation: "They knew this is trouble." The goat—in folklore and in fact—is the one that will eat anything. Although a relatively harmless animal, the goat also is associated with the devil. In popular belief, the devil is known to make appearances in the shape of a goat, which accounted for his horns and tail. Also, as a slang term for scapegoat, it signifies someone who is the butt of a joke; and as a Christian symbol, it represents how Jesus transferred the sins of man—for atonement—onto the sacrificing of a goat. In African and new world religions, such as Vodou, goats are sacrificed to propitiate a deity.

After one Sunday Morning Band program, as I was being escorted around and introduced to different heads of families, I noticed a particular interrogatory exchange: "Do you have any possum?" "No, but I know where you can get some goat." This esoteric query possibly is only to acknowledge membership, but it seemingly also includes the hint of an enigmatic password. As an outsider, when I asked about significance of the goat reference, the pat response was: "It's something you eat." In this neck of the woods, goat is a popular dietary ingredient. Yet, on these occasions it apparently signifies so much more. As bandleader Joseph Johnson explained to his sister-in-law, Sharoresier White, regarding passwords: "My password and yours are different. If you are a member of another band, I can ask you certain [questions] and you can ask me certain questions. By your answer, I'd know if you were a member or not." Moreover, in the recent past, the dinner baskets of the Henshaw band's initiates contained goat meat. As a mainstay of their Turnout skits, the goat functions an act of transubstantiation, perpetuating a root metaphor. As a symbol of burial lodges ritual experience, veiled allegory and allusive metaphors abound.

A few discreet details surfaced related to band initiations. Initiates may be blindfolded (hoodwinked) and exposed to eerie sounds, or an odd assortment of tortuous looking tools may be placed in plain view while initiates are being questioned. Similar to initiation by other fraternal orders, "Deprivation of sight placed the initiate in an unfamiliar and dependent state, mentally susceptible to false stimuli on his other senses, but better able to concentrate on oral descriptions." Apparently, these ritual acts prey on all five senses. As part of the initiation process, to "break" people in, one band leader explained: "Somebody would get out and sound like a goat and they would have a big bell or something and they would ring it and people would say: 'Get back, hold that goat!' They just bamming on the side and stuff." Beyond these stunts, I learned, "They used to put the belt on you years back, and you'd be sore for days." This ritual behavior corresponds to the ordeal, as a standard feature of initiation rites: "culturally induced suffering that dramatizes what might otherwise be a mundane physiological change." Secrecy is maintained to produce a fresh and unrehearsed experience for novitiates.

True to its name, a band's entire sacred–secular performance community turns out to feast on an array of sacred melodies interspersed with scriptural readings beginning with, of course, the traditional devotional period. Although Turnouts typically occur in local AME churches at the same time of day as Sunday worship service, they diverge in some significant ways. Instead, they approximate other church-related programs. After

Joseph Johnson, from Cottondale, is a Florida Folk Heritage
award winner and leader of Sunday Morning Band #363

"marching in," the Turnout evolves into the kind of pageant many associate
with Easter Sunday. Because all are not anointed to lead songs, poems give
them expression. So, the Turnout features the interplay of sacred music selections, blithe Christian poetry, and usually a recruitment skit. This ritual
act, too, is undergoing transition. At Henshaw Chapel, in 2007 the Juvenile
Department incorporated inspirational praise dancers, who performed to
prerecorded urban contemporary gospel tunes.

Joseph Johnson, the chairman of Cottondale's Sunday Morning Band
#363, is an x-ray technician, now living in Tallahassee. Each year, he articu-
lates the conditions for membership. Called "Duty of the Band," this segment is devoted to imparting details about the benefits of membership.

> *As I sat here, my mind reflected back on two young ladies, Sister Jenny*
> *and Sister Lizzie Pew. Many times . . . and also my dear mother . . .*
> *Many times that someone was sick, I remember the time they would*
> *take turns from the SMB [Sunday Morning Band]. They didn't place*
> *anybody in a convalescent home. They would take turns to help with*
> *the elderly and sickly in a particular home. I remember myself pitching*
> *in doing the yard work. I remember some of the older men gathering*
> *the wood. This is just some of the little benefits that SMB can offer*
> *you. If you decide to join one of the many Sunday Morning Bands in*
> *the state of Florida (and we're very happy to have the president of the*
> *state of Florida, Brother Morgan), the duty of the Sunday Morning*
> *Band has so many potentials. But we don't have time today to stand*
> *here a half-hour to a hour, and so I'll mention just a few things. It will*
> *assist you in burial. I'm not gonna stand here and say it's gonna bury*
> *you, naw. It wouldn't bury you completely, but it would make a start.*

And especially Sister Princess Johnson, and all the rest, anywhere from twelve to sixty years old we can take you in SMB #363. At this time and the next thirty days, it's only fifty cents. So if you're thinking about joining a band. If you want to join, the best band, excuse me, Mr. President. If you want to join one of the best, not the largest now (I didn't say it was the biggest now), but the best organized band, it is a good Christian band. We want you to know you're welcome. You can do it the next thirty days at the low fee of fifty cents. I don't know where you can get a fork of ice cream for fifty cents these days, Brother White, but we want you to feel welcome to join SMB #363. And we can tell you more in detail.

Expressed more concisely, he related that the duties are: "Five dimes, belong to a church, accept Jesus Christ as Lord and Savior. It's a holy band." In this manner, Johnson articulates "the Good of the Band," reiterating its affordability and rewards of membership. This sodality's enumerative list also corresponds with the AME church's motto: "God Our Father, Christ Our Redeemer, Man Our Brother." By performing these duties, as spiritual activists they demonstrate their commitment to living the Gospel Truth.

To further proselytize, as part of its membership campaign, Sunday Morning Band #363 is renowned for its Turnout skits. Annually, members humorously dramatize the abovementioned criteria. At one Turnout, wearing floppy hats and stereotypical country wardrobes such as bib overalls and a plaid shirt, the theatrical troupe utilized the minimal space before the pulpit as its stage. Playing on the mystery of initiation—riding the goat—it featured country bumpkin Jeb: "I have a feeling something's gonna go wrong today." Another year it satirized members who fail to attend meetings, who attempt to induct Jeb using bogus knockoff ritual acts. Then, one of the most hilarious skits featured a woman character shouting: "The band is coming; the band is coming," while another woman actor tried to interpret her frenzied cries. Playing on the assortment of connotations of the word, she asked for meaning: whether a marching band or American Bandstand or a jazz band. In this manner, they use slapstick comedy as a recruitment tool, depending on the audience receptivity to them often lampooning their elders. Then, officials dressed in standard Sunday Morning Band garb alter the comedic frame by authoritatively articulating again the benefits of membership.

In keeping with the aesthetics of this sacred–secular performance community, soloists perform most songs a cappella. In Wiregrass Country, of course, being a virtuoso soloist is not a prerequisite for singing

Turnout skit performed as a recruitment tool by Sunday Morning Band #363

unaccompanied. Besides, as they believe, everyone who has a song does not necessarily know Jesus. Although local churches have pianos, until recently the instrument was silenced throughout the Henshaw band's Turnout. For the more rhythmic songs, a low-key patting of feet by the audience was often the only accompaniment. Soloists, self-consciously aware of being before an audience, may issue such caveats as: "The devil is trying to steal my voice." At this Turnout, improvisation, too, was noticeably minimal. These occasions warrant sticking to the printed bulletin. However, unlike church worship, the audience is in motion, departing and returning at will. Because deemed to be a program, the audience commonly is comprised of more listeners and spectators than participants. Occasionally, singers prompt those in attendance to chime in: "If you can pick up, come on."

A lodge choir usually renders several popular gospel selections, such as "He's a Lily in the Valley" and "Jesus Will Fix It." By and large, songs facilitate transitions between discrete moments in the program. They foreground the formulaic welcome, introduce the solemn memorial notice and the honorary notice (which commemorate past and present members), aid the protracted offertory ceremony, and preface the sermonic address. Stylistically, the singing is perfunctory; no one is there to put on a show. They sing to fit the occasion. They sing to add a sacramental tone as well as filler. Their musical selections embody the voices of their ancestors, the foundation for their lives and experiences.

Based on my personal subjectivity, having attended over a dozen Turn-outs, I note that these sacred–secular occasions offer enough frames common to other worshipful occasions to allow the Holy Ghost, sporadically, to move. In 1994 at Henshaw, while emotionally and soulfully voicing the call for the song "Oh, Lord, Done What You Told Me to Do," spirit possession took the form of the lead vocalist catching the Holy Ghost. The song's repetitious structure allowed for spontaneity to take hold. As a consequence, the refrain, "Oh, Lord," followed by the same choral response buffered by handclapping, produced a form of spirit possession. The song leader placed both hands on her hips, rocked from side to side, began to leap in the air with hands raised in surrender, and bowed from the waist, bobbing in keeping with a polyrhythmic African-based dance vocabulary. Her fellow choral members surrounded her, waving a flurry of hand fans; otherwise, the audience remained impassive to the emotional display. Spirit-filled outbursts, while sporadic, occur no matter what style of sacred music (including a sedate rendition of the spiritual "Jacob's Ladder"), suggesting an idiosyncratic pattern. For this particular band, this song is rife with personal remembrance. Whenever sung, someone's entranced.

At a Turnout in 1997, I witnessed a more archetypal occurrence, ultimately, engaging sacred music. It happened during the customary call to discipleship, when those outside Christian fellowship have a chance to connect and to make amends. The minister preached an exuberant sermon that came to closure with him expelling a cacophonous, repetitious, preacherly chant: "Oh, Lord, My Lord." Instead of a pianist adding complementary music, approximating each of his pronouncements, the band's choir softly sang: "Something's Got a Hold on Me." Subsequently, the pastor began the call:

> *What I love about clocking in with Jesus—*
>   *you don't have to clock out.*
> *You don't have to worry about overtime.*
> *You don't have to worry about the overseer*
>   *talking 'bout you got too much overtime.*
> *Clock in with Jesus.*
> *Don't worry about clocking out.*
> *It's a lifetime job.*
> *If you don't have a job,*
>   *you may be seeking employment.*
> *If I was you,*
>   *I'd get my timecard today.*

Usually, at Turnouts, no one answers the call. It is only a church-related protocol or formality. The aroma of food wafting from the fellowship hall usually signals that it is time to bring closure. Everyone is anxious to bless the food and for the band to march out so that they might quickly partake of the generous portions. Turnout programs typically continue without a break, far beyond even the benediction at Sunday morning worship services. Turnout programs may last as long as four hours.

On this occasion, I witnessed an aberration when a young woman, probably in her twenties, approached the altar rail. There, she suddenly "fell out." Customarily, falling out is associated with entering into a trance-like state of semi-consciousness. Both in the North and South, I've witnessed many similar displays, including the forms associated with neo-world religions—Vodou and Santeria. I first noted that the supplicant's state was deemed demonic because the minister backed away. I remember my minister, Reverend Riley, admonishing worshippers not to rush to aid those in the throes of spirit possession. He explained that a demon can transport from one corpus to another. Eventually, a few younger women stepped forth to administer to her, but she still did not budge. Soon, reminiscent of Toni Morrison's novel *Beloved*, the assembled women folk began to raise a bevy of songs such as "Lay My Burden Down." I know that each song raised was spellbinding. During the pandemonium, I even forgot to flip the cassette tape in my audio recorder. It was the hat-wearing women, the prayer warriors, who spontaneously lifted up a series of timeless spirituals.

I realized, before my eyes, an exorcism was being waged. The scene continued without change. I recognized an older woman who finally stepped forward, Mrs. Heggs, who lives in Tallahassee and attends the church I now call home. She merely touched the human heap on the floor. Miraculously, the young woman immediately responded, allowing her to be guided to the front pew. Heggs sat directly behind her with an outstretched hand on her right shoulder until after the benediction. Afterward, overcome with the need to understand the depth of what I observed, I discussed the occurrence with a band officer and Joseph Johnson's wife, Catherine. Without mystification and as a matter of fact, she stated that to accomplish such a feat: "One needs to be prayed up."

Thus far, I have mainly been referencing the Turnout at Henshaw Chapel in Cottondale, Florida. With a population of 900, Cottondale primarily offers a tale of two bands, a so-called citified one and its country cousin. On the outskirts of Cottondale, the church founded by Rev. Henry Call before emancipation, Bethlehem AME, includes a settlement where Sunday Morning Band thrives. The brick edifice is designed in a modified Gothic

Revival style common to many AME churches nationwide. Its design, featuring a corner tower, marks its nineteenth-century origin. Locals brand Bethlehem's Sunday Morning Band Lodge #339, founded in 1899, as "country," not only due to its locale but its retention of a more folk cultural air. Social anthropologist Martin Stokes situated cultural performances as the embodying of specific alignments that "also enact in a powerful, affective way, rivaling principles of social organization." The chairman of one independent band estimates that ninety percent of local residents belong to a lodge.

Among bands, rules of decorum, ceremony, and the liturgy provide dynamic symmetry. Ritualization and celebration, however, frequently differ. Bethlehem AME is located along a dirt road, causing the rural band's tramping to lose some sonic resonance. Wearing the traditional white garb and walking two abreast, their signature tramping style features a jaunty strut as though to avoid kicking up dust. The lead stewards not only bear blue-and-white staffs, but this lodge displays a blue parade banner, requiring three flag bearers to support it. As part of the same reciprocal network, Joseph Johnson often acts as its grand marshal. Outside the sanctuary, his robust vocals enrich the sound because their band consists of mainly women and children. Once inside the sanctuary, Johnson forfeits any further leadership role. Later, in performance, narrative and memory often commingle. For instance, in 1995 he linked his rendition of a song to his deceased mother. Going back to a Sunday Morning Band Turnout in 1974, he recollected: "Right after the prayer, she would sing: 'Jacob's Ladder.'" He commenced to lead an affective congregational dirge. Others, too, transmit their remembrances using music as their vehicle. They dedicate songs such as "Serving the Lord Will Pay off after While."

While in the churchyard in formation, Bethlehem band members produce a ritual display entered into with solemnity and the greatest pomp. The long-term president was Inez White, until a recent ailment. Customarily, outside she would silently direct all the ritual acts, requiring kinetic movement. Especially interested in passing down this tradition, the youth auxiliary members break rank first to navigate down the middle pathway at the top of the line between paired adult band members. Then the adults follow, marching under the upright staffs positioned at the bottom of the line. Looping back to the bottom, the couple originally at the top of the line reverses positions. In total silence and facing their partners, gloved hands are raised palm up, placed across chest and, in sync, dropped to their sides. Repeated again, each individual clasps his/her outstretched hands, then grasps clasped hands first to their left side at the waist and then to the right. With strict coordination, this gesture is repeated. They unclasp hands to clap twice, and this also is repeated. Eventually, they resume their strut and the traditional theme song: "What Band Is This?" They "march in" the church while continuing their song, lining up across the front of the church and far aisles to complete their secretive, ritual gestures again in total silence.

This sacred performance community possesses a long history of overtly nurturing its youth. They partake in all the ritual events, and the Bethlehem band already has appointed one to be the future president. Opening with a juvenile program, it positions children (even toddlers) front and center, providing a stage for a barrage of them to perform. Literally every child gets to step up to the microphone. They perform solos, duets, and trios. Singing without musical accompaniment, the children occupy a platform that encourages them to take musical risks by changing vocal registers. For example, in one program they tentatively harmonized a popular Kirk Franklin release, "Why I Sing." The audience thunderously applauds each effort. They are being mentored into the future. As high notes are met, supportive phrases such as "That's alright," "Go 'head," and "Sang it, baby" encourage. As with Emancipation Day ceremonies, the home folks constantly seek ways to protect and preserve their core culture.

With two large bands in close proximity, the tale of the two bands speaks to continuity and change. As viewed in a 1993 video supplied by my student, once inside the fellowship hall of Henshaw Chapel, Sunday Morning Band #363 performed rhythmic tramping of their feet, letting them explode downward with abandon on the hardwood floor. The tables were already set up for the ritual repast, perhaps hindering another formation, so participants formed a square along the baseboard of the room. Since I have been in attendance, after its Turnout the band adjudged as citified lines up outside for a brief ritualistic exchange of patterned, kinetic hand movements above the waist. They execute a series of the customary enigmatic hand gestures while wearing the patented white gloves: holding hands above the head, two hands grasping from side to side, and a rolling-pin arm motion. They then promenade into the church's fellowship hall, maintaining a linear formation.

Comparatively, as captured for me on another video recording, after its Turnout program the Bethlehem band conducts its recessional. Upon entering its nearby lodge building (a vacated brick school building), it produces an explosive furor, encircling the room while tramping loudly upon the hardwood floor. Their movements fall within the sacred mode of dancing, as members never cross their feet. Unlike the renowned counterclockwise movement of the African American ring shout, however, dancers here move in a clockwise direction. Such an inversion traditionally signifies memory. Their enactment otherwise reconstitutes the ring shout, one of the oldest documented African retentions among African American in the United States. Musicologist Samuel Floyd described the characteristic movements as "the shuffling around in a ring, the upper-body dancing of African provenance, the ever-present singing accompanied by the hand clapping and thudding, repetitious drumming (of feet in this case), and the extended length of the activity." Much should be made of Bethlehem's band consistently shifting from its opening linear processional to a circular orientation at the close of its ritual event.

After its program, the rural Turnout transforms into a community celebration. Queues traditionally formed to sample Mr. Speight's lemonade, which he would ladle out of the traditional steel drum. By contrast, the Henshaw band introduced Kool-Aid, in a more sanitary, large plastic thermos, deviating from the regional elixir. These transformations perhaps speak to the self-proclaimed city band's self-reflexive sense of progress. Now, Chairman White's adult sons prepare the beverage for the Bethlehem celebration. The ritualization process still allots this chore to the men folk, and yet certain other men become tipsy (not from the lemonade). In a festive spirit, most delight by overeating. The Turnout becomes more akin to a family reunion, having attracted back those who migrated away but make the annual return. Unlike Henshaw, there is no buffet here. Various family groupings assemble around their vehicles, not to tailgate but to hoodgate. With the advent of more SUVs, this scene, too, is undergoing transformations. Prior, the hoods of cars were heavily laden with food dishes, transported in the traditional cardboard boxes. With the graveyard in such close proximity, one cannot escape a sense of the ancestors also being fed. As stated in general, "This is a day in which even the animals rejoice because they too participate by eating the leftovers." Both Bethlehem and Henshaw do not seek to stave off innovations. They adjust, intending to survive way into the twenty-first century.

While more populous, Sunday Morning Band shares the vicinity with other local burial sodalities, including one at nearby Antioch Church. In addition, two Independent Bands share the environs between Cottondale and the Alabama state line. Independent Band #1 is associated with Springfield AME Church, while Independent Band #2 only boasts a lodge building at what used to be Macedonia Baptist Church off Highway 231. It also surfaces as the most primordial of this pair. By this I mean that, without the relative glitz of the other lodge buildings, the Turnout of Independent Band

It is traditional for Sunday Morning Band #339 to transport mounds of food in cardboard boxes for the midday meal

#2 maintains an emotional tone rife with an insistent promise of a youthful orientation. Unlike the other bands, an abandoned church serves as its lodge and program site. As guests arrive, there's no other edifice to await the processional. Officials with inductees first must conduct their business meeting within the Turnout's primary structure. The church is but a shell of its past self. The number of sodalities and their various lodge sites are indicative of the tradition's will to endure.

Further west in the Florida Panhandle, the Independent Pallbearers Union holds what they call camp meetings every Fifth Sunday, which I will introduce in chapter 3. In the customary rotation from church to church, both Baptists and Methodists assemble. Camp meetings go hand and hand with revivalism. According to George Pullen Jackson, "Camp meetings were born in the South." During the summer months, while crops grew, revivals captivated white and black southerners alike. These camp meetings historically produced near riotous scenes of religious ecstasy, along with a secular undertone. AME Bishop Henry McNeal Turner indignantly referred to them as "scamp meetings," offering the "bellowing of watermelon, ice cream, lemonade, and different kinds of vendors, where tables and eating stands are rented out at enormous prices; and the assembly is carried on like a picnic." In light of their history, of course, most Wiregrass residents more positively associate them with their conversion as well as other good times. Camp meetings broke the monotony and were joyously exciting occasions.

Independent Band #2, lead by Raymond Dickens, demonstrates its stylized ritual movements

As relates to African Americans, folklorist Joyce Cauthen surmised: "Camp meetings provided an atmosphere of unprecedented cultural synthesis not only because they allowed and encouraged free religious expression, but also because they bore some similarity to African religious expression." Those who attended such camp meetings were simply referred to as *campers*. Therefore, it is not a big jump for those involved today to continue to refer to their small group formation as *camps*, while others prefer the term *band*. In addition, folklorist Art Rosenbaum documented a source, Jonathan David, as noting "the ongoing tradition of these 'bands' in the Chesapeake Bay area, trac[ing] the origin of the bands from the period of the Great Awakening: 'Further, camp meetings, then, as today, often ended with a grand march around the encampment, accompanied by singing.'" Rosenbaum interpreted this dance and song tradition to be a part of the syncretization process.

In keeping with its camp meeting tradition, on the last Saturday in October, rather than on Sunday, the Independent Pallbearers Union hosts its Annual Session. It is not like the Turnouts, however. Upon learning about this union, I shared photographs of the Sunday Morning Band Turnouts with one camp president, Willie Hutchinson. He prepared me to expect a less elaborate public display. Because I set out to document the full spectrum of sacred performance communities, admittedly, I anticipated an event robbed of folkloristics. Upon my arrival in Argyle, Florida, as anticipated no standing-room-only crowd assembled. I saw no choir in the loft, no musician at a keyboard, and no indication from the agenda that this would be anything other than a business meeting. In my pursuits, I have attended a few camp meetings. The only similarity with other bands was that the women wore fashionable white garb and the men wore the omnipresent dark suits. After the prerequisite Devotion, I began to evaluate how this session might fit into my overall interrogation. Soon, I discovered each frame was keyed by its own iconic flair.

Unceremoniously, the written agenda listed the following items: Finance and Disbursement Reports, Financial Secretary Reports, President's Annual Address, Election of Officers, and dismissal. The afternoon session opened with another devotional period. Deacon Willie Hutchinson recited a relatively short but exuberant prayer. The president of the union admonished them to "sing a song shortly. You do not have to sing the whole song." I discovered that the camp meeting schematized its ritual acts, but not at the expense of expressiveness. To my satisfaction, each report featured a subcommittee consisting of two or more individuals, who formulaically prefaced each report with a song, a prayer, and then its account.

Each collective body approached the podium, and each one performed a specific task. For instance, from the pulpit, two ministers issued the Memorial Committee report. Of course, a memorial ceremony would be a foremost staple of this kind of sodality. Reverends Broadus and Barnes, who formed this committee, read the names of five recently departed members. Before doing so, the Thomas Dorsey composition "Precious Lord Take My Hand" provided the essential musical prelude. Time-honored songs weather well within this context. Each song selection covered the gambit of the African American sacred music repertoire: a Euro-American hymn "Pass Me Not," a spiritual, and this archetypal gospel song. The longevity of these genres and their interlocking relationship affirms a selective repertoire to fit a multiplicity of contexts. Moreover, writer Arthur Jones asserted their purpose: "We sing one song after another; we feel our individual spirits intermingling. It is a chilling, ecstatic experience." In this way, their blended voices induce a communion of the spirit. As they sing extemporaneously, they evoke a community in harmony. This form of giving and receiving builds trust and enables others to thrive individually and uphold one another spiritually and emotionally.

For the most part, coed units filed forward to the dais. As part of the roll call, next the New Members Committee issued its report. Without proclaiming a song title, they offered up "What a Friend We Have in Jesus." It is as though they had memorized the entire *New National Baptist Hymnal*, a mainstay in churches in both the North and the South because Dorsey's song and this Joseph Scriven work abut one another (hymns 339 and 340, respectively) within this songbook. Annotating the best-loved sacred songs among African Americans, Gwendolin Sims Warren documented that Scriven first penned the words as a poem to comfort his ailing mother. It was later set to music; and, as with songs like "Amazing Grace," it developed a special meaning and ability to provide sustenance to a people once enslaved.

After his fellow committee member read that two camps report the addition of twenty-five new members, Deacon Waters commenced with an eloquent prayer. The camp meeting continued in this vein. The Time and Place Committee, with four members, including Deacon Hutchinson, launched its report with "Let It Be Real," gave a scriptural reading from the Eighth Psalm, announced the calendar of camp meetings for the upcoming year, and then closed with a prayer. The Finance and Dispersal Committee lead with "What a Time." As this hymn is much venerated, I want to annotate that Dixon, Godrich, and Rye's encyclopedic *Blues and Gospel Records, 1890–1943* listed perhaps more recordings of this song than any other title. Additionally, a roster of seven quartets recorded it: Dixie Hummingbirds, Golden Gate Jubilee Quartet, Golden Jubilee Quartet, Heavenly Gospel Singers, Old South Quartette, Richmond's Harmonizing Four, and Selah Jubilee Singers. The camp meeting session illustrates the extent to which spiritual songs, improvised standard hymns as well as traditional gospel tunes, commonly occur interchangeably and are socially conditioned. Instead of attesting to a linear progression, they assert themselves as more dialectical affirmations.

Perhaps to some, the membership fees are small and the burial payments slight, averaging two hundred dollars. One should not, however, diminish this communitarian outlook, with its parallel system of collective economics within America's capitalist economy. The charge I keep is to discern the "members' meaning," which might be quite distinct from my own. Eminent sociologist St. Clair Drake long distinguished a difference between African Americans who are "organized around churches and a welter of voluntary associations of all types" and those deemed "disorganized" whose dysfunctionality could be attributed to a lack of associational networks. And I would assert the role of collective economics as the price of admission. As I hear time and time again, "We were raised up like that, whatever we had, divide it." Besides, as is also often expressed: "When we're stretched out in a casket, we can't do anything for anybody." The impetus, as always, is never to lose sight of the harsh reality and what has carried them through.

Ultimately, these practices illustrate not the existence of cultish beliefs and practices among African Americans in the United States, but the constitutive planes of reality—material, verbal, and ritual—that pervade African American life into death. As the moderator of an independent band stated, "Company is good to the grave. Now, when you pass you need somebody at the graveside also. You need somebody there to prepare flowers, to let you down, to move you in and out of church and what not." In addition, Inez White explained that it is considered to be a "homegoing" service for a fellow Christian and is considered to be a happy occasion. According to Drewal, "Ritual journeys have a synecdochic relationship to the greater ontological journey of the human spirit in that they are nestled in 'life's journey.'" Via their Turnouts and Annual Sessions, these bands and camps reflexively experience the maintenance of a ritual identity as they complete another leg of life's journey.

These cultural performances, then, are a time of renewal and return. Sunday Morning Band officers claim to have an international as well as national membership, including not just those in the military but migrants who live in the North. In a dualistic role, Turnouts also serve as homecoming reunion events. They offer a designated time for relatives to converge on the homeplace for an exuberant celebration, featuring exquisite gastronomic excess and social overindulgence. To outsiders, however, the ritual activities of burial leagues are invisible. They speak volumes about the persistence of dynamic cultural practices, where there is an incentive to assemble in small groups, to share one's wealth, to respect ancestral forces, and to pass down tradition. For a usually marginalized, rural people, such obligations can fill up any personal void. The songs of old give expression to one as a sentient being on the way to glory: the final life passage rite.

CHAPTER 3

"There's a Meeting Here Tonight"
Baptist Modalities

Today, Wiregrass Country is a region in which many African Americans still attend Sunday morning worship services on a bimonthly basis. Whether Missionary Baptist, Primitive Baptist, AME, or Christian Methodist Episcopal (CME), church services are regularly held on either the first and third Sundays or second and fourth Sundays of each month. I soon learned that Fifth Sundays traditionally amount to a sort of wildcard, a time best used to unite various sacred performance communities. On Fifth Sundays, residents are mobilized to participate in ritualistic displays ranging from the denominational, such as Baptist union meetings, to nondenominational singing conventions and anniversary gospel programs. Most calendar years boasts four Fifth Sunday weekends, with musical activities usually commencing on the preceding Friday. Adherents consider five in one year a real bonanza. Doris Lewis, the district president of the laity for her AME church, spoke for most: "I enjoy every Fifth Sunday."

Fifth Sunday bespeaks the days of circuit-riding clergy, which is usually situated in the past. Yet, on these Sundays, today Wiregrass residents activate countless networks, having a clear notion about how best to observe the day. Lewis illustrates how sacred activities are firmly upheld. On Fifth Sundays, the lay organization that she heads meets. Lewis explained: "My church is on a circuit," and "one pastor tried to get us to meet on Fifth Sunday [for regular Sunday service]; but everybody say we got something else. You see I'm getting ready for the Lay and other one's getting ready for one thing or another." Despite the prevalence and longevity of alternate Sunday worship, research reveals virtually no documentation of this continuing phenomenon along with the musicality that it spawns. African American Baptists, foremost, persist in organizing a religious calendar to support Baptist district union meetings, which constitute a kind of modality. In Christian-based religions, modalities apply to fellowships that nurture congregational structures with an inward focus, rather than one of outreach.

SECOND WEST FLORIDA MISSIONARY BAPTIST
ASSOCIATION

5TH SUNDAY CONGRESS
NOVEMBER 29 & 30, 2003

TO CONVENE AT THE

SECOND WEST MISSIONARY BAPTIST ASSOCIATION
CHURCH
4110 HERRING ST.
MARIANNA, FL

THEME: "REDEMPTIVE PURPOSE AND POWER OF THE
MODERN CHURCH", II CHRONICLES 7:12-14 & ACTS 1:8

• •

Dr. H. G. McCollough, Moderator
Rev. William Harvey, Vice Moderator

Fifth Sunday bulletin of the Second West
Florida Missionary Baptist Union

For most Americans, the days of the circuit-riding preacher is evocative of a bygone era, but not for many African Americans in the South. It is only to the degree that imaginative literature makes common use of folk cultural traditions that such observances receive representation at all. For instance, African American creative writer Rita Dove overtly mentioned Fifth Sunday in a short story by this name: "The next day was Fifth Sunday. Whenever there was a fifth Sunday in a month, the young people presided over the main service. They ushered, provided music, read the text from the Scriptures, passed the collection plate—even led the congregation in prayer for the sick and shut-in. The only thing they did not do was give the sermon." I wish to correct this dynamic oversight by highlighting Fifth Sunday's mystique for African Americans in the Wiregrass. However, first, I will further contextualize their spiritual life.

To begin, the region provides a microcosm in which the diversity of core African American sacred experiences can be articulated. Other religious scholars and historians have comprehensively documented the conversion process for enslaved Africans to Christianity and variances in worldview. Where bondage existed within Wiregrass Country, enslaved Africans regularly worshiped in white-controlled churches, as elsewhere. Local Alabama historian Fred Watson indicated it was customary among slaveholders to furnish "a special wagon to transport [enslaved Africans] and places in the church were provided for them." Although Wiregrass Country's history is different from most of the plantation South, local historians furnish great specificity about the experiences of those enslaved. Accordingly, historian John Crowley mentioned Bethlehem Church in Quitman, Georgia, as the only local Primitive Baptist church with a slavery gallery. In this way, African Americans became indoctrinated about Christian tenets and doctrines, but they also synthesized this system of belief in accordance with a certain cultural specificity. As relates to African Americans, the term *Afro-Baptist* surfaces. As historian Mechal Sobel explained it: "black Baptists reached another level of integration (generally, not recognized) in which *a new cosmos was forged uniting African and Baptist elements in a new whole* [emphasis hers]." These constitute the root elements of African American spiritual activism.

Another prevailing viewpoint pigeonholes the South as the Bible Belt. Religious folklife in Wiregrass Country further complicates matters. A religious fundamentalism, which historically stigmatized southerners, really informs the stances of many people throughout the United States. Still, for many southerners the Bible and religion hold a position of centrality, contributing to biased stereotypes. Historically, worshippers chose religious affiliations in accordance with family traditions and a frugal lifestyle. According to historian Dickson Bruce, in accepting "frontier moral courts," all of the key denominations had systems of excommunication, although they administered them differently. Of course, dancing and drinking were forbidden, but one could just as well be expelled for playing an instrument at dances or handling alcoholic beverages. Institutions also imposed sanctions against profanity, dishonesty, and backbiting that caused grievances. Each had disciplinary bodies to oversee the salvation of its members. Thereby, a committee tried members if they divorced or were absent without a worthy excuse consecutively from church. The Baptists also did not permit their members to join secret orders such as the Masons.

What often goes unrealized is the degree to which enslaved Africans also had to comply with certain religious doctrines or face excommunication. As church members, they could be disciplined for not attending services and conferences; for breaches of the Commandments such as lying, cheating, and stealing; and for not living above reproach, that is, dancing, swearing, or fighting. In addition, they could be excommunicated for running away from their masters. In one instance particular to the region, "the church 'excluded' Madison, a colored brother, for uniting with a Pedo-baptist Church." In the nineteenth-century South, Pedobaptists emerged as an adverse denomination because leaders did not perform baptism, the foundation of Baptist belief. As Wiregrass historian William Warren Rogers suggested, "Certainly the Baptists, white and black, were doctrinally and emotionally concerned with what their name implied. For them the ritual of baptism was total immersion, and a baptizing was an event of inter-est: to the new converts, of course; to fellow Baptists pleased to call them brothers; and to just about everybody in town who enjoyed the drama and spectacle."

To further particularize Wiregrass Country, after emancipation Afro-Baptist churches cropped up throughout the region. Instead of continu-ing segregation patterns in white churches, separate churches grew during Reconstruction. Rogers further reported an example of what transpired in one 1865 Thomasville, Georgia, Baptist church: "While a division would have reduced membership over one-half, two important resolutions were adopted July 1, 1865. One asked 'that the Colored Church in conference be informed that it is their privilege and at their option to assume an inde-pendent form of Church government, or to remain as heretofore under the superintendence of this church.'. . . Blacks would have no claims on church property or right to sit in the white conference but were to help support the church." White members, apparently, acknowledge ambivalence toward a potential material loss along with the need to maintain the racial status quo. I note that this schism, paradoxically, occurred a few weeks after the first Emancipation Day on the Twentieth of May.

Curiously, in the case of the CME church, separatist white congrega-tions provided the necessary building or land. As one local history eluci-dated, "The exodus of Blacks into their own churches was in some instances voluntary, in other cases encouraged and assisted, and in a smaller number of white churches actually forced." For instance, the creation of the Col-ored Methodist Episcopal (later known as Christian Methodist Episcopal) denomination sprung from a mutual agreement by southern Methodists of both races and was made official in 1871. This new denomination repre-sented one of the last groups to splinter off. According to Rogers, "By the 1890s black Methodists were completely separate from the whites. If they did not match the latter in affluence, they did so in their dedication and in their numerous and expanding congregations." CME churches, however, are not very prevalent in Wiregrass Country. The exceptions are primar-ily located in Thomas County, Georgia, which is home to three: Clifford Temple CME, Hadley Chapel CME, and Midway CME. Midway actually has the distinction of being one of the few churches for African Americans in the region before the end of the Civil War. Thomasville even boasts a congregation of African American Anglicans. Thomas County was among the few locales in the Wiregrass with a plantation economy.

Historically, as a result of an earlier schism, Baptists splintered into two groups, Missionary Baptists and Primitive Baptists. Being Primitive Baptist was associated with censure. By adhering to a strict covenant, Primitive Baptist adherents customarily reject worldly things such as the playing of musical instruments. Such sanctions created a breach among early white Baptists. For these hard-shell southern Baptists, "Along with choirs, musical instruments, centralized denominational authority, seminaries, and Sunday schools, missions comprised one of the 'human inventions' that Primitive Baptists believed did not belong in the true church." By choice, the existing white Primitive Baptists continue to sing a cappella. However, this is no longer the case for African American Primitive Baptists. For example, St. Luke Primitive Baptist Church in Reno, Georgia, organized in 1874, may be representative. According to its historical sketch, "The church didn't have a choir, Elder T. L. Geter organized a choir in 1946 and he called it St. Luke Primitive Baptist Church Choir. The church needed a piano, so they brought a piano, during this time the Mr. Logan Milo was the musician." This example provides one of many departures from hard-shell doctrine by African Americans who bear the Primitive Baptist label today. Yet, folklorist Doris Dyen indicated there is a more "liberalized wing of the Primitive movement, called Progressive Primitive Baptists."

Regarding the Missionary Baptists, the general belief is that today only African American churches bear this name. Wiregrass Georgia native Deacon Tommie Gabriel reminisced: "I saw one. I remember one up near Bingham Lake, up in Georgia. One, and it's called Bull Missionary Baptist Church and it's white, but I haven't seen another white anywhere in Georgia. Anytime you see Missionary you can say that's a Black church. It's strange. I wasn't conscious of it until somebody called my attention to it. And I been watching it everywhere I go." These days, Wiregrass whites show more denominational diversity. They become Free Will Baptists, members of the Assembly of God as well as the Church of Christ, or join other charismatic ministries. While recognizing gray areas, as pertains to the Wiregrass, the general belief is that African American "faith is expressed through invocation, whereas in white Christianity it is expressed by adoration." This results in not much crossover denominationally, racially speaking, with the exception of the Church of Christ and Jehovah's Witnesses, which reach out to Latino believers as well.

With the arrival of newly emancipated African American migrants, the need to establish a church ensued immediately. Local African American historian Agnes Windsor of Slocomb, Alabama, elaborated: "It was Adeline Adams that said that she desired to have a church and her husband Shade gave the use of the land for the church and cemetery. And it's still out there." So, historically, new churches were no longer founded out of friction but out of spiritual necessity. Vital communities developed, configured around the stability of a community church. Additionally, women frequently were key figures in the establishment of churches. Mary Lou Henderson related that Willowhead Baptist Church evolved from her mother's vision:

> *That church started in our home. It was a vision of my mother. And she started it from a Sunday school. She said that she had a vision of the Lord of a long arm came down and it had a large arm of books. And it told her. She didn't see the man, just saw the arm and heard the voice. It told her to take these books and distribute them among the people. And so my mother rose up (and it was three of us), and she said: 'I'm going to have Sunday school this morning.' And she began to tell the vision that she had, and she sent us around to tell some of the neighbors to come to our house that we are going to have Sunday school. And the Sunday school grew so large until my father decided to have prayer services in the home. And the prayer services grew so large. It was a vacant house right next to our house, and they moved over there in that vacant house. And they tore the petition out and it was a stacked chimney in the center and the Bible rested on that chimney . . . . Afterwards, it was organized as a church on July 14, 1914, the third Sunday.*

The church gained its name from a nearby willow tree with characteristic drooping limbs. Henderson recalled "rallying," selling fish to buy the present lot and finally building the church with the congregation ceremonially taking occupancy while singing "We're Marching to Zion."

At this juncture, I would like to state that many renowned theologians charge African Americans with being overchurched. This charge stems from the relatively larger visibility of churches within African American communities. The tendency is to politicize the proliferation based on their supposed failure to contribute toward a strong social justice movement as relates to the Black Theology Movement. Critics are quick to surmise that fewer churches could function more efficiently to bring about social and political change. Such views signal a gap in understanding of what prompts such a growing magnitude of churches. I insist that the bountiful number of churches reflects the richness of African American folklife. Instead of being excessive, this wider range of churches speaks to the multiplicity of ways to "make church." Individuals and families seek congregations that fulfill their ideal worship experience. As both sodalities and modalities indicate, when embarking upon a spiritual path, it is important to engage in practices suited to the nature of interbeing, which connects the individual and the collective.

Along with belonging, walking in faith is a shared religious principle. Those who profess to be Christian combine many religious interpretations. Within the Wiregrass, church members typically reject strict denominational divisions. Local residents are prone to interject: "She's a Methodist, and I'm a Baptist. I'd rather be known as a child of God." Understanding this very foundation among African Americans in Wiregrass Alabama, Dyen further stipulated: "At this level, each church is seen as a 'child' of God, and so churches are 'brother' and 'sister' to each other, are 'part of the family' and are expected to act toward each other—and each church's members toward those of other churches—as members of a blood-related family would act. Thus, any one person is involved in a network of 'family connections' beginning with his own blood-related nuclear family, then including the extended family . . . and finally, through the church and to other churches, embracing a fairly wide geographic area, in this case the six contiguous counties in southeast Alabama (plus Jackson County, Florida)." Professing a communal spirituality, then, pastoral days are reciprocally supported, engaging an explicitly elastic ecumenicalism.

Nevertheless, each congregation maintains its own set of frames for the keying of its Sabbath church service. Their host religious institutions offer the backdrop for enacting their homegrown principles of spirituality, the most meaningful being that God gave them instructions to take care of one another. In actual practice, many African Americans continue to live their theology through open, affective expression. As writer Ray Funk documented it, "The basic aesthetic is not to entertain but to bring the spirit to the participants and audience." Others may pay lip service to this level of spirituality, but African Americans within the Wiregrass tend to abide by it. Like their northern counterparts, whom folklorist Glenn Hinson positioned as performing a duty, "a holy obligation to follow the Lord's bidding," folks here also sing to grant Him the glory. These close-knit sacred performance communities assume that all within the sound of their voices already are true believers. Therefore, their musical selections and ecumenical church-going stand to dramatize how they practice what they preach and sing.

In general, it was easier to organize a Baptist church than any other denomination, and the democratic tradition of individual church government
lent itself easily to the mindset of newly freed ex-slaves. As expressed in *A
Baptist Manual of Polity and Practice*, "the most prized doctrine of Baptists is 'the autonomy of the local church.'" The interpretations of religious
doctrine proved to be the domain of all involved, not just the preacher. Few
of the laypersons, or home folks, as they are called, are passive participants
when it comes to their church and its teachings. For African Americans, in
particular, the home folks control Sunday school, the weekly prayer meeting, and so forth—everything except Sunday worship on pastoral days.
These roles speak to the absolute conviction of spiritual activists about
what they do.

The worship services in the Wiregrass's African American churches
are patterned and reciprocal. With pastoral days being on alternate Sundays, despite attrition, the doors of many downsized houses of worship
graciously spring open on schedule. The common mindset is to attend precisely because only a few members remain. Even with small memberships,
church leaders manage to attract a minister to hold forth at least monthly.
Since most pastors work fulltime jobs, preaching commonly constitutes
a devout avocation. Besides the ones nearby, these clergymen frequently
commute some distance to pastor as many as three other churches. Another aspect of their religious life reveals these Wiregrass Christians to be
transdenominational. When their own place of worship is not in session,
after Sunday school, churchgoers traditionally visit and support other congregations regardless of denomination. Locals generally profess by stating:
"All of us are on the same road to heaven. The denomination, that doesn't
mean nothing."

Baptists of all persuasions are known for their protracted meetings. Of
these, revivals are the most often delineated. Although not the only denomination to hold revivals, historically the Baptists were notorious for the
fervor of their revivals and camp meetings: "And those songs look like were
so good. You would start to revival, and you hear one of the deacons singing: 'Bye and Bye I'm Going to See the King.' And you'd break out and go to
running because you wanted to get up there to hear that particular fellow
sing that song." Dating back to the Great Awakening, enslaved Africans
were given the day off to join in the services. Baptists and Methodists "endorsed (unevenly and not without wrenching internal debate) the view that
blacks ought to be proselytized, thus spurring the tepid commitment of
owners and overseers to extend the religious franchise." African Americans
then maintained numerous African-based retentions, making Christianity

their own. Yet they appropriated the organizational structure and appara-
tus of mainstream Baptist denominations, advancing them according to
their own ethos.

Quitman pharmacist and preacher Terrell Hollis provided a testimony
that conveys the typical ministerial bent. When I met Reverend Hollis, he
was a former drugstore owner and is presently employed by the State of
Georgia as a pharmacist in charge of substance abuse programs in six counties, while the pastor of two churches. Hollis finds ministry to be therapeu-
tic: "I get a kind of satisfaction that I can't get nowhere else. It uplifts me. I
feel good. I have revelations from the Lord that you just don't get without
being attune and working in His vineyard." Besides Bethany Missionary
Baptist Church in Quitman, home of the local Twentieth of May festivities, he pastors another church in Moultrie, Georgia, forty miles away. As
a case in point, when the reverend undertook these pastoral duties, the
church only had six members and averaged twenty dollars in revenue. He
is proud that three years later the church grew to fifty members, committed to tithing. Now, this church's membership and finances are the envy of
other small churches.

In the South, after religious revivals, union meetings are the most ubiquitous of Baptist calendrical events. Baptist union meetings are when church
members within an assigned district convene at one site. These meetings
traditionally occur on Fifth Sundays. In Slocomb, Alabama, Countryline
Missionary Baptist Church was named for a church left behind when its
members migrated there, founding this small rural town. Lay historian Agnes Windsor explained that her home church is fortunate to be among the
few African American Wiregrass churches to meet weekly. Well, it meets
almost weekly. She elucidated that pastoral days were "set for the third Sundays in each month. But now we have it every Sunday, except the Fifth. [On
the Fifth], we just have Sunday school and we go to what you call a union,
a district union." In this way, long established Fifth Sunday rituals remain
sacrosanct.

Constituting rites of exchange, each network's primary underlying principle is to generate revenue. Such calendrical activities ensure the survival
of an entire group of modalities. Their survival, as sites of memory, depends
on the perpetuation of a perceived collective idea, connecting the past and
the present. Surprisingly, little has changed for a core of African American
Baptists. For them, the repetition of events complies with having a cyclical orientation. Their cultural performances constitute the "everyday" for
African Americans who have ritualized social life into a repetitious cycle
through an adherence to phenomena such as union meetings. Accordingly,

ritual is a "strategic form of cultural practice." Past scholars predicted a reduction in ritual density in contemporary life. Yet, ritual is the only way to describe the repetitive and stylized nature of predictable cultural performances that occur with cyclical regularity throughout Wiregrass Country. As ethnomusicologist Charles Keil defined it, in passing, to suit secular musical forms, ritual engages "processes that insure the opportunity for participation and catharsis to each member of the community." As part of the African American Christian calendar, members may easily enumerate a schedule of forty distinct ritual events. For example, most maintain Pastor's Anniversary, Church Anniversary, Men's Day, Women's Day, Youth Day, Choir's Anniversary, and Homecoming Sunday.

Baptist polity is also predicated on national and state conventions, local associations, and district unions. Here, I document Baptist district union meetings within this tri-state region. These meetings traditionally occur on the Fifth Sunday, as a legacy from the white Baptist associations. The following is how Georgian folklorist Mariella Hartsfield delineated them: "A typical Baptist church might hold, in addition to the regular Sunday service(s), a weekly prayer meeting (usually Wednesday), revivals (protracted meetings) twice a year, class parties, and fifth-Sunday meetings (a joint meeting of several churches on the fifth Sunday of a month, lasting all day and including 'eating on the grounds' and all-day preaching)." The earliest Baptist associations were regional organizations. Of course, over time and space, African Americans adapted and continue to maintain many of these conventions. Yet, they enjoy their own variation.

As a means of regulating their routine social interaction, African Americans adhere to only select structural conventions. For instance, dinner on the ground is a quintessential southern tradition. In their printed bulletins, African Americans may not always reference the midday meal by using this vernacular term. Speaking specifically to church-related activities, Dyen observed: "It is the duty of the women members of the host church or host district to 'bring boxes of dinner'—enough to feed, collectively, all the people who come (it is expected, of course, that the event will draw a number of people from other congregations who will come to show support for the host church). It is also these women's job to serve the food, and to make sure that everyone is 'enjoyin' their dinner' (as they would in their own smaller families)." A great deal depends on accommodations. With fellowship halls and air conditioning, few African Americans now venture out, literally, to picnic outdoors on the grounds. The tendency is for men to venture out to mill around in the shade, conversing in groups.

Many rural Baptist churches exist as monuments to the past. Seldom cathedral, their physical structures conform to more of a vernacular architectural plan. Most are frame or concrete and fit a box design with two doorways on either side of the pulpit, which is centered in front of a choir loft. Today, these side doorways usually lead to restrooms and/or a fellowship hall. Many originated as brush arbors outdoors, known as invisible churches, sites where African Americans congregated to worship with only branches overhead for shade. Home of the longleaf pine, the interior designs of many churches support luscious knotty pine beams, altar railings, and walls. Depending on their membership size or network strength, gratefully, air conditioning is a recent addition. Hand fans remain prevalent, too, as the service heats up. In some, the pews, pulpit, and preacher's chairs, being roughly hand hewn, showcase exquisite carpentry work by artisans. Most sanctuaries are decorous, with ornate ceiling fans and plush cushioned pews with matching carpeting in bright royal blues, splendid maroons, or radiant red. From the looks of their exteriors, few passersby would guess the quaint opulence inside.

As pertains to African American churches, in general, many scholars affix a compensatory role for officials in various church leadership positions. For example, as relates to an urban Chicago church, in *Feeling the Spirit*, anthropologist Frances Kostarelos wrote: "Church members are given an opportunity to work on committees and boards and in offices and thereby gain respectability and status as they fulfill their spiritual aspiration to serve God." Given this interpretation, many Wiregrass church officials would really be overcompensating. They fulfill countless duties in a range of sacred performance communities. If seeking status were the mere aim, then one might ask: Why the motivation to duplicate a multiplicity of roles entailing so much of their time, energy, and money? Instead, I surmise that individuals aspire for leadership roles to befit their spiritual identity. They accept that life has a spiritual purpose in all that they strive to do. Often, it is the same people fulfilling these roles due to their explicit sense of duty, where others may falter.

Historian Gregory Wills accurately declared the function of associations: "Baptist tradition permitted local churches to act alone but in the interest of unity they sought the endorsement of other churches." Activities for these church-related organizations generally commence on Fridays and last for three days. Conventions denote a statewide or national meeting when all associations send delegates to discuss issues pertinent to the entire membership. Conventions, associations, and union meetings mirror regular worship services but also include structural frames uniquely their own. Each of these organizational endeavors demands the presence of not only ministers but also church choir members and ushers. Because congregational bodies blend, the attendance by unfettered members is more voluntary. To decide to accept a leadership role is a real time-consuming, arduous commitment.

Louise Sapp, a Baptist church leader, confirms by reporting the local arrangements that her home community organizes around: "What they did up there. They had four churches that united together. Our church had fourth Sunday service. Saco had first Sunday service; New Hope was third Sunday Service; and Blooming Light was second Sunday service. And then, when the union meets, all those churches belonged to the union meeting. Every Fifth Sunday they would go to the union meeting. And in October the second weekend in October starting Thursday coming up to the second Sunday was the Home Mission Association meeting. And all those churches that were combined in the union would go to that. That Sunday they would go to the association. And that was a big day." She is actively involved in them all, including the singing conventions. Unlike district union meetings, which are universally held on Fifth Sundays without customarily necessitating any church closings, associations require church bodies to shut down to worship as one. Usually occurring in October, now, some churches balk when it affects their regular pastoral day and, possibly, revenue.

The Baptists organizations in each state and district in Wiregrass Country are relatively autonomous. Although many churches have "cut back," they manage to meet on Fifth Sundays, if not the entire weekend. Many churches in southeastern Alabama are no longer affiliated with these larger Baptist infrastructures. In the Florida Panhandle, I found that much of these union activities are centered in Marianna and Crestview. In southwestern Georgia, church modalities adhere the most to old Baptist traditions. For instance, in Wiregrass Georgia I regularly interacted with at least four rural districts: the South Georgia Local Church Union out of Grady County, the Blue Springs Missionary Baptist Union near Albany, the Western Division of the South Georgia Baptist Association in Cook and Lanier Counties, and the Third District Union Meeting out of Bainbridge. Baptist district union meetings still commence on Friday nights. These musical services are stirring and well structured, rotating church choirs in a pattern established long ago. There is a pride of place evident in the choirs, whether wearing colorful robes or attired in black and white. The ushers, too, may simply wear crisp white tops and black bottoms, or they dress uniformly in other colors ranging from purple and white to red and white. Seldom do they wear actual church usher uniforms.

What most beguiles me about Wiregrass singing is that, while frequently performed in church settings, in essence, these gatherings are recreational. Being the only institutions under their control, African American churches historically served multiple functions, including secular ones. Historian Arnold Taylor suggested: "In the social sense, the church also provided respite from the monotony and drabness of everyday life." An understanding of Wiregrass religious folklife should go a long way toward explaining why these home folks sing with such gusto and diligence. The sacred songs that they sing are not mere relics but testimonies to God. Adherents relish any opportunity to engage the Gospel Truth. By doing so, they formulate a divine partnership with God.

The first district union meeting that I attended was the South Georgia Local Church Union, hosted by a Primitive Baptist church in Beachton, Georgia. Primitive and Missionary Baptist churches sometimes coexist within the same associations. Knowing the Primitive Baptist denomination's white stoic, hard-shell history, it was a revelation that the most bluesy encounter occurred in this context. The pianist played in a barrelhouse blues manner with a hard-pounding style as a lead guitarist sat unobtrusively on the side. The president, Elder Jimmy Simmons, dispensed with offertory matters soon after the opening frame "to save time and to have a good time." The choir of the host church, Oak Grove Primitive Baptist, then opened the gospel-singing portion of the evening's ritual activities. I noticed that it performed the same song at the next week's Sunday School Convention at St. Luke Primitive Baptist Church in Reno. Nine churches make up the district, and the "A" and "B" rule was in effect. However, their second number demonstrated some jitters, getting off to a false start. Before a standing- room-only crowd that had waited three months to convene and a church body that had waited more than two years to be in charge, musical mishaps add to the momentum. Sacred listening entails bringing your heart, soul, and compassion, which means more than any melodious mishap.

Baptists, essentially, are independent polities that form tacit agreements to associate with one another. In rural sectors, there often are no addresses or public phone directories as such. For me, to find these churches requires the best of verbal directions and sometimes ingenuity. It was by virtue of being taught by the folklorist whom I call my dean, Roland Freeman, to drive figure eights along unpaved roads in rural communities that I located Reno and Elsie Smiley, with her yard full of artistically constructed airplane whirligigs. For comparison, after attending her school convention and union meeting, I gravitated next to Alabama. While in Opp, I also attended a family reunion picnic, and a minister explained that local Baptist churches tend not to have district meetings anymore. For sure, it took awhile to find an active union meeting until I encountered a member of the Rural District in Ashford, Alabama, which abuts the Georgia state line. Sheryl Melton of Gordon, Alabama, reported: "I participate in the Rural District Association. Fourteen different churches get together. I'm the advisor over the youth for the junior hour. At Fifth Sunday meeting, we go to the churches out of the fourteen churches. Time allows us to rotate and so we associate together. We combine the program. Most of the people that got positions in the Rural District come from our church, Antioch. They have a district choir." This association along with St. Mary, in the same vicinity, introduced me to some illustrious and assertive Christian women, a few of whom I discuss in chapter 7.

Melton was the first to relate to me the significance of the Old One Hundred. Anthropologist Walter Pitts clarified that "Although each new generation of Afro-Baptists creates its new sacred songs, the older songs are not so easily forgotten." Furthermore, one of his key informants, Sister Odessa, explained: "They will live on. There'll always be somebody to come along and keep them alive." They live on now by virtue of being both gospelized and syncretized like the spirituals and European-based hymns into the gospel blues. At Baptist union meetings, Old One Hundred hymns ring out grandly and with great enthusiasm, often taking the place of the fairly sedate lining hymns. Sung with full percussive effect and accompanied by the stomping of feet to syncopated rhythm, they resonate:

You better run on
You got a race to run
All God's children got a race to run.

(incorporating a stanza of "Amazing Grace"). As here, a common feature of such hymns is their hybridity, the ready pairing of different lyrics from disparate songs. They deem the Old One Hundred, like the spirituals before them, to be religiously sound because biblically based.

The repetition is hypnotic but the rhythmic pace becomes intoxicating as the multitudes find a blues-inflected fit for each voice, released "in synchrony while out of phase." As a result, the subsequent prayers gain in antiphonic impulse. The expected "amens," "wells," and "yeahs" flow en masse, as a great act of solidarity. Each sacred performance community established long ago what tonality would shape its sessions. In one sense, the choices may be infinite, although the core song selections remain the same: common meter, Old One Hundred, standard hymns, and the downhome gospel blues. To pace their singing, they also intersperse select prayers and scriptural readings. For them, the musical selections connect with the people's interior.

For example, Blue Springs Missionary Baptist Union Meeting is one that excels at congregational moaning. During a typical Devotion, a deacon arouses Sunday's meeting with a spirited prayer and this introduction:

We gonna sing that old common meter.
I feel something.
I believe you feel something.
I feel like a son of God

The accompanying moaning is immediate and primordial. Despite it being stereotyped as fueling emotionalism, moaning does not escalate into shouting the house. Instead, antiphony reigns, seldom taking the form of spontaneous combustion. From the members' perspective, the Holy Spirit moves to "outwardly express an inward feeling." Collective moaning occurs when the fellowship gains a certain energy and feelings deepen. Ethnomusicologist Willie Collins positioned such moaning in a "hot" context: "I reckon they moaned to see if they could get comfort or something; I think they [sic] moaned so that they could receive the gift of God's power; sometimes you can feel good through moaning and that have to be the power of God." One of its functions is to "unite congregants with the fire of the Holy Spirit." They act as supplicants sending a joint invocation. After one effusive display, the presiding officer exhorted to great acclaim: "All of us feel a little better! You've got to feel a little better!"

Moaning also sets up a special relationship between the song and worshippers. Collins constructed the moan-and-prayer as constituting a communicative event, "a ritual occasion where specific entrances of parts interplay to create a dense counterpoint of moans, verbal phrases, responsive musical phrases, underpinning a prayer which might move from speech, to intonational chant, to occasional chant levels." In the text accompanying the audio tapes from her *Wade in the Water* National Public Radio series, a cappella style singer, folklorist, and scholar Bernice Johnson Reagon intoned: "The song leader 'raises the song,' but if it is to go anywhere the opening lines has to be joined and expanded by the group." The moaning operates in this capacity, being enlarged through the vocal consent of all. Unlike merely singing spiritedly, moaning can prolong rejoicing. Pitts likened the Afro-Baptist ritual process to a ship that "also transports the worshipper along a continuum of spiritual uplifting from the moment Devotion begins until the closing benedictory prayer." Seldom do congregants enter transfixed. Some Fifth Sunday union meetings, however, quickly escalate to a zealous pitch, chiefly privileging righteous moaning, not the shout.

The Blue Springs Missionary Baptist Union incorporates ten rural churches from the surrounding Albany, Georgia, area. To transcend the everyday, moaning is the code used for progression into a higher gear. The spontaneous transition into moaning, en masse, denotes an optimal experience. As also positioned by Reagon and applicable to this attendant moaning, "Our singing tradition announces the presence of our community. It is a way in which we nurture and heal ourselves. It is an offering to the celebration of life and the lifting of the spirit." The vocal response derives from the sheer profusion of congregants who augment the usual seating capacity on Fifth Sundays. To close out the first frame that entails the moaning, then the choir must virtually bellow its lyrics to squelch any residual murmurings. In this way, it becomes apparent the extent to which "moans and groans were the balms to repressed spirits that soothed and ensured longevity and survival." For this sacred performance community, union meetings are fetes, denoting their quest for an abundant and holy spiritual life.

Within such a context, chanting can also spill over into every ritual act, including the various financial offerings. Baptists are typecast for their multiple offertory rites to raise funds for the Missionary Department and to defray the costs of the host church as well as to fund the association. For instance, the Blue Springs Missionary Baptist Union Meeting, over the course of the three-day weekend, appealed for seven monetary collections, including two Freewill ones on Saturday along with the usual complement of public offerings. Consequently, individuals tend to dole out monetary gifts piecemeal, often a dollar at a time. Anticipating the numerous offertories and with limited personal finance, it is seldom that a single offering produces more than a couple hundred dollars. Attendance is fluid as well. These Christian realists recognize that a little bit does, indeed, go a mighty long way. Needless to say, dividends incrementally add up. In this manner, modalities showcase their sense of reciprocity, the price of belonging to a collective economy and demonstrating gratitude for countless blessings.

After the Devotion, the welcome constitutes another ritual act, the rite of hospitality. The acknowledgement of visitors and announcements from the floor allow for the greatest level of participation. Visitors and members alike are greeted with overtures such as: "Glad to have each and every one of you. Whenever our doors are open feel free any time you see fit to come and share." For those sessions, which privilege musical flow, sometimes the welcome more specifically addresses the occasion: "We are glad that you are here where we can share in learning more about our Lord through song. This musical service is planned for participation and enjoyment for you as we praise God from whom all blessings flow. 'Welcome' seems such a small word to express the big feelings we have tonight for your being here—not just tonight, but for any other time you desire to come." On the other end of the eloquence scale, it is more de rigueur to simply declare: "Welcome, welcome, welcome!"

Additionally, multiple sermonic texts infuse these Fifth Sunday weekends. By design, unlike the singing conventions, Baptist union meetings are very logocentric. Although upward of a dozen churches typically belong to any district, most ministers pastor several churches. This proclivity slightly diminishes the number of possible ministers present. Still, there is a large contingency of them. In southwestern Georgia districts, on Sundays different ministers preach during the morning and afternoon sessions. In keeping with traditional structure, a choir sings a musical interlude prior to the preaching. As an epilogue to his sermon, the preacher usually incorporates a song from within his repertoire. Commonly, it is a spiritual such as "Steal Away," which (when sung with vibrato) can lead to near pandemonium. These ministers know the aesthetics of their audience, seldom having to request an "amen." As their aesthetic community is very participatory, often from the start, they allocate a surge of singsong responses that flood the air with a continuous wave of ecstatic utterances. These Fifth Sunday union meetings provide the best indicator of the festive mood these calendrical events can evoke. Today, home folks have other leisurely options. Yet many still elect to attend the best cultural performance in town. Fifth Sunday rituals occur in a multiplicity of sacred and secular spaces.

Initially, in the Florida Panhandle I met with much frustration trying to find the locus of the Baptist union meetings, since AME churches tend to predominate. In November 1997, I finally experienced a breakthrough. I happened upon a program announcing an annual banquet hosted by the Brotherhood of the Second West Missionary Baptist Church. Luckily, the announcement contained a calendar of November events including its "Fifth Sunday Congress." As it turns outs, the Second West Florida Association possesses a long, venerable history. It was formed in 1874 and is headquartered in Marianna. Originally, it only included churches in Jackson and Gadsden Counties. Reverend Richard Ellis of Greenwood served as its first moderator. It then extended its territory as churches developed in adjacent counties.

The Jackson County Association building is immense. Probably four regular box-style African American churches could fit within it. All of the pews are filled to capacity by an alert, congenial body of worshippers actually covering at least two counties, from Marianna to Bonifay. It also has

A women's praise team ministers music to usher a Fifth Sunday congregation into the presence of God

the distinction of being the largest association in western Florida, with an affiliation of thirty-six churches. The event's structure chiefly follows most church bulletins, beginning promptly after Sunday school. Unlike other unions, its larger functioning requires a moderator, a minister appointed in an executive role. Since being introduced to this body, it has changed moderators three times. The present moderator is Reverend Doctor H. G. McCollough of Bascom, Florida. Reverend William Harvey, one of the past moderators, is now vice moderator. Such leadership changes are relatively unprecedented within sacred performance communities, as I will further analyze later. Still, a different church serves as the parent body for each Fifth Sunday meeting, which begins on the Saturday before with an array of sessions. Such a physical structure is being erected in Crestview, Florida, as well.

Jackson County union meetings are not without innovation. The structure allows for a devotional period led by the usual full complement of men and a praise team comprising five women. The collective of finely arrayed women are attired in primary colors. Some women wear braids, otherwise nary a one is without an ornately trimmed hat. Especially in the more urban churches, praise teams are usurping the role of the traditional devotional period. Therefore, it is interesting that in Wiregrass Country the transition is not complete, relying on both. It comes as no surprise that all the ministers and deacons are male. Only afterward does a long line of well-wishing clergy, shaking hands and embracing one another, indicate the true number in attendance. However, only the host preacher wears full clerical garb.

On Fifth Sundays, local churches commonly brim over with congregants, representing home churches with names like St. Mary, Pleasant Grove, New Mt. Olive, New Provisor, Shiloh, Bright Morning Star, Mt. Moriah, Blue Spring, St. Paul, and Antioch. Their names speak to biblical texts, saints, the natural environment, and the capitals of ancient kingdoms. The church names, no doubt, were chosen with care and hold specific meanings. Most are almost archetypal because similar names are so widespread. Some in the North gained their church's name as part of a migration wave, causing new emigrant communities to transfer the names of the churches left behind. I cannot speak to what degree union meetings remain intact there. I know Baptist conventions and associations remain of significance, but I do not see how district unions survived, especially since Fifth Sundays are not usually set aside. This phenomenon tends to be overlooked in scholarship by folklorists, anthropologists, and sociologists alike.

On Saturday morning, the emphasis is totally on the Youth Department, which conducts most of the activities, including youth volunteers conducting the Devotion as well as featuring a youth choir and later a showcase of its "Children on Parade." After lunch, the adults form focus groups called "Ministries at Work," highlighting every conceivable church support unit: Junior Women, Senior Women, Brotherhood, Ushers, and Ministers. As if at their home church, the host furnishes the uniformed ushers, the choir and its selections, along with the morning's sermon. Unlike most of the others, the parent body is not responsible for serving dinner. Instead, everyone disperses, some to local restaurants.

Union meeting Sundays glorify diversity, yet the term *union* is quite apropos. Union meetings are like a regular church service but also are organic, with a life of their own. Sacred performance communities have a bond that traverses the ages. These sessions originated within the southern Baptist tradition. On Fifth Sundays, local residents flock to be part of the mass crowd, achieving spiritual release. Given my background, it is awe inspiring to witness small children participating fully, standing alone and vociferously singing. Not only are the children given intermittent duties to perform, they are an actively engaged part of each energetic performance community. Certain districts only host Saturday and Sunday sessions, as occurs in Ashford, Alabama. The emphasis quite often is to magnify the youth, and there are innumerable ways to do so. In Crestview, Florida, due to the sheer number of young people, the Saturday session occurs at a separate venue than the adults. In the Southwest Georgia District Union, the tendency is to allocate the Friday night session as the time for the Young People Program, highlighting a song, reading, or solo performed by representatives from each participating church. They imprint their youth to take their place as orators, song leaders, ministers, deacons, and deaconesses.

Far from being fundamentalists, many African Americans whom I interviewed possess a dialectical understanding. For instance, these Christians emote a kind of tolerance, which entitles young people to investigate the secular world without rancor. For example, Deacon Richard Lawyer Jr. expressed:

> *I learned that you have to grow in this thing. You veer away from the church. At certain ages you get wild. I veered away for I imagine ten or fifteen years before I really went to work; and since I've been in it working, I've been working. And I enjoy working. I didn't know what a good time was until I began working. It is better than it is when you're out in the world. A lot of people in the street they forget where their help comes from; and I also did the same thing. That's why I don't have too much problem with the children now days. They have to do certain things, sometimes. They have to grow through their stages. Sometimes, we want children to grow up like we are today, and we done just about burned out. I like for all of us to have a little break on the children because they only do what we've did in our lives. They have to grow through that stage just like I did. I give them a chance to grow to have fun, too. You can't just stop jookin.' You have to go through that stage. That's what I had to learn the hard way.*

Being reality-based, they moralize in ways seemingly at odds with neo-conservative Christians. They demonstrate a greater understanding, refusing to be hypocritical. By so doing, these Wiregrass African Americans internalize "the word" in ways not often articulated within metaphysical dualistic ways of thinking.

In keeping with tradition, Baptists rely on union meetings to indoctrinate their youth and to supplement their public school education. These youth gain an expressive forum to fit them not only for a Christian life, but, once fully grown, to achieve in the real world. Unabashedly, the Third District Union meeting at Pine Hill Missionary Baptist Church in Bainbridge, Georgia, proclaimed this youth hour theme: "Regaining the Strength of Our Ancestors." The intention clearly is as Wendy Haight asserted, "to promote the development of resiliency in African American children." Resilience and fortitude are needed to move forward in the real world. In this way, spiritual activism is not about protesting; it is about self-empowerment and commitment to a higher vision.

To illustrate further, in Ashford, Alabama, as the director of the Youth Department, Sheryl Melton moderates each performance. After the perfunctory devotional service, starting with the host church, the director interjects: "Do we have any youth that would like to take part at this present time?" After each recitation, they receive glowing applause and approval.

The objective is to "pick 'em up," add voices to fill in any perceived gaps in the performance, and offer them praise and encouragement. The afternoon progresses in this way as a few youth, representing each home church, come forth. Singing a cappella is terrifying enough for adults. The tentative voices of children develop aplomb, learning to worry the lines and expand syllables with melisma. Young lead singers practice the call-and-response trope, singing in parts. Popular gospel songs such as "Silver and Gold," hailing from contemporary urban gospel, become constants. I cannot begin to count how many times I have heard youth choirs and ensembles sing "Shake the Devil Off," a song popularized by gospel singer Dorothy Norwood. Each performance is met with the obligatory accompaniment of applause and earnest "amens."

The Youth Hour is a bit of a misnomer, as their segment seldom lasts the entire allotted time period. Although printed bulletins situate the ideal proceeding, the reality allows for much improvisation. To compensate, adults may segue their way into performances, utilizing a common statement: "I'm a youth in the sight of God because I'm certainly still growing in His grace." Saturdays at 1:00 p.m. is not always an optimal time to convene these sessions. With this eventuality, "Wherever two or three comes together" is the pronouncement in effect. So, youth programs are not well attended. Most participant churches send only a few delegates to represent them. As a matter of convenience, Alabama districts may eschew joining associations. Fifth Sundays never lack for sacred activities. Yet, on this day and at this hour, a multiplicity of union meetings is unfolding across the Wiregrass. By enculturating their youth, these modalities—and by extension their aesthetics—are not destined to die out soon. Frequently, tradition bearers from a core family predominate: Sheryl Melton shepherds the youth; her husband, Deacon J. J. Melton, represents the laymen; and Reverend E. Melton speaks for the ministers.

Moreover, the time frame is never a real factor. No one is a slave to the clock, and being there is a choice freely made. In Gordon, when the host preacher finds himself nearly one hour ahead of the ideal programmed schedule, he acknowledges this factor: "Sometimes we fly when we get too far ahead." Instead, he implicitly begins to stall by concentrating on a recurrent motif: how to get one's prayer answered, taking time to demonstrate points drawing on both sacred and secular experiences. The dean in charge of the service, Reverend J. D. Flowers, provides an extemporaneous sermonette. In keeping with a cyclical orientation, his spontaneous act is designed to allow more ministers to arrive for the appointed 3:30 segment. The next segment is more male-centered, including a full-fledged devotional service led by deacons—relying on perennial meter hymns such as "A Charge to Keep I Have" and a spirited prayer—with a rousing sermon to follow. This sermon will be the first of several to be heard. Therefore, although the Rural District in southeastern Alabama does not feature a Friday night songfest, it engages much spoken word. The two tend to go hand in hand at union meetings.

The Progressive Baptist District Association of West Florida holds what it calls a Quarterly Congress, although its session always occurs in conjunction with Fifth Sundays, and these can occur back to back, as sometimes happens during a leap year. Its Friday session features the host church choir supplying all selections. There is no choir rotation. With a youthful choir director playing keyboard along with one of the few guitarists, Ralph Rice, I anticipate innovation. The fact that this district attracts members from nearby military bases clearly influenced its urban contemporary repertoire and introduced some distinct variants. The choir director acts as a praise team leader, an innovation that is replacing the traditional devotional service. More or less, the praise team is a music band to invigorate worshippers more expansively than the traditional Devotion:

> CHOIR DIRECTOR: *Come on and give God another handclap of praise.*
> *Congregation applauds.*
> CHOIR DIRECTOR: *Look at your neighbor and say, "Neighbor."*
> CONGREGATION: *Neighbor.*
> CHOIR DIRECTOR: *Come on let's praise God.*
> CONGREGATION: *Come on let's praise God.*
> CHOIR DIRECTOR: *Come on. Look at somebody else and say, "Neighbor."*
> CONGREGATION: *Neighbor.*
> CHOIR DIRECTOR: *Come on everybody.*
> CONGREGATION: *Come on everybody.*
> CHOIR DIRECTOR: *Let's praise God.*
> CONGREGATION: *Let's praise God.*
> CHOIR SELECTION: *"Come on Everybody, Let's Praise God"*

Moreover, this union meeting also comfortably incorporates both the traditional Devotion and the praise team. Within this ritual context, however, urban contemporary gospel dominates. The choir loft is overflowing with a transgenerational mass choir, literally including all ages from small children to older adults. While other union meetings cleave to and gospelize the traditional Old One Hundred, no tension exists here regarding recent popular compositions. Adding another twist, there is no Fifth Sunday service.

Due to a well-traveled military presence, the Progressive Baptist District Association's quarterly musical is quite dynamic

Crestview area churches are among the few Wiregrass districts where Sunday worship commonly occurs weekly.

Wiregrass union meetings assist in characterizing the African American sacred music experience. To build and to fortify interdependent communities, each reciprocal support network relies on sacred singing and listening, reflective of their values and spiritual reality. Each Baptist modality is "not just a conservator of evolutionary cultural behavior, but a generator of new images, new ideas, and new practices." It bestows new meaning to a spiritual like "There's a Meeting Here Tonight." Its social commentary is obvious. When enslaved and denied the right to assemble, the creators of this song subversively encoded their nocturnal activities that granted them unity, wholeness, and serenity. The "invisible" churches of this era continue to influence present-day spiritual activism. Baptist union meetings constitute a current means by which African Americans overtly order their spiritual lives, train up their youth, and collectively support a host of small home churches. The temporality of Fifth Sundays and spatiality offered via worshipful sites affirms a real God Time.

CHAPTER 4

"On the Way to Glory"

The Shape-Note Tradition

While training to become a folklorist, I heard mention of Sacred Harp music. But like certain grown-up words overheard by a young child, I possessed no reference point. With its European origin, I could not fathom this musical form's religious appeal or how African Americans engaged in its aesthetic value. Simply put, nothing I read prepared me for the day I finally heard it performed live by the Wiregrass Sacred Harp Singers of Ozark, Alabama. Wiregrass Alabama is the last stronghold of four-shape music sung by African Americans. In 1991, I agreed to transport bluesman Neal Pattman from Athens, Georgia, to perform at a festival in Columbus, Georgia, where the singers also performed. Having their own Sunday morning television show in Dothan, the Wiregrass Sacred Harp Singers enjoyed a wide, local following. They gained national recognition when the group performed in 1970 at the Smithsonian Folklife Festival and later at the Newport Jazz Festival. They have since traveled extensively, contributing to a revival movement among whites in places like Chicago and Tallahassee. White Sacred Harp singer Steven Sabol validates that such exposure usually resulted in "creating a network of friendly and accepting people of varied religious, educational, professional, and musical backgrounds who are united by a common love for this musical genre."

Two years later, I finally traveled into the heart of Wiregrass Alabama to bear witness to this long-lived, but remotely known, African American tradition in its natural context. I attended the Fifty-Eighth Annual Memorial Singing Honoring Judge Jackson, which customarily occurs the third Sunday in April. It so happened that a New York–based production company attended to document this rarified African American tradition as well. Their recording sessions resulted in the release of *The Colored Sacred Harp: Wiregrass Sacred Harp Singers*. I could not have been introduced to this tradition's singing conventions under more dynamic circumstances. That

The Wiregrass Sacred Harp Singers gather for a group photo at a Judge Jackson Memorial Sing, April 1993

Sunday morning, outside Union Grove Baptist Church, I intermingled with a coterie of folklorists from Alabama, Mississippi, and Georgia. Unlike me, most had direct roots connecting them with this music. Chiquita Willis gathered data for a shape-note directory for the University of Mississippi Folklife Program. Cheryl Johnson, a young freelance folklore consultant from Atlanta, had already conducted research historicizing this phenomenon and accompanied me. Joey Brackner still directs the Alabama State Council on the Arts, and in his position he is indispensable to the preservation and exhibition of this landmark tradition. We milled about as the photographer Lauren Piperno set up an iconic group photo of the Wiregrass Sacred Harp Singers for the album cover. We extraneous public folklorists prolonged the start while the mainly African American assemblage patiently waited inside.

By all appearances, I belonged there with the throng of African American singers and supporters. However, I felt like an interloper, since I had never attended a singing convention before. By then contracted to write *Wiregrass Country*, it was my first full-fledged site visit as a folklorist new to the region. In keeping with their professionalism, the crew from New World Records spent much of the previous day prerecording these singers, many of who were physically frail or infirm. I overheard them say that the recording session had been a rigorous and challenging one. The singers committed to recording all seventy-seven songs in *The Colored Sacred Harp*, a tunebook of original songs by African American composers, which was something they had never done before. As a consequence, some openly expressed being a bit sluggish and fatigued. The reason they gathered to sing this day was because of their patriarch, Judge Jackson, who is responsible for the publication of *The Colored Sacred Harp*. It first appeared in 1934 at the height of African American shape-note singing activity in southeastern Alabama. The achievement extended to the number of African American composers, their ability to overcome internal strife, and to do so full of faith. I felt privileged later to interview the two recent patriarchs, Japheth Jackson and Dewey Williams, in their respective homes.

Much has been written about these singers and Sacred Harp. I intend here to update some of the latest intricacies related to shape-note singing, filling in some gaps. Among African Americans, the Sacred Harp tradition experienced its heyday long ago. Its sheer survival is extraordinary. People continue to assemble, as if by rote. As Steven Sabol presented it, "While 'harp' is an old word for a hymnal containing music, in a broader sense, the 'sacred harp' is the human voice or ensemble of voices." The questions for me were: Why did the first generation of African Americans out of slavery still commit to this style of music, and what does their continuous commitment ultimately signify in relation to its future among African Americans?

In the popular culture, without attention to it musical diversity, African American sacred music traditions are often represented stereotypically as hyperemotional. No doubt, Sacred Harp singing is perhaps one of the more obscure genres of sacred music surviving among African Americans today. Two systems of shape-notes coexist in Wiregrass Country. First, Sacred Harp, the four-note fa-sol-la system, can be traced back to Elizabethan England, with African Americans in the Wiregrass tracing their participation to the mid-nineteenth century. Second, the seven-note system known as dorayme evolved from the introduction of a new variant and the publication of William Walker's *Christian Harmony*, outlining the rudiments of the do-re-mi-fa-so-la-ti scale. As the name *shape-note* suggests, different shaped note-heads are assigned to musical notes. Each note in the fa-sol-la song tradition is a different shape: fa is a triangle, sol is a circle, la is a square, and mi is a diamond. Dorayme added three geometrical shapes—a pyramid-shaped triangle, a half-circle, and a cone—to add do, re, and ti. Folklorist Lynwood Montell further explained: "Shape-notes are used to teach a system in which the pitch of each note corresponds to its shape, independent of lines and spaces on the musical staff." The music is sung in four-part harmony: treble (melody), alto, tenor (soprano), and bass. Both men and women sing tenor and treble, but men often sing treble in a high falsetto voice. A white East Texas singer, Judge Ross, suggested: "For example, these black singers always sang at a much higher pitch than the whites would ever attempt. It seemed to me that the black keyer tried to pitch the song just a tad higher than the best treble singer in attendance could reach. When he knew that treble singer would have to strain to reach the highest note in the song, then it would be keyed just right! Admittedly, the songs were keyed out of my range about ninety percent of time." Scholars trace falsetto, too, as another African retention appealing to African Americans. It is when a male singer vocalizes in a range above his normal voice.

The southern Sacred Harp has a most interesting conception. Although the practice originated in Elizabethan England, Sacred Harp did not accompany the nation's early pioneers to the South. Instead, in the early 1700s the tradition first arose in New England and branched out as an instructional means of teaching the poorly educated how to sing religious music harmoniously. Sung a cappella, this folk music thrived throughout rural America. Its entry into the African American lexicon of songs and continued importance represents an intriguing conundrum. Due to the role polyrhythm customarily plays within African American music, it is noteworthy that this relatively staid form gained sway. As an undercurrent, however, African-based rhythms still manage to punctuate the melody of these singers. Potentially, as described by white Sacred Harp singer Steven Sabol, it is the appeal of the "'dispersed harmony' which, while creating some dissonance, produces a beautiful perception of multiple simultaneous melodies." Therefore, this European-derived notation system syncretizes well with an African-based preference for antiphony, call-and-response.

Cross-culturally, four-note Sacred Harp singing is now a relatively unique cultural product. While singing dorayme constitutes a mainstay throughout the South, including Texas, Sacred Harp singing survives significantly in the Wiregrass from the Cooper edition, and for African Americans, chiefly among these singers. *Wiregrass Country* contains more in-depth details about the various songbooks. It further explains, "The Cooper revision of the Sacred Harp continues to be the primary book for African American and white Sacred Harp singers in southeast Alabama." As relates to another stronghold for shape-note singing in Kentucky, Montell wrote: "The extent to which the four-note system was utilized in south central Kentucky will never be known." Some might adjudge its sound to be unpleasant, but it is not intended to sound polished. Although most note a difference in performance, the structure of African American singing conventions do not deviate far from their white counterparts: "A number is usually called (most singers will remember each song by the number rather than its name). Someone sitting near the front of the sing will usually carry a pitch pipe to set the first note of the lead line, the third line from the top in four-part harmony, if you have not the notion to set it yourself." Ultimately, the pitch is negotiable. Rather than seeking perfect pitch, the pitcher's role is to locate a comfortable range that will not strain voices, especially those singing treble. At many sings, if in attendance Japheth Jackson functions as the tuner, or keyer, a position that usually goes to the one with the most familiarity with the music and greatest confidence. At conventions, many officers defer to him, stating: "The better the keyer, the more music we make." Having suffered several strokes, limiting his mobility, Jackson still keys tunes vigorously although wheelchair bound.

Among African Americans, honorary or memorial sings comprise a goodly portion of current Sacred Harp conventions. Originally begun as tributes to certain singers during their lifetime, they function to memorialize them after their death. Until his death, the Judge Jackson tribute celebrated his birthday with a family reunion. I have now attended numerous commemorations on behalf of Judge Jackson. As a sign of the times, the *Revised Cooper Edition*, which these singers revere, remained segregated until the 1992 publication. That year, the publication of the long-awaited revised Cooper edition created a general sensation because for the first time it published a tune from *The Colored Sacred Harp*, "My Mother's Gone" (519), breaking racial barriers. From another vantage point, I could not avoid noting that of the seventy-odd compositions, half address the Jesus theme. The titles of many speak to the Christocentrism of their composers: "Jesus Calls for Thee," "Jesus Calls," "Jesus Lives in my Soul," "Jesus My All," "Jesus Saves," and "Let Jesus Lead." This array is in keeping with theologian Walker noting the endurance of the Christ theme, "mirroring the centrality of Jesus in the Black religious experience." For instance, related to the crucifixion, at sings "Jesus Rose" often warrants an encore. After one rendition, Reverend John Jackson proclaimed: "This was no fairy tale. It was true."

I would be remiss not to mention how these memorials, as with burial leagues, prop up the belief in ancestral forces. Today, Sacred Harp is a tradition primarily performed by African American octogenarians, for whom remembrance precludes doing things as they were always done, never compromising the musical quality. To celebrate their living kith and kin and to respect their elders, these memorials serve as a homecoming for younger nonsinging family members. Knowing the history, the family members

return with a sense of continuity and pride of people and place. As part of
the program, they traditionally assume center stage to offer remarks and always there is the tentative hope that they will also deign to lead a song, as is
traditional. Their elders encourage them to seize the occasion momentarily
to sing, to stave off fear of the encroaching possibility of its demise.

By conducting a longitudinal study, I began to note subtle, deep structural features. For example, a call of order is standard frame at the Jackson
singing. In 1993, after his prerequisite opening prayer, Reverend John Jackson remarked: "We're going to quit talking and start singing." Yet instead of
the usual quintessential Devotion, the Watts' composition "At the Cross"
operates as the favored opening hymn. "Amazing Grace" is another staple.
Few singing conventions occur without number 45 being sung from the
Cooper edition. As part of his formulaic opening, prior to his death, Elder
John Jackson often led this song loudly with bravado and great conviction,
highlighting the third verse: "This is the verse that suits me." The verse begins "Thru many dangers, toils and snare I have already come." Upon their
father's, Judge Jackson's, demise it became traditional for Reverend John
Jackson, his oldest son, to "open up" the session. Japheth Jackson once acknowledged that he would be next in the line of seniority to perform this
duty. Today, he functions more like the informal emcee: calling for song
leaders, pitching songs, and directing singers to the correct announced
page whether in *The Colored Sacred Harp* or the Cooper revision. So far,
another surviving brother, Reverend Shem Jackson, administers the opening and closing prayers.

The Jackson family's history consolidates and creates a strong bond.
Judge Jackson had twelve children, with one dying young. When I began
my sojourn into this tradition, most were still living. Much is written about
the men folks; however, the women are accomplished singers as well. Dovie
Dee Jackson Reese is now deceased; but I remember how, even with osteo-
porosis, she walked the square sans book, waving her hands heavenward as
she sang. Pauline Jackson Griggs is the sixth child and third daughter. She
officiates over other singing conventions. With her outstanding personality,
Ruth Jackson Johnson is still referred to as the baby of the family. Performing with vigor, she usually receives a great round of applause. Once after
leading "Service of the Lord," her brother John remarked with pride: "That
was my baby sister just sang." As a testament to this clan, a federal housing project in Ozark, the Judge Jackson Memorial Homes, is named in his
honor.

Although the singing intends to commemorate Judge Jackson, most select
songs from the Cooper edition, not *The Colored Sacred Harp*. Musicologist

David Warren contended: "Singers regard Jackson's book more as a source of community pride than as a source of active repertory." Some speculate, along with the Bible, that the Cooper book is the one most readily found in most rural southern homes, especially in Wiregrass Alabama. Early musicologist George Pullen White explained the region's steadfast commitment to this text: "In southeastern Alabama the Sacred Harp singers have a distinct organization. Their separation from their brethren to the north is due partly to their geographical remoteness and partly to the edition of the Sacred Harp, by W. M. Cooper of Dothan, Alabama, which they use." In 1902, the first new edition in over thirty years was published and created an undying loyalty.

Ideally, there are no onlookers at Sacred Harp events. It is a very egalitarian tradition; anyone present may elect to lead a song. Participants also take special requests, usually from those too infirm to sing themselves or longtime supporters who never learned to lead a song. Without the aid of a signup sheet, attendance list, or arranging committee of any kind, methodically, everyone seated gets "to sing around" the square. They begin with bass (usually all men). Each leads one song, relinquishing the floor to the next person in that section, thus proceeding until everyone forming the hollow square leads a tune and eventually asking those in pews to participate. Each song leader stands in the middle of the square and directs singers first through the notes to the song and then through the lyrics. To facilitate the process, they are asked "to hold in mind" their selection prior to their turn. Most singers do not require prompting. They have a lifetime preference for the same song.

The square utilizes the usual spatial arrangement almost universal in African American churches. Congregants establish the "hollow square" customarily by relying on the two sets of side pews, usually constituting the "amen corner" in most African American churches. The deacons occupy the ones to the left of the pulpit while those facing them are reserved for women church dignitaries such as the church mothers' board or deaconesses. Now it is the bass and treble singers who occupy these side pews. Folding chairs are added immediately in front of the pulpit area, facing the tenors seated on the front pew to complete the square. Each song leader takes turns entering the middle of the square to direct and stylistically "walk the square," stride in tempo with the music. Doris Lewis, daughter of W. Webster, one of *The Colored Sacred Harp* composers, yielded this description: "a leader on the floor—they can strut and step so the correct way—you start in the center; walk first to the right; and walk to left and end in center at same time you're beating your song." The African American

Song leader Ed Snell marking time.
Photo by Henry Willett, courtesy of
Alabama Center for Traditional Culture

variant relies on greater heterophony and marcato, creating an undulating, percussive sound. In music, marcato refers to strong accentuation. Finally, after navigating the square, Jackson will ask: "Who we miss?" or "We done got around?" Part of the tradition is to be hospitable and not to overlook anyone desiring to sing. As tardy arrivals appear, they are informally urged to "come on up, close by."

Oblong songbooks are unwieldy for neophytes to cradle in one arm while customarily beating time with their free hand. For those with great competency to sing by rote memory, their songbooks are mere props. Often, as a public display of devotion to a tune, singers walk the square with books closed. Yet, from their appearance, they are obviously well perused. The first thing I noticed was the number of well-worn book covers. One cover in particular showed significant age, bound with duct tape. To describe the sound, I will defer like others to the Atlanta Bureau Chief for *Newsweek*, Joseph Cumming Jr., who described a traditional sing: "In the center of the hollow square, the leader calls out '32A' and 100 or more singers—men, women, and children—shuffle through their songbooks. Like a sudden gale, they burst into song. The volume is turned all the way up, as if God might be a little hard of hearing; the pace of the majestic hymn is breakneck, as if God's patience were exhaustible." The numbers correspond to the page number of selections, rather than their titles. Japheth Jackson used a biblical analogy—the story of Abraham and Isaac—to assert: "It ain't gonna die." The belief is that divine intervention will ensure its preservation by future generations of African Americans. In today's high-tech age, I do not foresee an African American–prompted revival movement. As music critic Nelson George indicated, arguably African Americans "create and then move on. Whites document and then recycle."

For singers, perhaps, the music's call-and-response pattern offered an earnest appeal. Theologian Riggins Earl Jr. spoke of call and response as "the dialogical narrative self," meaning it functions as a means of communicating with both God and one's community. Although everyone in the square gets to lead a song, they are not song leaders in the usual sense of the word. For they launch the random selection to be sung, but the songsters sing in surging parts communicating one to another. A former graduate student rooted in the tradition, Wendy Coleman, furnished an apt description of the operation of vocal strands: "The contrasting sounds of the strands combine much like the music in a gospel musical piece, with the sounds sometimes blending and at other times sounding as if almost clashing. There are often solo lines included at various points in a composition of vocal music. The solos are not, however, sung by an individual. They are instead sung by an entire section or strand." Although a musical form based on participation, no one outside the square usually sings along. Therefore, though congregational in a sense, this tradition does not promote full congregational-style singing.

Given the secular shift and performance style of today's contemporary gospel music, shape-note singing remains conspicuously tame. In performance, shape-note resists most of the African characteristics professor Pearl Williams-Jones famously attributed to African American gospel music. Nonetheless, the antiphonal interaction between vocal parts is delivered in a relatively percussive fashion. For example, certain selections such as number 335, "Return Again," warrant remarks like "That's a good one," seemingly because of its accentual-syllabic beat, which lends itself to a polyrhythmic flow. The strongest percussive sounds are still those supplied by patting feet or the heels of singers' shoes, as they walk the hollow square. The varying vocal tones associated with gospel music are mostly absent. Instead, one hears a cacophony of voices as these elders sing in the most convenient key. Yet, as Japheth Jackson explained the musical objective to me: "When we get to singing we want our voices to blend in together." They do, but with a degree of heterophony favored by African American voices. Drawing on the expression of longtime chairman of the United Sacred

Harp Musical Association, A. M. Cagle, who likened singers to people in a community: "some were good, some were gooder, and some not so good." Yet, within this context, commonly one hears: "Everybody sounding good." A song such as "New Jerusalem," with its slurred notes, generates spontaneous applause.

During my very first morning session, I noted that the singers championed more than thirty tunes, from both Sacred Harp texts, without a break. This portion of the program is called a "singing class," with their song selections constituting lessons. Of these I note "Service of the Lord," "Jesus Is Willing," and "Struggle on" to be perennial. Seldom is there a singing in which these songs are not sung at least once. Especially over the course of a county singing convention, it is not exceptional for a song like "Cleansing Fountain" to be selected by various songsters three times. No one objects. As the informal emcee, Japheth Jackson, might wittily interject: "Don't give them all the singing they want. They won't come back." Still they do come back to the same settings and same tunes for a lifetime.

Many consider emotionalism to be a by-product of African American religious expression. It is easy to dismiss shape-notes' ability to spark an emotional tone, given its dependence on a Western system of notation and its steadfast lack of triggers: improvisation and repetition. Based on my observation, memory is the vehicle that compels some to shout or, more generally, to whimper. "Sweet Morning" and "Newman" are songs with the ability to incite some to audible tears. Supporters reserve applause and pronounce "amen" for the culmination of songs that delight them because they are led with enthusiasm and passion. Sung to perfection, favorites elicit strong, affective responses.

Even greater fanfare ushers in the ubiquitous dinners on the ground. Another key element is the desire for sociability. What Ted Olson wrote about white Sacred Harp songsters applies equally to their African American counterparts: "Shape-note singing is nearly always performed as part of a complex, recurring celebration that weds a challenging religious song repertoire to a food-sharing event with important social ramifications. And I knew that no other American choral music tradition so effectively balances its spiritual and social rewards." Undoubtedly, the durability of this musical tradition among African Americans in particular extends to the degree to which the sacred and secular converge into a quotidian spirituality. Engaging the music itself, local historian E. W. Carswell opined how singing conventions represent the epitome of sociability: "Several of the singers had been meeting periodically for a lifetime to sing—loudly, joyfully, and without inhibition."

Likewise, music is not the only catalyst drawing African Americans to this tradition. As with their white counterparts, they obtain "a sense of spiritual fulfillment, the pleasure of sharing in community, and the satisfaction of musical accomplishment." Moreover, as part of reciprocal support networks, there is an element of fair exchange, as participants donate to one another's coffers. The Jackson singing features two offertory rites, and all present give generously. To place these cultural performances into proper perspective, sentimentality runs high: "I don't do this for the money, you hear? I don't do it because I'm looking for something. I do it 'cause I loves ya'll and cause I love the music. Don't think that if you don't give me nothing, I won't come. I'm going to come every time you call, if I'm able and the Lord says the same, and I'm going to come 'til you tell me not to come no more. It ain't the money, you hear?" No, it is not just the money. The monetary incentive helps defray costs, while perpetuating a beleaguered tradition.

Furthermore, I've learned that, foremost, such enjoyable singing expresses unconditional love due to its continuity as a form of social fellowship. The Jackson singing also constitutes a family tradition, a time to relay personal experience about Judge and his wife, Lela. Each is given equal weight. The afternoon session includes a tribute and memorial service in which Japheth Jackson's children and grandchildren play prominent roles. Herman Jackson usually presents the family history. He described his grandfather as "firm, but fair," a religious man who patterned himself after the Lord, bestowing on his children biblical names. He also narrated several humorous anecdotes about his grandmother Lela. Later, Ruth, exhibiting the skills of a raconteur, gives an impromptu embellishment on relevant themes about her mother. She highlights her mother's singing ability, ending with her favorite song, "There's a Great Camp Meeting." Japheth Jackson's son, who is named for his grandfather, Judge, and who actually is one, leads the memorial service. Finally, during these frames, the Jackson family gathers to sing from *The Colored Sacred Harp*. A few mainstays include "My Mother's Gone," "Jesus Rose," and "It Is Finished." Judge Jackson composed the tune "Florida Storm," commemorating the 1926 Miami hurricane that stalled over Pensacola and devastated southeastern Alabama. It is an omnipresent selection, too, especially in light of the sustained threat hurricanes engender throughout the region.

Regarding hospitality, it goes beyond that associated with southern regionalism. It bespeaks the African American communitarian outlook. Hospitality conforms to a social ritual that makes doing otherwise an abomination within traditional West African contexts. These songsters travel at great lengths to sing and perhaps like "the Igbo know how a guest or a traveler appreciates being made welcome in a 'foreign' country." Such events begin auspiciously enough with the omnipresent welcome. At his father's memorial singing, one of Japheth Jackson's granddaughters, Traci, usually fulfills the role of the official greeter and bestows the welcome. As the youngest child in the Jackson clan, Ruth originally performed this role. Newcomers, like me, as well as regulars from neighboring communities all receive heartfelt acknowledgement as well. None will conclude until all have been granted a platform not only to sing but possibly to speak. The expression used is: "We don't want to overlook anyone." My days as a novice folklorist in African American communities of Philadelphia prepared me to expect such recognition. When transcribing field recordings, I still cringe in anticipation of hearing how my words never quite do justice to the hospitality and warmth each performance community extends to me.

As part of my longitudinal assessment, I attended this and other singing conventions religiously for five years. Then, as my research expanded, I attended more intermittently. After the initial treat of attending a Jackson sing, I had to wait two more years to experience the sing under routine conditions and without it being part of a major recording session. Even in 1995, the singing was being documented. This time the Alabama Folklife Association videotaped a field recording of the proceedings. Nonetheless, this format seemed less intrusive, and the Jackson sing seemed to come alive with more participation from songsters than I had yet to experience. It was an Easter Sunday and the Sixtieth Annual Memorial Singing Honoring Judge Jackson. All but a couple women positioned along the square wore splendid hats as their crowns. They wore white, turquoise, navy, beige, rose, gold, and combinations in between. Traditionally, singings began by 9:30 a.m. However, due to their advanced age and, as a concession to contemporary lifestyles, to attract more spry adults, the Jackson decided on new time, which is now 11:00 a.m. The expressed purpose of these occasions is so that "Judge Jackson's children, grandchildren, and great grandchildren are at the forefront of efforts to preserve interest in and the practice of Sacred Harp Music."

Dewey Williams was born on March 6, 1898, and began singing at the age of seven. With his passing in 1997, I regretted witnessing his birthday celebration sing evolve into a commemorative event. On March 5, 1995, I first observed one of his birthday singing conventions, which was every first Sunday in March. The only important commemoration I never got to attend is the one for Pokey Kirkland's mother, the Louise Holmes Sacred Harp Singing in Samson, Alabama, on the fourth Sunday in March. It is

Dewey Williams, recipient of a 1983 National Endowment of the Arts National Heritage Fellowship, lived to be ninety-seven years old

now defunct. Accordingly, Japheth Jackson stated to me, "Most of our best singers are dead." Given his advanced age, Williams was practically an institution. In 1983 he was awarded the NEA National Heritage Fellowship. Williams was the organizer of the Wiregrass Sacred Harp Singers, which went on to achieve national and international acclaim.

After William's death, his daughter, Bernice Harvey, assumed more of a leadership position. Harvey routinely plays a formidable role during most sings. In performance, her fervor never wanes. It is a custom to fulfill requests by those infirmed and anyone lacking the rudiments. Foremost, I observe Bernice Harvey and Pauline [Jackson] Griggs lead on behest of others, especially frail family members. Harvey usually leads with amazing gusto her mother's favorite, "Bound for Canaan." "Blooming Youth" appears to be her own signature song, because she leads it consistently. Ironically, after her father's demise, on March 2, 1997, his home church (Church of God by Faith) permitted Sacred Harp songsters to grace its sanctuary. While the contempt of some ministers is legendary, it was church members, who dismissed shape-note singing. Consequently, Williams' sing chiefly occurred in secular spaces such as the Perry Recreation Center in Ozark. His birthday memorial customarily generated a very diverse following of family, friends, Sacred Harp enthusiasts, and local white politicians. While living,

Williams selected to lead some of the Cooper revision's more complex pieces such as "Blessed Lamb" and "Loving Jesus." Moreover, the Jacksons would defer to him as their elder: "He's the oldest man in the house. When he speaks, we must listen."

One of Williams' close family members presently lives in Gary, Indiana. In an interview, Clementine Williams Du Bose provided several familial anecdotes: "He [Dewey Williams] amazes me about all the things that he know about music and mathematics. They were sharecroppers and farmers, when I was growing up. And he knew exactly how much speed it would take him to produce however much crop that he wanted to produce, and he only had a six-grade education. And he could read that Bible from front to back, pronounc[ing] all the words correctly. And I even have problems with some of the words even now, and I have a master's in education. So he learned a lot without on the job training or a lot of schooling." She also recounted information about family genealogy, including a grandmother who lived to be 107 years old.

As part of Sacred Harp history, after the Civil War a number of county conventions began to spring up. Segregated, African American singers adopted this model as well. Every convention, at all levels, offers another excuse to come together and sing. African American and white styles of singing shape-notes reportedly diverge, but not to the detriment of the two uniting. Customarily, white convention members sing faster. As Jackson articulated it, "They turn [words] loose it seems like a little quicker. They go through it a little quicker," which he attributes to feeling. He also attended a convention in Houston, Mississippi, once and expressed that they hold words even longer. Once at a Jackson singing, while leading "New Jerusalem," white songster Stanley Smith commanded: "Let's pick it up just a little bit." Nevertheless, all adherents welcome any opportunity to convene and demonstrate a willingness to accommodate everyone.

If not for segregation, one might wonder how the music tradition might have fared. Now, a sprinkling of African Americans attends white state conventions. However, a coterie of white Sacred Harp songsters is more likely to attend African American memorial singings, but not their standard singing conventions. These meetings can be quite protracted and esoteric. The segregation of texts that prevented Judge Jackson's and other African American composers from being included in B. F. White's *Sacred Harp* spilled over into their everyday lives, although downplayed today. According to James Bagwell's archival research, singers of an earlier era equated the death of Sacred Harp to the disappearance of segregation: "Not while the God fearing, Bible reading, and the song praising people practice the obedience of *nature, harmony and sentiment* [emphasis his]. Those attached to the Denson Edition remain virtually all white, although a possible enclave of African American singers may exist in northern Mississippi."

About a decade after attending my first Sacred Harp convention, in 2004 I witnessed the greatest crossover at both the Williams and Jackson memorial sings. This eventuality, perhaps, is the most unlikely answer to the survival of African American Sacred Harp singing. Along with other researchers, I find that although African American and white songsters use the same songbooks, the songs they revere differ. Although not empirical, I base this inkling on several suppositions. African American sacred music specialist Reverend Wyatt Tee Walker first asserted: "Black Christians, in response to their religious, psychic, and social needs in America, were selective in their use of Euro-American hymns." Williams' daughter, Bernice Harvey, nonetheless, found it especially gratifying when a contingency of white supporters filled out the square in tribute to her father. It was not the first appearance by Ozark songsters Tommy Spurlock and Stanley Smith; however, other white newcomers came to Ozark, traveling from as far as Baker, Florida. Whites comprised nearly half of those assembled to sing. Their presence invigorated this flagging art form among African Americans. Although attired chiefly in dress shirts and ties, eschewing the fancy aesthetic in effect among their counterparts, the white songsters introduced some new social and musical patterns. For instance, the white singers were more apt to request permission to lead two selections in a row. I also recorded a greater compunction to be raconteurs between songs. When conducting songs, the tendency was to assume a fixed position while "beating the song" in a more precise fashion like a choir director, rather than walking the square. To say the least, these are superficial distinctions, but even the white songsters noted introducing novel elements into this repertoire. Tommy Spurlock indicated as much when he articulated: "This is a song [146] you may not be familiar with, and we'll add 'Amazing Grace' at the end."

In 1994, I also attended a white Sacred Harp convention in Tallahassee, occasioned by the publication of a new revised Cooper edition of B. F. White's *Sacred Harp*, first published in 1844. In author John Bealle's terms, since the 1960s a virtual Sacred Harp revival emanated, influenced by folksong supporters. While experiencing a revival throughout white America, African Americans revitalize their music and seldom revive. Ironically, the African American Wiregrass Sacred Harp Singers influenced the revival among whites throughout the United States. Yet they stick to their conviction as stated by Dewey Williams: "If God didn't want this, he would have cut it off way back then." So, ironically, its appeal broadens to locales worldwide not originally known for singing conventions while facing an unknown fate among the African American Sacred Harp Singers. Besides commemorative events, African Americans host county Sacred Harp singing conventions throughout Wiregrass Alabama, including Dale, Barbour, and Henry Counties. The Dale County convention is the second Sunday in September. Also, African Americans host their own state convention the fourth Sunday in September, beginning the Saturday before. Their reciprocal support network is in full effect as the same voices people the halls of countless churches and conventions regardless of their residency. Systemically, there is always a business component. As Bealle noted, most Sacred Harp conventions entail: "elected officers, an adopted songbook, designated geographic domain, independence from civic and religious institutions."

The Alabama–Florida Union Singing Convention is a noteworthy one because it is, unofficially, led by Doris Lewis, as I will explain more in chapter 7. She is the descendent of another composer associated with *The Colored Sacred Harp* who contributed fourteen songs. Moreover, her mother, Florence Woods, penned the song "Doris" in honor of her child. Due to Lewis' leadership, St. Phillips AME Church in Madrid, Alabama, where her father served as pastor, is a hotbed of Sacred Harp as well as contemporary gospel activities. The church is a veritable museum, being one of the few remaining with original handmade amenities such as pastoral chairs, pews, and pulpit. Yet singers do not take umbrage about coming to this space without air conditioning, carpeting, or other ornate luxuries. The Alabama–Florida Union Singing Convention, a relatively small convention, generally used to meet there annually on the fourth Saturday and Sunday in August. On Saturday a handful of officers gathered for a business meeting and to kick off the singing convention. By Sunday's sing, a couple dozen songsters arrived to enjoy a full day of singing in keeping with tradition. The business component of a county or state singing convention is what distinguishes them the most from a memorial event. Another big distinction is that visitors are rare at singing conventions because memorials are similar to family reunions and homecomings for some and a form of cultural tourism for others. The year 1996 saw the Ninety-Fifth Session of the Alabama–Florida Sacred Harp County Convention. It also marked the first time in my life that I stood before a body and sang. I selected "Amazing Grace," figuring at least I knew the words, one less thing for worry. I stood flatfooted, though, daring not to lose focus by attempting to walk the square.

Taking session minutes is a mainstay of singing conventions. Dating back to B. F. White's early conventions, Bealle assessed: "By recording singings in the form of minutes, B. F. White likened them to public meetings and thus observed conventional documentary restraints designed around democratic discourse." African Americans are as copious as their white counterparts when it comes to recording the minutes of their singing conventions. Such conventions are very orderly occasions. Although the white Sacred Harp source sang from the Denson revision, I thought it might be interesting to conduct a brief comparative analysis. The first noteworthy mention is the convention's attendance appears to match that among African American Wiregrass singers today. Perhaps the speed of white songsters can be attributed to each conducting two, sometimes three, lessons—a group of songs. Each participant was allotted fifteen minutes. Moreover, these conventioneers impose a number of ten-minute recesses, whereas, in the Wiregrass, other than the break for the midday meal, there are none. Then, too, the white singers customarily maintained an early morning schedule, commencing as early as 8:30 a.m. Also, theirs included a Sunday morning sermon, another distinct feature.

Singing schools constitute a loosely formed institution within this tradition. Although virtually extinct now, singing schools used to occur in the summer. Historically, these sessions were conducted all day, five days a week for two weeks and were a form of recreation. The singing school teacher spent most of the class time reviewing the "rudiments" of music printed in the *Sacred Harp* book, practicing both major and minor scales and teaching how to mark time and lead songs. The itinerant singing schoolmaster was a common phenomenon in Wiregrass Country. A singer herself, Chiquita Willis affirmed: "Community leaders and singers came together and organized singing bodies to promote fellowship while providing inspiration. These leaders—and the conventions they organized—provided hope and relief from day-to-day struggles. The conventions were a shelter and refugee [sic] in the midst of chaos and disruption. Not only did children learn shape-note rudiments, they were acquainted with role models within the community. The lessons of these community elders prepared others for leadership responsibilities in the future." Moreover, they assembled ostensibly to improve the quality of their singing, but in reality these schools offered an additional social outlet. Moreover, they were designed to cultivate voices to fit within this musical tradition's frame by teaching young singers how to "run the scale," which is considered a fast way of reading music.

The singing schools were taught at local churches during "laying-by time," the period when the cotton bolls matured and cultivation ceased.

Musical instruction usually lasted from ten to twenty days. Then, the church was more than likely a one-room, white-clapboard building that sat upon rock pillars. The whole family would attend the singing school from mid-morning until mid-afternoon. Each family brought a picnic lunch to spread under the shade trees at noon. Perhaps other African Americans readily turned to seven shape-note singing schools due to this form's extensive publication of new songbooks, putting into words their desired praise. Du Bose attributed learning to read at an early age, without her family knowing it, to attending singing schools. These singing schools offered a multiplicity of functions while alleviating life's tedium.

Local singers tout Judge Jackson as one of the most notable teachers of Sacred Harp. W. Columbus Sistrunk, who chopped cotton with Jackson, instructed him about the rudiments of singing Sacred Harp after hours. According to Joe Dan Boyd, "They'd have a fire in the fireplace and he'd go over the notes and rudiments and teach him the notes. By the time he was twenty-one, Jackson demonstrated his accomplished by composing his first song, 'Alone'" (*The Colored Sacred Harp*, 18). This song precipitated the breach, which led to the publication of *The Colored Sacred Harp*. Whites thwarted Jackson's attempt to have the song published in the Cooper edition. Ironically, the song recently gained acceptance, with the Revision Committee not knowing of the song's turbulent history. Another irony, African American Sacred Harp singing may have escaped public awareness had Jackson not submitted a copy to the Library of Congress, where a researcher later happened upon it, located present-day singers, and invited them to the Smithsonian Folklife Festival. The group's name, Wiregrass Sacred Harp Singers, sprung up due to promoters needing a professional sounding appellation to call them.

Following in his father's footsteps, Japheth Jackson is a formidable teacher as well. Growing up, Sacred Harp was so popular he assumed that everybody knew how to sing it. As one of eleven children, he started singing at about age five. He remembers his family not waiting for the convention; they would sing Sacred Harp nearly every night. The vocal parts were evenly distributed among his siblings. In its rudiments section, *The Colored Sacred Harp* emphasizes musical keys, the general "rule for pitching or keying music." During our interview, using perfect pitch, Jackson explicated how children would be taught the four notes, followed by the major scale: fa, sol, la, fa, sol, la, mi, and fa. There are seven keys, which are indicated on the page by sharps or flats. As the current patriarch of the music attests, while explaining this element to students at a university in Ohio, when asked what he meant by "key," Jackson humorously and metaphorically responded: "Well, it's a small instrument that unlocks the door." Although he occasionally may teach a local singing school, he admits having difficulty attracting students lately, though not giving up hope of a future revival. Among African Americans, dorayme continues to flourish.

Several African American masters such as J. W. Sykes have gone relatively undocumented by researchers yet are fondly remembered. Since singing school teachers were called "professor," the entitlement certainly communicated a deep-seated respect. Students paid ten cents for the privilege to acquire and pass down this tradition. According to one participant, Mary Lou Henderson, "We were taught the shape-notes in the class; that's where our choir started singing doraymifasolatido. Right here at Willowhead. Reverend G. T. Martin he taught us. He was the main principal of that and then he would have teachers to go around (Sykes among 'em) to go around and teach the notes. And we'd have a week of study classes and then we would wind up into the main singing convention, which would be as far as Moultrie and Bradenton and all around. We would be delegated to this convention. And that's the way that our choir started." Chiquita Willis also established that the function of singing schools was to teach the rudiments: "reading a musical staff, singing by syllables, singing harmony parts, and reading rhythm." By all indications, unlike white adherents, African American singing schools did not exist simply to "improve the quality of congregational singing." Even with the popularity the Old One Hundred and the advent of traditional gospel, shape-note music coexisted, enriching participants' spiritual lives with added vim and vitality.

Appreciably, both shape-note forms privilege the musical rudiments over the texts. Nonetheless, Japheth Jackson disclosed to me: "The one thing that makes [music] so good is that the words of the songs are out of the Bible." Many four shape-note singers habitually cross over, supporting the dorayme system as well. The term *Sacred Harp* is not usually used interchangeably for those who sing dorayme. Remember in the dorayme system, instead of four notes, seven notes are sung. Only the shape of the notes distinguishes dorayme from the standard notation system. The genre of sacred music does not matter. By rote, most singers can line a hymn with equal competence. Their repertoires are comprehensive. The greatest reward for the majority of these singers, who also sing in church choirs or gospel ensembles, is that singing enables them to wed the music and text as part of a dialectic continuum. Given the significant shift in singing styles, it amazes me that a song such as "Crown Him Lord of All," can be sung by the same individual in common meter, Sacred Harp, as a hymn of improvisation, and even gospelized.

As part of an evolutionary chain, Sacred Harp music is conterminous with many other forms of African American musical traditions. It also is not performed in the absence of these styles. Common meter, the Old One Hundred, and gospel may be heard at the conventions, too. All styles of sacred music gain attention without establishing a hierarchy. What Steven Sabol indicated as the essence of Sacred Harp music applies to these sacred performance communities: "Greater importance and personal satisfaction lie with singing the spiritually meaningful words, creating powerful music together in a friendly and accepting atmosphere, building friendships among other singers, and remembering deceased and sick-and-shut-in singers."

African Americans engaging in the seven shape-note system are far more prevalent throughout the South. Although raised in Mississippi, former student Wendy Coleman also recalled: "The fifth Sunday was, and still is, the day of the singing convention. When I was a child, it was the day when we visited other churches, sometimes with few young people like us. But what was there was a spirit of praise and vocal thanksgiving that charged the air and excited even we children who had little if any idea of what real experienced-berthed praise was about." Such singing conventions represent a holistic, recreational vehicle. Spiritual activists, vis-à-vis their music making, systematize their own heaven on earth.

I also have now attended a number of seven shape-note sings: the South Alabama Seven Shape Singing Convention in Greenville as well as a Fifth Sunday Seven Shape Singing Convention in Brundridge, Alabama, and another in Banks, Alabama. The environs around Troy, Alabama, are a breeding ground for such activity, as is Wiregrass Georgia from Bainbridge to Damascus. Of these, I consider the ones in Greenville, Alabama, the most engrossing. Conventioneers trek to a special place, the Seven Shape Singing Convention Center, every Fifth Sunday. Although founded in the 1920s, the South Alabama Seven Shape Singing Convention did not acquire its own edifice until 1973. Mother Elizabeth (Lizzie) Bedgood donated two acres of land specifically to build a site to ensure her convention's longevity.

The cavernous building's interior is quite Spartan in comparison with the ornate and plush interiors found inside many rural churches today. Imitation wood paneling, instead of the common knotty pine, grace its walls. The wood-paneled wall behind the pulpit showcases a photo gallery of esteemed past officials. The building features hand-hewn pews, and its concrete floor indicates the stark functionality of this space. It is bare bone, without ornamentation or air conditioning. Possessing such an autonomous site brings order into contemporary lives, offering a designated site without the encumbrance of locating and recollecting disparate venues. Prior to its construction, in keeping with formality, the convention rotated from church to church, traveling in a set pattern within their bailiwick. The Seven Shape Singing Convention Center stabilized a constituency that might have otherwise fragmented had individuals lost their compulsion to journey to each remote site. With the creation of this one space, this sacred performance community guaranteed its very survival. As Roger Abrahams stipulated about rituals, they provide "traditional ways of momentarily binding the opposing forces within the community and tying together the past with the present." By creating this ritualized space, this community of singers granted itself a future. Called a singing building, outside of Fifth Sundays gospel singers and their entourages gather on a regular basis to host anniversary programs there as well.

Lizzie Bedgood's family continues to play pivotal and precise roles. Her grandchildren are the elders now and continue to orchestrate each session. When I first located this convention, twin brothers Esau and Jacob Bedgood brought a special verve and vivacity to the music. They conveyed an amazing team. One could only speculate about how spectacularly they sang during their youth. In 1997, to show appreciation, members honored Esau's thirty-six years as vice president and nine as president. Replete with a sheet cake, they presented the award in absentia because illness prevented him from attending. When in good health, he acted as emcee, announcing who will sing next, pitching songs, and, relying on a microphone, amplifying his own robust voice to accompany more tenuous singers. His brother, Jacob, frequently led requests and raised hymns while stylistically walking the hollow square. Despite his age, Jacob is accomplished at leading any selection. For instance, singing "Turn Around and Go Back to the Lord," he dramatized the lyrics, whirling around while making wide, sweeping gestures with his outstretched arms before an appreciative convention. Voluble lyrics strengthen each presentation. When performed expressively, the level of approval is immense. Jacob's competence in performance garnered much admiration. Rosebud Bedgood Hamilton is another of the grandchildren who is an embodiment of this family's history. Her esteemed presence exacts much deference all around.

Although four shape-note singing waned considerably among African American southerners, dorayme continues to enjoy the widest following. This form of shape-note music allows for greater innovations and material resources. As folklorist George Pullen Jackson observed regarding this form of singing in general: "They use the seven-shape notation and have their own little thirty-five cent manila-bound song books, their own singing schools, conventions, teachers, composers, and, to some extent, publishers." Presently, the number of songbooks used is astronomical. In Wiregrass Alabama, singing conventions continue to conform in structure to a Sacred Harp convention with individual songsters conducting hymns. However, the choice of songbooks requires participants literally to tote an array of satchels from flight bags to briefcases. In Greenville, one book predominates, *Heavenly Highway Hymns*, but everyone arrives loaded down with a cargo of books just in case. Other popular songbook titles include *Matchless Love, Notes of Praise, Ceaseless Praise, Heavenly Sound, Divine Joy, Matchless Grace, Convention Classics, Getting Ready, Springs of Glory,* and *Holy Praise.* Comparatively, I noted at a white shape-note singing convention in Dothan, Alabama, that the favored texts on hand were *Heavenly Harmony, Matchless Grace, Songs We Love, Good News,* and *Kings Praise.* The titles mainly signify the state of grace, love, and praise these Christians struggle a lifetime to achieve. Besides being well worn, these texts often symbolize heirlooms passed down among generations of singers.

Many familiar elements traditionally associated with singing conventions remain intact. They continue to sing strictly a cappella. Badges, now costing fifty cents, continue to be a mainstay of this tradition. The badges are usually strips of ribbon cut in small swatches and affixed with a straight pin and, emblematically, worn as a sign of belonging and contributing. You purchase them at the door as if paying the price of admission. In 2003, after the World Trade Center tragedy, a patriotic badge emerged with a small icon of the Statue of Liberty and the words: "In God We Trust." Along with the singing, the collection of enrollment fees and a monetary offering before the midday luncheon break are all accomplished with precision to the beat of the clock. It remains customary not to deviate from the written program. Although conventioneers no longer circulate to local churches, the system of rotation is still in effect. Customarily, four churches get to host a convention annually. Their churches have lyrical names such as Star Hope, Spring Hill, Indian Hill, Sweetwater, and Goshen. One is an AME Zion church, another distinct African American denomination. All of the proceeds go toward the maintenance of the singing building (bank loans, electric service, gas, insurance, including fire service) given in the name of the church scheduled to host the convention. The host church also is responsible for catering and serving the midday meal.

The last Fifth Sunday of the year (usually November or December) results in a two-day annual session. As in the past and in keeping with Sacred Harp, the Saturday session is relatively mundane. It is devoted to organizational business: the collection of enrollment fees; reports from all officers,

Bennie McDonald conducts a song at the Seven Shape Singing Convention Center in Greenville, Alabama

missionaries, and trustees; and a memorial service. In addition, it involves an election of officers. There is a singing workshop, not to be confused with a singing school, as no rudiments are taught. As a testament to the commitment of this sacred performance community, Saturday's session begins at 10:30 a.m. with an intermission for lunch. They reassemble at 1:30 p.m., hold another brief recess, and resume again at 6:30 p.m. With several perfunctory monetary offerings, this day's session is usually the most lucrative, paying most of the bills. For this event, I noted that the badges issued were more elaborate. They were two-inch-wide red ribbon embossed with: "Welcome to the 77th Annual Session of the South Alabama Seven Shape Singing Convention," listing the date, president, and secretary.

Singing, eating, and fellowshipping are the three powerfully reinforced ingredients. Furthermore, to situate this more business-oriented frame as outside of the singing convention proper, intermittent congregational style singing reigns, without making use of the hollow square. Saturday evening appropriates elements from a regular church function: someone states the occasion, a child reads the Twenty-Third Psalm, and someone else renders a humorous religious poem. Perhaps to attract a youthful following, a gospel ensemble sings a cappella. The day's program is reminiscent of the Baptist youth department meetings. The annual closing program instills longstanding values and absorbs the next generation, institutionalizing singing conventions as a recreational and spiritual activity. The evening program is one of the few occasions at this site when I have witnessed a minister delivering a brief sermon. Signifying that this occasion is an ally of but not the singing convention itself, the program returns to a robust exhibition of virtuoso gospel singing, sung by soloists and without congregational participation. Even the handclapping is restricted to those performing, marking the event as occasional. Thus, the shape-note musical frame is held in reserve until the next day, bringing a climatic finale to their year in song.

Seldom does a network assemble to sing without a reference to Psalm, in passing or as an overt theme: "I will praise Thee O Lord among the people, and I will sing praises unto Thee among the nations" (Psalm 108:3). Besides an appropriate theme for their programs, as with most sacred and secular performance communities, this southern Alabama convention also selects an appropriate theme song: "Lord Give Me Just a Little More Time." The repetition of themes and songs across performance communities speaks volumes about their shared spiritual communalities. These collectives wish to uplift. Unlike Sacred Harp, moreover, seven shape-note singing attracts more middle-aged singers. Although this participation is no insurance of the form's preservation, it buys them time. Moreover, although they do not predominate numerically, there is a recognizable presence of younger adult males.

I must accept that my family history exists outside so many core forms of African American artistic expression. Because we are from Gary, Indiana, in hindsight, it still frustrates me to encounter visitors from our hometown at these conventions. This awareness acknowledges African American cultural diversity. I still envy how emigrants from my hometown (and elsewhere in the North) time their visits to coincide with these singing conventions. During remarks on the Saturday before the Fifth Sunday in November 1997, a visitor expressed: "I enjoyed myself while I've been here, but I'm going back up that way." The industrial North claimed a lot of the convention's children. Yet they constitute a large portion of the nonsingers at these cultural performances. Giving testimonial to an appreciation of shape-note, someone else remarked: "I can't sing, but I love it and am glad to come to hear anybody else sing." Their returns speak to the push and pull factors that have long cross-pollinated African American culture. In March 2003, during its eighty-third annual session hosted by Sweetwater Missionary Baptist Church, families visited from far and near: Etta Thomas from Detroit, Michigan; Weetha Mc-Cant from St. Albans, New York; and Bernice Du Bose Ethridge and Lillie Hughes from Montgomery, Alabama.

As is customary, remarks conclude the singing. Some songsters return after years of absence and testify: "I got rusty. I laid out twenty-five, thirty years but decided to come back but I ain't got right yet." On the other hand,

I overheard another gentleman state that he had only missed three conventions since 1948, when he was without transportation. Someone else commented: "I haven't been here since the '30s, used to come in a truck, people change and things change. We don't talk about singing [conventions] in our churches anymore." This convention, indeed, is representative of a community demonstrating its fluidity and cohesion, the ebb and flow of those attune to this tradition. Many, no doubt, would concur with the following sentiment: "I wouldn't walk across the street to hear Sacred Harp singing, but I'd walk two hundred miles to help sing it. Sacred Harp is singers' music; it's not a listeners' music—you have to participate to get the good out of it." Yet, as previously expressed, things change and the listeners who come return to claim an inheritance.

Regardless of which sacred music tradition is performed, by design, the evangelical message remains the same. According to Dewey Williams, the first time I heard him sing in Columbus, Georgia:

> *God got two places for us after we're dead.*
> *One of them is in heaven,*
>   *and the other one*
>   *you know where it is.*
> *All of us gonna get together down there*
>   *or up there.*
> *We ain't got but two places in the Bible.*
>   *You know what I'm saying?*
> *Since there's only two places*
>   *let's get together here.*
>   *Why don't we?*

Historically, observers referred to Williams and his constituents as God-fearing people. In practice, it is not just fear but their trust in the Lord. Their theology speaks to survival and their survival depends on much reciprocity to accompany them into eternity.

As a folklorist, it was redemptive for me when, upon the passing of John Jackson, the family thought to notify me in time to attend his funeral on August 31, 1996. His homegoing celebration lasted upward of two hours, and I never observed such a cross-section of sacred performance communities come together so tightly. Along with an extensive network of family, friends, Sacred Harp singers, and fellow church members, of course, a full complement of local folklorists and political dignitaries attended. He ministered Allen Temple Church of God in Christ in Dothan, Alabama. His wife,

Mary, known as "Hon," was among the first in the Wiregrass to embrace me, indoctrinating me about local traditions. She always enthusiastically welcomed me at Jackson memorials, and I developed a special allegiance to her. One of my fondest remembrances of John Jackson is how he publicly and good-naturedly acknowledged me for traveling from Tallahassee, by saying he "just did beat [me] here this morning. We appreciate that and God do too." In an interview with the two, John whimsically conveyed how his church could "jazz up" sacred music. After hearing the Allen Temple Choir gospelize one of his favorite hymns, it is now mine: "God Has Smiled on Me. He has set me free! God has smiled on me. He's been good to me!" In their inclusivity, Wiregrass African American spiritual activists welcome such lyrics, ensuring the good that they share is returned, increased, and multiplied. They magnify God by animating a spiritual life—well spent in song.

CHAPTER 5

"God Has Smiled on Me"

Traditional Gospel

I now believe it was divine intervention that called me to trace the Thomas-Grady Counties Singing Convention, leading to this larger research project. In fulfillment of my early research agenda, I confess often being very dependent on the kindness of strangers, serendipity, and some say divine unction. There is an elusive quality about documenting African American folk culture. Success often depends on timing.

Historically, a canopy road lined with majestic oaks met you upon crossing the Georgia–Florida state line. In Tallahassee, hardwood trees chiefly have dominion over the more scraggly longleaf pine. Botanist Roland Harper found "that this region has been longer and more extensively cultivated than any other area of the same size in Florida," as Tallahassee had been the homeplace for generations of American Indians until its abandonment. Just as I almost reached the canopy road, in 1993 I espied Mr. Willie Johnson posting a sign to direct guests the next day to his church for the Thomas-Grady Counties Singing Convention. I drove past him for about a mile. Then, responding to a nagging intuition that I had come to trust, I made a U-turn.

This stop opened up a totally new vista as Johnson briefly explained that his church, Piney Grove Missionary Baptist Church, was hosting a singing convention that weekend. Located approximately twenty-five miles north of Tallahassee, in clear view, I drove past Pebble Hill Plantation without ever noticing the church tucked away down a narrow lane from the highway. I also assumed that convention meant shape-note singing. I came to find out otherwise. At the time I was conducting research for *Wiregrass Country*, but it was this chance meeting that convinced me to commence this project. Given the intensity of the interest in singing sacred music within this one little hamlet, I followed the path laid out before me. I let the folk and what they do dictate my future fieldwork initiative.

Piney Grove Missionary Baptist Church
located on the Pebble Hill Plantation in
Thomasville, Georgia

I soon attended the 383rd Session of the Thomas-Grady Counties Singing Convention. The number of sessions indicated that this organization
had congregated every other third Sunday for more than sixty years. Following instructions, I turned right on one of the first dirt roads after crossing the Florida–Georgia border. In the pitch dark, fixated on keeping to
the winding red clay-surfaced road, I noticed evenly spaced "No Trespass"
signs tacked onto trees the length of the road. Like Piney Grove, Mercy
Seat Missionary Baptist Church occupies land off a dirt road on a hunting
plantation. I passed several sporadic houses; but unlike the squat dwell-
ings for workers near the luxurious Pebble Hill Plantation, these were not
grouped into quarters. Immediately upon emerging into a clearing, as directed, it amazed me to find myself in Metcalfe, right at Mercy Seat. The
throng of parked cars provided full assurance of this being the place. Imagine my amazement to find, instead of songbooks and an assembly seated in
a square, a full-blown traditional gospel fete.

As I noted in chapter 1, southern plantations were an anomaly in Wiregrass Country. Even more of an anomaly is the extent to which, by the turn
of the twentieth century, northern industrialists came to own a few of the
existing plantations around Thomas and Grady Counties. This changing of
landowners granted descendants boasting rights to a distinct history within

the larger southern context. As descendants, it is this elaborate history that most of these choral singers uphold. Jack Hadley is their official historian. According to his publication, "Beginning in the 1880s, African Americans benefited economically as Thomasville became a haven for wealthy northerners and sportsmen seeking pleasure in the supposedly restorative airs and winter climate of Thomas County's pine forest." The turn of the century saw the establishment of quail hunting plantations. During Reconstruction, by offering wage labor the plantations possibly could have served as a model for the New South. The general testimony is that African Americans who lived on these plantations had an advantage over African Americans elsewhere. Besides churches, their employers also provided schools and encouraged them to send their children to college. As a result, these families tended quickly to acquire a higher socioeconomic status, many becoming professionals themselves. Unlike many who aspire to attain a middle-class status, these home folks consciously held onto their traditions.

The kind of insights that Hadley and his key interviewees brought disrupt previous conceptions about southern plantation life and sharecropping. Pebble Hill Plantation is still a stately showcase and a historic landmark. Purchased in 1896 by industrialist Howard Melville Hanna of Cleveland, Ohio to become a quail hunting lodge, over time it possessed its own dairy, laundry, fire company, dog hospital, and a certified nurse for the workers. Hadley documented: "Every morning, fresh milk would be delivered to the home. Hot breakfast and lunch were prepared for the workers as well as the uniforms done at the plantation laundry. Those who lived on the plantation did not have to pay rent." They all worked as wage earners so that even the plantation maids had maids, women whom they paid to clean their individual homes. They also had land allotted for sharecroppers, too, allowing them to advance financially as well.

Holidays were especially memorable occasions because the landowners granted the workers leisure time, refreshments, gifts, and other surprises. On Easter, festivities like the traditional Easter egg hunt were held on the lawn right in front of the big house. Later becoming Reverend Washington, the buck dancer they called Mutt grandly performed on the tabletops. He would make dramatic entrances, for example, in a wheelchair. According to Washington, there are fifty-two steps in buck dancing, and he could do them all. The St. Thomas Harmonizing Choir also regularly performed, suggesting the local existence of another pre-gospel tradition—the barbershop quartet. It is out of this environment that local singing conventions grew as a dynamic force. Accordingly, the conventioneers' own documented history expresses: "The loving spiritual atmosphere of the sessions made the time not pass fast enough. In the fields conversations were about the singing convention. In the wash tubs and over the wash pots singing convention songs were song [sic]. In the homes and at church services conversations were about the singing convention. The singing convention was an inspiration to the community. A time when people could see each other young and old from various churches to sing, socialize, and feast." These singing conventions perhaps supply the missing link related to the history of Black southern gospel music.

Later, in an interview, Willie Johnson recollected that his mother was a member of Piney Grove's choir when the singing convention started. Back then, they sang shape-note. Innovation within a tradition is another hallmark of African American cultural expression. In southwestern Georgia, singing conventions, which began in the dorayme shape-note tradition, brought about their own transformation with the introduction of traditional gospel music. These conventions started as a class singing one tradition but quickly adapted to the gospel blues sound endorsed by Thomas Dorsey, the Father of Gospel Music, who organized the oldest gospel music convention. Dorsey was born in Villa Rica, Georgia. As a blues composer and musician, he was known as Georgia Tom. Although not from Wiregrass Country, he shared with most southerners a familiarity with shape-note music. He wrote: "The shaped note singer didn't want no accompaniment; they wanted to blend their harmony. They wanted nothing but pure harmony. The shape of the note gave you the tune and the pitch. And I mean every man and every woman knew their place [i.e., part: soprano, alto, tenor, or bass]. It was beautiful singing. You wouldn't hear any better singing now than those folks did in those days." Members of the Thomas-Grady Counties Singing Convention followed Thomas Dorsey's progression. They pinpoint him as being instrumental in their own transformation to choral gospel music, making them among the first to answer his call. According to local singing aficionado Tommie Gabriel, "Dorayme was the main thing; but after a period, they finally got away from it." With the rising awareness of gospel blues circulated, "everybody thought that they could sing without going through that route" (learning the shape-note fundamentals). He went on to say: "The young people don't know do from ray, but they can show you how to sing." Thus, Sacred Harp was my primary context for the region's singing conventions. Structurally, the gospel singing conventions are organized the same, having evolved from this venerable tradition. Today, however, strictly gospelized choral music prevails.

Upon entering Mercy Seat Missionary Baptist Church, in keeping with the shape-note traditions, I purchased a badge. Later a banner was given

Thomas-Grady Counties Singing Convention dinner on the grounds, circa 1950

to the church choir enrolling the most members. Banners are awarded to inspire competition in order to raise more funds to benefit all the churches. Here, choirs only sing one selection each. They magically assemble in the choir loft with precision and descend with a processional as the final notes conclude, and then the next choir dutifully mounts the loft without any spoken fanfare in between. During the singing session, few words are spoken. Listening to field tapes, the transitions sound seamless and as though one holistically inspired choral concert. Choruses understand their traditional roles, operating in unison and without egotistical displays.

At African American shape-note conventions, song leaders are mainly predetermined by the order in which seated around the square. Thomas and Grady Counties' choruses follow a prescheduled progression. For the longest, fourteen choirs comprised this convention; and, as customary, each hosted a session in rotation. The former host sings last, appearing at the bottom of the printed program. To demonstrate group unity, most choir members wear standard black skirts or pants and white tops. A few don actual choir robes. I want to emphasize that choruses are not organized just to sing at conventions. They actually are part of their home church's membership and choruses. Beginning on the Friday night before the third Sunday and every other month, the Thomas-Grady Counties Singing Convention convenes. On Sunday, since these conventions do not coincide with

Fifth Sunday and to avoid conflict for those enjoying a pastoral day, the convention reconvenes at 1:00 p.m. In addition, the fancy aesthetic is more apparent on Sundays. On Friday nights, the women singers are more casually or uniformly dressed. They may wear denim dresses or the ubiquitous black and white, while men usually wear conservative dress suits.

Another personal discovery was the extent to which these singing conventions habitually advance congregational singing. The tremendous, melodious sound can be attributed to the assemblage of some of the locale's best songsters. Sometimes, only one, solitary soul enrolls to represent a church's choir. Undaunted, a handful of members from other choirs spontaneously materialize to fill the choir loft. This arrangement merely masks the degree to which most selections dissolve into "pick up numbers," with everyone in attendance singing along. As singer Bernice Johnson Reagon defined congregational singing: "This is the tradition in which the singing for a gathering comes from those who fill the pews. Songs are raised by a song leader and survive and fill the air and the hearts of those souls who with their voices, hands, and feet give it life. One learns this style in performance by being in church." The Thomas-Grady Counties Singing Convention bequeaths another enduring context.

Residents of Thomas and Grady Counties founded the singing convention in 1929. This convention consciously decided to privilege local church choirs. According to the history printed for their fiftieth anniversary: "A soul is not mature until he has learned how to work with another. A skillful Violinist [sic] is better for having been part of a great symphony orchestra. A singer is better for having sung with a concert choir, a group or church choir. A house is erected by men working together." When gospel came into being, everybody thought that they could sing without going through the rudiments. Foremost, the defection did not cause them to waver from principle community values. By singing together, harmoniously, they engage in an infinite flow, serving as divine vessels.

Upon the death of its original president, Walter Baidy, in 1939, Tommie Gabriel ascended to the presidency, a post he was to hold for more than fifty years. He most recently served as the president emeritus. Gabriel, born in 1911 on Pebble Hill Plantation, revealed a less-romanticized view of hunting plantation life. The overseer expelled his father in 1926 because he bought a Ford that year from wages earned out of season laboring in Miami. Southern plantation superintendents served as the gatekeepers of regional mores, which dictated that African Americans remain a wrung below all whites, including the lower class. His father breached local protocol. On the other hand, Willie Johnson loves to narrate how families fared on the hunting plantations during the Great Depression. He noted: "During the Depression, the plantation people really got over because they were never laid off. My uncle came down from New Jersey. He lost his job up there, and he worked down here until jobs were available again in New Jersey. So, blacks on the plantation never experienced any hardship. People were talking about soup lines and that sort of thing, but they never knew anything about that kind of thing." The collective identity of many of these singers is derived from the values they learned growing up on past sites of demeaning oppression, transformed into buffer zones from most overt symbols of racial discord.

Furthermore, traditional gospel music did not originate in a vacuum. Many scholars center its provenience as part of the urban migration experience of African Americans. They do not recognize the extent to which radio broadcasts influenced rural sacred performance communities, too. Rural African Americans also read northern newspapers such as *The Pittsburgh Courier*. These communities sent representatives and delegates to Dorsey's National Baptist Convention. The great migration wave was not strictly unilateral. Many Wiregrass residents vacationed in the North or lived there for an extended time. Tommie Gabriel, as a delegate to the National Baptist Convention, attended conventions in Washington, D.C., and Brooklyn to network and learn the rudiments of this new form of sacred music. Therefore, choral group members made informed choices when shifting to the traditional gospel music they sing.

In historicizing it, one master narrative situates gospel music as antithetical to earlier African American churchgoers, especially in the South. With its connection to secular music, gospel blues was not considered the right kind of spiritual music. Singers in this part of Wiregrass Georgia, however, gravitated to its nascent sound. Dorsey himself recognized: "By March 1933 many other churches in Chicago and throughout the country began organizing gospel choruses to serve simultaneously with the so-called Senior Choirs . . . .Then gospel singing began to spread like wildfire to other churches and in twelve months almost every church throughout the country had a gospel choir or wanted one." Thomasville's singing conventions provide hard evidence to support his contention. After all, shape-note is a form of a cappella choral singing, with collective lyrical interaction emanating from around the square. Changing to a gospel format and relying on congregational singing appropriate well elements from this more archaic tradition. Moreover, they came to privilege the piano, the mode of instrumentation introduced by Dorsey's gospel blues. At first, the churches lacked pianos and musicians to play this kind of music. Impervious, they purchased the sheet music and adapted to singing the gospel blues vocally. Melisma, elongating several notes within one syllable, is the musical element they used to transform even standard hymns.

Thomasville, Georgia, is the nucleus for a host of these neoteric singing conventions. In the beginning, the Thomas-Grady Counties Singing Convention convened only every other third Sunday. Originally, only five churches belonged to the convention. Their church names speak volumes about their locality, spirituality, and quest for brighter hope. Ochlocknee was named for a local river, St. James, a book in the Bible; the others rely on more abstraction: Paradise, Friendship, and Providence. They met with a mission eloquently expressed in their history:

Up the hills to Ochlocknee these officers sung. In the lane at St. James these officers and followers sung. Thru the mud and in the rain to Paradise they sung. In the cold to friendship [sic] praises by officers and the convention were sung. On the corner and avenue at Providence these officers and convention sung:

Traveling shoes, Lord; I got on my
traveling shoes; Traveling shoes
Lord I got on My [sic] traveling shoes.
I can travel now, cause I got on my
traveling shoes.

Traveling, in harmony, united with a common goal and purpose. The goal was to help each other raise money to aid their churches' finance. Their purpose to render unto the Lord by giving time and singing [sic]. Taking advantage of every opportunity to use their talent.

In addition, this resource proclaims, "Many voices singing the same song has a far reaching effect in church services; also in a community. The choir next to the minister has the most influence upon church membership and listeners." They ask the rhetorical question: "How can you sing in the choir without a song in your heart?" This set of commentaries portrays a people who liken the performance of sacred music to a spirit of excellence and ministry. They internalize their lyrics as being at the core of their sentient existence.

In a prescribed order, convention sites alternate in accordance with arrangements established decades ago. Sort of like the pyramid system, each choir ascends to host a singing convention (within a three-year cycle) and benefit by keeping a portion of the proceeds. At its inception, on average, they might raise one hundred dollars a session. Yet they deemed this sum glorious during the decades of the Great Depression. The funds garnered come from choir enrollment fees as well as individual donations. The only thing met with disapproval is when a choir wants to change its place within the rotation. Calendrical events are practically engraved in stone, and to do so would be like the moon changing its phases. In addition, no group wants possibly to postpone the receipt of its share of the proverbial pie.

Additionally, the 1940s saw the inclusion of many traditions that continue to be mainstays of today's convention. With the growth of membership, due to time constraints choirs began to sing only one song. As part of the fundraising initiative, Bible verses were to be recited each session alphabetically. If a member did not recite one, he or she had to donate five cents. Also, for five cents, each choir member had to purchase a badge. Officers also received a meager salary. In 1941, due to advances in modes of travel, the convention added the Friday night session, which not only increased revenue but their musical outreach. During the World War II era, African Americans in the rural South finally became more dependent on automobiles. The collective spirit extended to transportation so that: "Members happiely [sic] and freely picked up those who did not have transportation of their own." Choirs would make arrangement for their members' transportation. By the conclusion of the decade, host churches Willowhead and Rebecca raised over a thousand dollars each, meaning post–World War II prosperity trickled down into the region.

By the close of the decade, the convention membership embraced fourteen churches, including Piney Grove, Rebecca, Willowhead, Mt. Pilgrim, St. Paul, Mercy Seat, Shiloh, and Pleasant Hill. By 1956, membership consisted of approximately twenty choirs. As a result, it took a little more than three years to complete the "circle of visitation," and membership had to be limited to this number. The new church choirs enrolled were Aucilla, Antioch, New Jerusalem, Oak Grove, and Mt. Zion. While waiting their turn, they lent financial support to the others. The kind of organizational skills this entailed perhaps presaged individual success during the post–civil rights era.

Each choir also is formally structured with its own officials. For example, Louise Sapp is president of the St. James Baptist Church choir. The Thomas-Grady Counties Singing Convention is only one of the affiliations with which her choir associates. It belongs to other active singing conventions: the City-Wide Choirs' Union and the United Singing Convention of Georgia and Florida, which convenes every Fifth Sunday. In addition, there is also the Fellowship Service, which meets every second Sunday at 3:00 p.m. Unlike most, her church worships only monthly, on every fourth Sunday, leaving more opportunities to ecumenically commune with other churches. Moreover, Sapp is president of choir #1, meaning that the church also supports more than one choir. At the time of our interview, including her, the choir had just seven members. It never had more than eighteen. They fellowship via song, bringing communal exuberance, and total numbers do not matter.

With the growth of its membership, the Thomas-Grady Counties Singing Convention instituted some additional changes. Leadership roles grew beyond the essential officials of president, vice president, secretary, assistant secretary, and treasurer. Noting the significance of monetary incentive to this group, the duties of the secretaries became more pronounced and the group of officers consisted of a recording secretary, financial secretary, as well as the regular treasurer. Their history asserts the officials committed to a divine role: "They thought deep [enough] to reach beyond the fact that not merely the singing convention elected them, that God's work must be done and this was their way of fullfilling [sic] their promise to Him and serving on His program. They nurtured the fact that sure the convention was depending upon them for superior leadership." Therefore, service to God and community constituted an important part of their spiritual activism.

The changes from 1959 to 1969 bear witness to the civil rights era and openness to greater organizational possibilities. The Thomas-Grady Counties Singing Convention established the only credit union of its kind, being founded by a rural singing convention. Its convention bulletins issue the following announcement to supporters: "Remember to: Join and support your federal credit union." Apparently, local residents do not need coaxing, for at one of its annual credit union banquets I learned it has reached an endowment totaling over one million dollars. For rural home folk, who often still farm, this accumulation is no small accomplishment. As a charitable movement, through the U.S. Department of Housing and Urban Development, a local church developed subsidized housing for senior citizens. Most of this venture was funded by the tried-and-true way, which is now often maligned, selling fish dinners. These achievements speak to the power of collective economics and this community's desire to spread its benevolence. Such ventures also speak to the economic savvy and vision of those generally deemed unsophisticated.

Undeniably, a system of collective economics also fuels their singing sessions. Usually eight choirs sing, and then time is allotted for the obligatory offering. The presiding deacon will request that a member from every church choir stand before the entire assembled body for "the long march." Then everyone remaining in the pews walks single file forward to deposit their donations in one or more of the proffered baskets. While surging along, they sing something inspirational such as "We Have Joy." Afterward, the deacon in charge of ushering the assemblage through this process officially turns the program over to the president. The president eloquently will make an address like the following:

> We want to thank you
>   for being so nice tonight
>   and walking.
> A lot of people want to walk
>   who can't walk.
> A lot of times I don't feel like walking.
> I'm not able to walk;
>   but I thank God I'm able to walk tonight.

The singing soon resumes with the remaining six groups, followed by the financial reports. Based on my observations, the host averages five hundred dollars on Friday nights. On Sundays, attendance usually escalates, as with Baptist union meetings, producing a greater windfall. Members refer to these singing conventions as rallies. On average, such a rally might net nearly three thousand dollars. Although the sums may not appear impressive to most, according to Gabriel: "They had no other outlet wherein they could raise any funds."

This form of reciprocity strengthens the community's overall economic base. Therefore, as with Sunday Morning Band, singing conventions mask traditional West African cultural practices. In *Culture, Politics, and Money Among the Yoruba*, researchers Toyin Falola and Akanmu Adebayo indicated that "The type of institutions for saving money which were developed among the Yoruba and which are still in operation in many places today, were those that suited the economic pursuits, social organization, and cultural setting." As rotating savings and credit associations, as extensions of *esusu*, this economic system operates as a monetary system in which members contribute and take turns as the principal recipient. Accordingly, President Emeritus Gabriel stated: "The same conventions got kitchens, air conditioners. Some of the only air conditioners that they would ever would have [are] from these choirs, that money like they're raising. Kitchens, air conditioners, rugs, on the floor—all that seating—that they got—[are]

comfortable. The church couldn't do that ordinarily with a one or two Sunday church." By uniting and working together, the choruses rally to improve the aesthetic and functional qualities of churches where they allocate so much of their time as well as being the sites for the recovery of so many memories.

The same communal spirit invigorates most aspects of their everyday lives. As with any system involving money, abuses can occur. From this standpoint, the spiritually motivated chanteuse, Mary Lou Henderson, made clear this potential: "Singing conventions used to do pretty good, but most of it is a racket. Raise a thousand dollars . . . if you don't raise money they don't leave no money there. Then, you're feeding them free. Now, the congress, we buy our food." With so many different singing conventions within this small town, some have created mechanisms of control to ensure that all of their memberships pull their own weight. Henderson exposed some shortcomings and how one church organization worked to greater satisfaction by paying for its refreshments upfront. Willie Johnson provided a few additional fine points: "A lot of time, most of us won't give unless they know that you're doing something. If you plan to buy new pews, if you plan to buy a new piano or what not, they will give liberally. But if you're talking about just about building the treasury up or to take care of things that may wear out or replace stuff, you won't hardly get a whole lot for just that. But if they can see a need, and you have gone and bought a new piano, and say you've got to pay for this piano, they will give liberally or whatever. But they want to know where it's going." Therefore, within this sacred performance community, reciprocity is not enough just for its own sake.

As a consequence of their successful fundraising, these sacred performance communities' churches boast luxurious infrastructures compared to some other small, rural community churches. Appearances can be deceiving when viewing them from the road. In some respects, from the exterior they may all look alike: cinder blocked, no stained glass windows, and set low to the ground. However, once inside, Thomasville's African American churches can be relatively opulent: fully carpeted, upholstered pews, glittery chandeliers, modern kitchens and restrooms, and most importantly: air-conditioned. Willie Johnson explained how all this came into being: "We needed [funds] more in the past because people weren't able to pay much in churches back in those days. The little money that you were getting it took all of it just to give it to your pastor, and you didn't hardly have anything to do any building with." As a result, the community devised these reciprocal support networks to improve collectively a multiplicity of home churches.

Louise Johnson, member of the Thomas-
Grady Counties Singing Convention and
wife of the late Willie Johnson, a key
informant

Always with an eye to the future, these conventions attract a more youthful constituency by discarding dorayme singing for the gospel sound. They
also garner larger community support and rely on other inducements. The
City-Wide Choirs' Union grants scholarships to high school seniors who
join them a total of twelve times, six months during their junior and senior
years. The requirements allow the students some agency, asking they attend
at their own discretion half the time. The greatest hope is that these youth
will become tradition bearers themselves. These gospel gatherings also allow for greater instrumentation: piano, organ, drum, and guitar. Although
older members like Mother Henderson embrace the transformation, they
also acknowledge a lost aesthetic: "You were singing a cappella. . . . They
didn't have no music then. When you're singing a cappella, you're singing
then. You see the music helping you now. You can't sing without the music now. Before you didn't have no piano then." All the attendant changes
enter Henderson's scrutiny, she added: "This younger crowd don't know
the notes. [Demonstrates shape-note] You pitch a song . . . and they catch
it . . . you sing the note and then you sing the words. . . . When they get up
there and start to rocking . . . I move with the spirit . . . I move by the spirit.
. . . The time they get up there they start a-rocking and a clapping." What
Henderson is critiquing is how this swaying, footpatting, and handclapping
have been appropriated as stylistic devices rather than affectively ingrained
responses. However, her remarks are intended as an observation, not as a

criticism. From her perspective, rather than choreographed clapping, all that is called for is to "Open your mouth and give event to the spirit by saying amen." Members are ever conscious of paradigmatic generational shifts but seldom in the spirit of directly opposing change.

The elders delight in recounting past and present differences. Sapp reminisced: "I grew up in a singing family. They mostly sung from the floor. When they were singing those shape-notes, they didn't go up in the choir [loft] singing. They sang from the floor. They got up and sang on the floor. Individuals would get up and lead, then everyone would sing along." Despite their condemnation of certain changes wrought by the shift to gospel music, Henderson and Sapp remain instrumental in ensuring the survival of singing conventions. They hold several official positions and belong to multiple singing unions. Moreover, Deacon Grimes, the longstanding vice president, leads the devotional period and often reproves everyone about the purpose of singing conventions—to have a good time. He cautioned:

> *I always say*
> > *that you don't have to have*
> > > *a house full of people*
> > > > *to enjoy the Lord;*
> *but you do have to get in the spirit.*
> *If you don't get in the spirit,*
> > *then the house can be packed*
> *but you won't enjoy a lot.*

For this singing convention, spirit does not mean shouting. Rather spirit entails singing together, energetically participating, and allowing a godly aura to come alive.

Deacon Grimes engages a body that believes that prayer changes things. Unlike the prayers rendered by deacons at the Baptist union meetings or even regular Sunday worship, his prayer at the Thomas-Grady Counties Singing Convention is spoken with greater specificity:

> *I pray that you will sound a little better. I pray that you will loose yourself, get into the service.*

As a deacon at his church and an officer of this convention, Deacon Grimes is responsible for raising the opening hymn to inaugurate the frame shepherding them into the next binary frame: the choral singing. Instead of common meter and lining a hymn, his choice of opening devotional selections commonly include "Come Go to That Land," a song popularized by the gospel quartet The Soul Stirrers and "I'll Fly Away," a song written and arranged by African American composer Albert E. Brumley. A typical devotional period will end with a hymn such as "Leaning on the Everlasting Arms," a favorite standard Baptist hymn. Musicologist Gwendolin Sims Warren noted: "A common saying in the African-American church, even today, comes from this song. When someone asks, 'Sister So-and-So, how are you doing today?' the answer is often, 'Oh, I'm leaning on the Lord!'" Ritualistically, relying on these standard hymns functions to stabilize the assembly before it diversifies into a cacophony of sounds.

Initially, I anticipated more emotionalism. With the Thomas-Grady Counties Singing Convention being my first exposure to singing conventions, I admit to expecting more stereotypical, rapturous behavior. Given all the component parts associated with these conventions, they are the most unlikely performance communities to experience the Holy Ghost. As already reported as relates to memory, even Sacred Harp conventions exhibit the propensity to demonstrate tearful sentiments. Based on the ensuing performance, John Storm Roberts' assessment would seem to hold: "All in all, when early black Christian music used existing white material, this material was immediately subjected to a molding process, bringing it in line with established musical practices developed from African sources: call-and-response, increased rhythmic flexibility, the use of handclapping for percussion (which can lay claim to being the major African percussive practice, and which was reported in black U.S. religious music by the eighteenth century), and the emphasis on possession states as a form of worship and a sign that the spirit was present." Perhaps researchers overstate the extent to which African American's privilege the shout. I have duly learned that singing conventions are worshipful occasions. They may sing with fervor and clap with ferocity, but these hypnotic moments do not trigger spirit possession. The same songs and the same chords being met along with great repetition and handclapping galore may lead to emotional displays in church worship. Yet, at these conventions, they are about God's business—making a way out no way, for all. The spirit is present, but it moves multivocally, fomenting a collective, spiritual identity and is not reducible to a community shouting the house. According to group leader Henderson, shouting did not fuel worship services much in the past either. She attributes such behavior as learned responses from television evangelism.

Of course, since the formation of these singing conventions, gospel music, too, has evolved. But members generally eschew the more popularized contemporary gospel music, preferring the traditional early gospel sound.

Many favorite songs are standard Euro-American hymns. Once again, I cite Reverend Wyatt T. Walker, who noted their transitional use by African Americans, who "blackened" them. As part of the blackening process, the foremost transformation is the addition of melisma. Deviating from the musical score is the hallmark of gospel music. Musically, within the Thomas-Grady Counties Singing Convention sacred performance community, if not performing a cappella, singers rely heavily on piano accompaniment. Not everyone who plays piano can play the organ; therefore, organs are rarified fixtures within these churches. Nor did performances normally incorporate electronic keyboards and drums. However, with their introduction, shouting is not uncommon. Seemingly, instrumentation permits the experiencing of greater spiritual empowerment. The Thomas-Grady Counties Singing Convention allows for a great deal of musical flexibility. Probably thanks to the money raised at these conventions, every church possesses a piano; however, it is not unusual for it to remain silent either. Some choral ensembles may sing a cappella, others attend with their own pianists, while still others may accept accompaniment from another choir's musicians. It all depends on available personnel and inclination, without compromising their aesthetic community.

Their musicianship is steeped in the traditional gospel style established by Roberta Martin, Willie Mae Ford Smith, and others from the Dorsey era. Deacon Gabriel reported that upon returning from a convention with newly purchased sheet music, local pianists could not play it. Speaking to their persistence in upgrading their style, choirs still sang it vocally. Even today, singers in this part of Wiregrass Georgia sometimes find it difficult to perform with musical accompaniment. As Sapp indicated, "They want me to sing like they play, and some people can't pick you up singing in your tune. They try to put you in their tune, the tune they playing in. What they learned how to play because the majority of the musicians now don't know one thing about round or shape-notes. No doubt, they don't know what a rudiment is." Those without shape-note singing experience are judged as lacking. Nostalgically, shape-note is looked upon as the singing of music with vocal finesse, the blending of notes and words delivered a cappella.

Larger area churches now have choir directors as well. The directors also play a dual role, sometimes also performing as song leaders. In performance, choir directors add a stylistic element, turning to face the pews, singing as though speaking the lyrics to the audience, or relying on broad gestures such as outstretched arms to accentuate the lyrics in songs like "Jesus Can." The audience response is not resounding as when a lone song leader makes similar kinetic gestures, but instead they sway and raise their hands high in surrender. Within choral music groups, lead singers emerge to carry most selections. The preferred vocal range for female song leaders generally is contralto. At most, there is only one male in attendance per choral unit to sing the still lower scales.

The predominance of women speaks to the role female singers played as gospel performers from its inception. Singers such as Rosetta Tharpe, Mahalia Jackson, and now Shirley Caesar are their role models. Song leaders customarily initiate a song and their vocal role often fades, blending in with the other voices and occasionally adding vocal dexterity and sonic, acrobatic lyricism. Due to the repetitious nature of most selections, the song leader improvises by furnishing the next repetitive vocal thread. Others see this as another distinction from the shape-note tradition: "Then they used the books all the time. They never sang without the books; but now everybody's got so famous singing, they don't need the books." Unlike gospel programs or fetes, as part of the turn taking at these singing conventions, each selection is completed expeditiously without the typical full-blown spontaneity.

Advancing a congregational style, the excitement seems to evolve from the randomness of the selections, as at a shape-note convention, with the audience finding voice along the way, with the usual patting of feet, clapping of hands, and other body movements. On Friday nights, the audience customarily consists primarily of other choral group members. Singing to a roomful of vocalists who eagerly participate produces sensational music. For the most part, because they also sing together at their home churches, there is generally no need to rehearse: "Once you kick off and get it warmed up, everybody can go on about their business [singing]. All they need is a lead." So, these gospel choruses depend on antiphonal triangulation. Their song leaders transmit the verse (the call) while other choir members render the chorus (the response), which is ultimately taken up by all present as one larger rejoinder. Beyond the common call-and-response patterning, this triangulation privileges joint familiarity of existing repertoire.

I reiterate that only one representative from a church choir is enough to constitute an enrollment. I should also note that these are not mega choirs. The average choir size is seven members, usually the majority being women along with a male vocalist or two. One church, Rebecca, recurrently enrolls the same duet, whom rely on sweet harmony, blending voices dolce. In conjunction, the audience typically hums softly along; then, more vocal chords gently arise from among them. Their dismount from the choir loft signals a hymn's conclusion. While singing a hymn of improvisation, "Were You There," one Easter weekend, the duet dismounted, continuing to harmonize.

The audience responded voluminously, escalating to demonstrate support. By garnering their full participation, stylistically, the selection was among the few to elicit earnest applause. Sometimes, choral groups combine into one mass choir, such as Piney Grove and Ochlocknee. When this occurs, with about a dozen people assembled, the tiny loft reaches near capacity. Also deviating from the norm, two selections may then be sung. Such arrangements do not generate any noticeable dialogue in garnering accord.

Moreover, textually, this convention features a diversity of sacred music genres. Unlike the other sacred performance communities, this singing convention does not approximate the structure of Sunday morning worship services, anniversary programs, or other religious celebrations. It conforms mostly to the shape-note singing conventions of old, except for the choral format. Although one might encounter an admixture of genres within different frames of even shape-note singing conventions, at these events, the main frame is keyed traditionally by one genre of music from their tunebooks. At the Thomas-Grady Counties Singing Convention, however, the enrollees determine each selection, without regard to generic form. Although they sing only one selection, they gospelize every selection, including a spiritual song such as "Wading in the Water," with great improvisation. When this happens, where the average selection is approximately four minutes, by prompting a congregational surge of enthusiasm, a song might last up to ten or even fifteen minutes. The song leader orchestrates the ending by initiating the processional to exit the loft while, ordinarily, the singing continues until the last musical chord is struck and everyone's once again seated in the audience.

These choral groups make their transition with unequaled precision. This convention is a rarity with its ability to mobilize an assemblage of people in an orderly fashion without fanfare. Only the slightest delay may occur when pianists switch positions. As an outgrowth of shape-note singing, in which song leaders emerge from around the square, the tradition here is that as one listed group mounts the choir loft, the next in succession takes its place. Seldom does any choreography enter into this level of performance. The processional from the pews to the choir loft creates the most pomp in terms of kinetic movement, and some choreograph their exiting moves. Stylistically, some gospel choruses may add a vamp as they exit by repeating a section or slipping in a few bars of a different song. One thing that distinguishes this form of gospel event from the rest is that no one acts as an emcee might, encouraging participation or interpreting lyrical content. Everyone knows the order of their appearance because, long ago, their ancestors engraved the sequence each church choir follows.

Handclapping operates as a specialty within this singing convention as well. Adding a percussive element of style, it is a mainstay of most African American musical performances. Because most of the songs are up-tempo, one can witnesses the many ways this collective responds percussively. The handclapping is an instrument and a part of a song's polyrhythmic display. Traditional gospel depends on creating a syncopated effect. May I say, there are rhythmic songs and *rhythmic* songs. As Boyer indicated: "And gospel song regardless of its text may be performed as a slow song, with a dotted quarter-note at M.M. 44–60; a fast song, with a quarter-note at M.M. 77–200; or as 'without rhythm' (performed in the lining out hymn traditions, w[ith] quarter-note at M.M. 50–60)." For some selections such as "Let Us Go Back to the Old Way," the handclapping pattern becomes more accentuated. Once the devotional frame ends, because spoken words are kept to a minimum, handclapping is the most unrelenting expressive component. It also represents the nearest thing to percussive instruments, as drums and bass guitars generally fall outside this performance community. Relying on their hands, percussively, in keeping with tradition they supplement their joyful noise, knowing how to get their musical invocations heard through the expressive amplification of sound. They insist that you don't get as much out of the music if you don't put yourself into it via some kinetic movement.

I often asked choir presidents, who usually also function as song leaders, about their favorite songs. Henderson cited the following songs: "Now, this last song that I like: 'Is Your Grace and Mercy' [narrates entire text]. And then we have this song I used to sing all the time: 'Never Grow Old'" (narrates for me):

> *I've heard of a land*
> *On a faraway strand*
> *It's the beautiful home of the soul*
> *It's built by Jesus on high*
> *There we never shall die*
> *It's the land where we'll never grow old.*
> *Chorus: Never, never grow old.*

According to her, the appeal is that they all transmit a meaningful literal message. Sapp, too, selected an evocative song: "I like that song ["Trouble in My Way"]. It got a lot of meaning in it, 'cause trouble do get in your way. And you do have to cry sometime." She acknowledged that in performance she usually improvises the words to this song. Musicologist Oral Moses documented spiritual texts as a source for traditional gospel music. Consulting his list, it substantiates the degree to which many songs in current circulation originated as spirituals. For instance, one of the first songs I heard sung chorally, "Why Jesus Is a Rock in a Weary Land," is appropriated from the spiritual "Jesus Is a Rock." The transformation appears to uphold the sentiment that traditionally spirituals spoke to God while gospel to one another.

New ministers can be notorious for disrupting the flow of traditional activities. Because they play no role, some schedule other events such as the usher's anniversary program in conflict with times when their church is to host the Thomas-Grady Counties Singing Convention. To avoid shifting hosts, the options are to only meet on Friday or consecutively for two months. One church leader demanded his choirs no longer participate. When its members refused to obey his command, he enjoined them to desist from using the church's name, nor could they host the convention there. On the printed bulletin, instead, it is generically listed as Gospel Chorus. Once again, it is the classic case of a minister expressing dominion over the spiritual life of his flock. At the time, Deacon Gabriel was serving his fiftieth year as Thomas-Grady Counties Singing Convention's president. As with Dewey Williams, the respect they elicit from throughout their community fails to impress some men of the cloth to waver. Gabriel expressed this stance: "You're still an individual. You still have some rights to go wherever you want to. You're not enslaved." His church actually has five choirs, including its youth choir, and the minister wanted them to form a mass choir, a recent trend. They never did. Eventually, the minister did relent, although they have yet to shift back to using the church's name.

With this kind of commitment, Thomas-Grady Counties Singing Convention has convened every February, April, June, August, October, and December for more than eighty years. On occasion, the convention coincides with Good Friday and Easter Sunday. As with documenting Fifth Sunday activities, on holidays I sometimes found myself in a quandary as to which ritual event to attend. In 1995, I spent Good Friday in Thomasville and Easter Sunday at the Jackson singing in Ozark. By doing so, I sought to witness how holidays might influence cultural performances. One big difference at the Thomasville convention was how the season affected attendance. As per tradition and part of his plenipotentiary role, Deacon Doster Grimes commenced the Devotion while evidently stalling for time. After leading a couple more hymns than usual—"I Have a Savior over in Zion" and, of course, "Leaning on the Everlasting Arm"—he communicated: "Hopefully when we finish this one everyone will be in." Being a voluntary association, attendance is always a concern, which is aggravated around holiday times when many may commit to a cornucopia of other options, including the familial.

Following an elongated Devotion, during the felicitous welcome Easter emerged as the dominant theme:

> *We think about what the hymn writers said.*
> *Some say: 'Well, I can't sing.*
>   *I can't sing like this one*
>   *and I can't sing like that one.'*
> *We may not be able to sing like angels.*
> *We may not be able to preach like Paul,*
>   *but one thing we can do is:*
> *we can tell the world that Christ died*
>   *for all of us.*
> *And in this season,*
>   *when he arose from the dead,*
>   *the main thing is*
>   *to know that Christ arose*
> *in us.*

Easter informed the closing prayer as well:

> *We're in that time of the season*
>   *that everybody*
>   *that confesses to know Christ*
>   *ought to be in celebration.*
> *I don't mean*
>   *just buying new clothes now*
>   *and planning far away trips.*

The president of the convention, Clifford Williams, also commented on the slack attendance, expressing for those in attendance to "act just like this might be the last time." Most poignantly, he experienced a stroke before the next official meeting. Although he survived to sing again, his perfunctory response upholds his stated beliefs.

The president's church, Mt. Moriah, is always remarkable. Rather than black-and-white attire, choral robes, or street garb, typically they appear color coordinated—all dressed in maybe royal blue with the men attired in yellow shirts. Audience reception is great due to their exceptional wardrobe, which triggers heightened anticipation. As soon as the pianist strikes the first note, with full recognition, President Emeritus Tommie Gabriel is known to exclaim: "That's a beautiful one." President Clifford Williams claps thunderously, while leading "Call on the Lord, He'll Come." It should be mentioned that Williams is one of the few participants who also performs regularly with an amateur quartet. Everyone gravitates to the repetition of the call-and-response patterns he ordains. By the end of a five-minute song, he compels most in attendance to their feet, in one accord, and without the usual congregational participation. Everyone listens enraptured.

Surprisingly, on the opening Friday nights, this performance community can conduct all its business with great speed, considering that more than a dozen choirs perform. I have timed performances. Most are actually quite brief, approximating the three- or four-minute length of most commercial recordings. At this rate, if all choral groups attend, about half the appointed time is devoted to singing. The opening remarks and offertory rite consume the majority of the time. As late as 9:30 p.m., there may be a couple groups remaining to sing. Yet no one leaves prematurely, as is the case at gospel anniversaries. This is a highly supportive and routinized sacred performance community. However, after the benediction, the church is quickly vacated. No one mills about because the Sunday session will be the culminating event and they'll meet again. In total, the first night of the convention takes slightly more than two hours. This time frame is remarkable in comparison with other performance communities.

When sessions reassemble on Sunday, it is broadcast over a local AM radio station, which results in a different dynamic. The singing convention starts at 1:00 p.m., allowing those with pastoral days to attend both. Within an hour, they recess for lunch, then the public broadcast begins at 3:00. To lend a greater amount of artistry to the radio program, they showcase their best song leaders, such as Bernice Lurry, who is also always among the most fabulously attired on these Sunday afternoons. A member of Shiloh's choir, Lurry reminds me of Onett Meeks when I was growing up. She is the kind of vocalist who rivals Mahalia Jackson, not only in vocal range, but the ability to translate her faith through song. She sings many songs from Jackson's repertoire such as "Last Mile of the Way." Traditional gospel reigns supreme within this performance community because there are singers among them who can interpret and deliver it, relying on melisma, to maximize the emotional appeal and heighten their awareness of the Lord. They may not have the musicianship that contemporary gospel enjoys, but they know how comforting and inspiring it is to know the Lord as well as join hands with their ancestors of faith. Such singing links their foundation to the past.

The Willing Workers is one of the more curious singing conventions. According to one official, Grant Revels, the Thomas-Grady Counties Singing Convention is one of its offspring. Ostensibly, there were too many churches interested to maintain efficiently just one convention. It meets every other first weekend of the month on Friday night and Sundays at 12:30 p.m., operating as an offshoot from dorayme singing. Originally, a teacher from Moultrie, J. W. Sykes, taught singing schools using a Stamps and Baxter tunebook on one night a week, giving instruction at different local churches. Conforming to the norm, he charged ten cents per student. He used a blackboard to teach the rudiments. Several of these churches then organized the Willing Workers singing convention. Nine AME and CME churches mainly comprise the membership of this convention. However, a choir from Providence Baptist takes part as well. I observe women are less visible, except in predictable roles as the secretary and one of the youth advisors.

Revels began singing school in 1925, at the age of fifteen. These members, too, no longer sing shape-note; but the convention continues in the spirit of the older tradition because singers rely on songbooks. Revels imparts that the death of Sykes, the only instructor, acted as the catalyst for them to discontinue shape-note singing. Thus, the convention conforms more to a memorial sing to J. W. Sykes. It features crooning a hymn composed by him, "When I Cross the River," which is also its theme. Ironically, they enact a reinterpretation of the earlier singing conventions. The Willing Workers convention now deploys mainly Euro-American compositions, as notated on the page, first calling out the page number as if singing shape-note and cradling the hymnal as if a B. F. White tunebook. Referencing choirs is also a misnomer; without the hollow square or pacing, individuals select a hymn and lead all singers. It also has a convention pianist who is paid a salary but, if tardy, the absence does not impede the convention's progress. Most of these churches possess a piano and organ. Those gathered generally sing without melisma, handclapping, repetition, or any of the characteristics associated with the gospel sound. Some elusively subtle footpatting occurs; and after each selection, there is usually polite applause. Their repertoire privileges "Amazing Grace," "I Have Decided to Follow Jesus," and "Blessed Assurance." These are songs that resonate from my past and with the same tempo and timbre. Uncannily, the ambiance most sends me back to the church of my youth.

The youth involvement was an afterthought. By the time of my introduction, the Senior Department had met consecutively for 585 sessions, while the Junior Department held its 425th session. But young people receive a great deal of focus. As an incentive for young people to continue their education, they are eligible for scholarships based on participation. Still their attendance is spotty. On Friday nights, the Junior Department is comprised of seven churches. After the ever-present offering, the Senior Department concludes with representation from nine. On Sunday, the convention opens with the Junior Department presiding over the Devotion with a song and prayer. Here, young people are overtly positioned in authoritative roles. Revels' expressed sentiment is: "Those are some future convention leaders. They came right out and did what was told of them. We have to instill in our young people that they've got to learn how to do it; and we have got to pick 'em up and strengthen them because they're learning. It takes something to get up here and do that." I suspect that there is no generational cleavage within this convention because participating youth, as I remember first hand, are expected to be compliant beings. Based on attendance, I would conjecture that this sacred performance community intends to persevere on it present course. From my perspective, this convention signifies why African Americans are charged with being overchurched. There can never be too many conventions either.

The City-Wide Choirs' Union is also relatively complex, due to its meeting schedule and mission. This body is very business-oriented, promoting college scholarships for its teens. City-Wide Choirs' Union meets monthly expressly after the fourth Sunday, on Wednesday nights, the night many churches reserve for Bible study. Like other area assemblages, it has survived for several generations. Deacon Gabriel considers its ability to survive and to keep moving a mystery because people generally don't like to go out on weekday nights. This arrangement speaks volumes; in the scheme of things, it is a virtual newcomer. Significantly, it has gathered for more sessions than the others because it convenes more often. Originally founded by three choirs in the 1970s, as many as twenty groups once belonged. Furthermore, this network is the one that caters to having youthful participation. Today, twelve choirs comprise the union, but two churches—Willowhead and St. James—enroll adult and youth choirs. Young people are integrated within the remainder. Organizers reserve the first six pews specifically for each choir.

This union features a binary structure. But unlike the accustomed pattern (beginning with a Devotion), before a note is sung, its president presides. As the longtime president, Ossie Robinson (the Willing Workers youth advisor) outlines the upcoming calendar and explains the scholarship guidelines along with making other announcements. Economic rituals, replete with the previous month's financial report, occupy the first frame. Other than a musical interlude rendered by the host choir, congregants set aside the musical frame for up to an hour. The City-Wide Choirs' Union convention probably owes its structure due to meeting on a weekday, to ensure that they do not tarry too long. Also, although rare, when hosted at Willowhead there is a ministerial presence. Instead of a sermon, however, Reverend Brinson of Willowhead recites a long prayer. He fully supports this union, and his church's adult choir bears his name.

Another singing convention unique to the region is The United Singing Convention of Georgia and Florida. In 1953, a small network of churches that once navigated across state lines occasionally in support of one another decided to formalize their obligation. Borrowing temporally from the Baptist union meeting structure, they rally on Fifth Sundays. The United Singing Convention consists of eight Georgia and three Florida home church choirs. Its name is an indication that its members are hardy wayfarers who will go to any length to sing. As with past singing conventions, these sessions function without a ministerial presence strictly to sing traditional gospel. Mother Henderson, who's also active in several other local singing conventions, often leads its Devotion. When situated in this role, women often bring their own dimension. Henderson is a powerhouse when lining hymns. According to Henderson, once rather than leading the ritual act with an individual prayer, she "had something else up her sleeves." She introduced a different form, Sinner's Prayers, with different attendees giving a short prayer.

These singing conventions share personnel, meaning choir members consent to spend many otherwise leisurely hours singing sacred music. Cumulatively, they commit to sing every Fifth Sunday, on Fridays and Sundays every other month, and monthly one Wednesday night. Especially because their churches do not worship on a weekly basis, the time allotted could balance out. But these conclaves add up. Moreover, most choir members belong to and hold leadership positions in other voluntary associations, including Freemasonry. The salient point is, as a lifestyle, singing is "musically nourishing." What they privilege most is a musical rite, which is a sign of belief whenever it comes alive.

Many commonalities link these singing conventions, besides the sharing of personnel. These are forums in which the latest in contemporary gospel music never seeps into a choral performance. They believe in the old time church, singing from a repertoire that may be archaic elsewhere. During an interview, one singer expressed: "I don't want no studio style, I want church style." The prevailing objection is that contemporary gospel contains objectionable lyrics that do not coincide with scripture. In other words, as the saying goes: "You can sing a lie as well as tell a lie." Singers must make sure music selections conform and strong lyrics are an important means of conveying God's word. To be frank, I propose that because overchurched, so to speak, each congregation cannot sustain the musicianship and vocalists to support contemporary gospel styles. Moreover, they sing for the collective good, and traditional gospel continues to suffice for now.

Rather than octogenarians, the general population constitutes members from the civil rights generation or a bit older. Participation in choral singing conventions is not predicated on a fundamental understanding of certain musical rudiments or a denominational orientation. Moreover, they do not veil the heightened role of women who populate their executive boards. During Devotion, Mary Lou Henderson periodically lined hymns, a role most church bodies and shape-note groups only extend to men. The song leaders and pianists most commonly are women. These bodies collectively represented the most egalitarian and efficacious sacred performance communities. Bealle also historicized how, as an extension of revivals and Sacred Harp, such singing communities represent a transformation: "extract[ing] hymn singing from the world of liturgy and doctrine and releas[ing] it to the community, to the home, and to the unfettered hearts of its singers." The church supplies one context, but sacred music belongs to all realms.

In this way, shape-note singing conventions evolved into several hybrid forms. The abundance of choral singing conventions emanating out of Thomasville represents an impressive evolution. Scholars, who create a North–South binary regarding the rise of traditional gospel music, tend to generalize the history. Southerners accepted gospel music and participated in the transmission of this tradition, perhaps before many northern churches such as my own. Admittedly, these neoteric Wiregrass singing conventions are relatively idiosyncratic. I have not heard of others that operate chorally, as they do. And the sheer number of them in one locale speaks to not only the desire to praise the Lord in song but the magnitude of their collective economics. Their lives are sustained each day by a spiritual activism, which translates financially. The Thomas-Grady Counties Singing Convention, City-Wide Choirs' Union, Willing Workers, and The United Singing Convention of Georgia and Florida did not grow out of a vacuum. The seven shape-note tradition allowed for the expansion into a range of significant sacred music communities. The next chapter describes those networks that, via reciprocal support, engage quartets and more contemporary gospel performance styles. Therefore, the "Gospel Train Is Coming" signifies the arrival of yet another distinct response to the region's communitarian outlook and communal exuberance.

CHAPTER 6

"The Gospel Train Is Coming"

Wiregrass Contemporary Gospel

For me riding the contemporary gospel train turned into a mesmerizing experience. Not having grown up in a church or household that privileged gospel music, I really embraced interacting with some spectacular networks. Gospel performances are ubiquitous throughout the region. Whereas certain sacred performance communities may be limited to a particular pocket of Wiregrass Alabama, Florida, or Georgia, contemporary gospel music is omnipresent. Its performers depend on actively belonging and regularly contributing to their networks year round. This pattern holds true nationally as well. According to the preeminent performer and historian Bernice Johnson Reagon: "In African American communities, gospel music remains a way of developing and asserting a sense of individual and collective identity—of finding one's individual and collective voice in one's own time, and speaking through one's heart and soul for all to hear." Additionally, amateur gospel performers in Wiregrass Country provide their own fiscal and musical twists. They engage in a level of spiritual activism that requires perpetual motion.

To reiterate, reciprocity gains full expression through the traditionalizing and maintenance of support networks. Mechanisms to ensure the survival of the group, such communally defined networks constitute the heart of rural African American social and spiritual life. As I have explained, these reciprocal support networks depend upon both secular and sacred performance communities to provide the rationale for regular social interaction. They act as an outlet not only for artistic expression but support a communal identity based on collective economics. As scholar Melvin Williams stated, community can be defined as "patterned interactions among a delineated group of individuals who seek security, support, identity, and significance from their group." With membership, in times of crisis an abundance of financial resources materialize in accordance with their communitarian outlook. Performance communities agree to network, that is, to pool their finances periodically, to affirm one another. Whereas a larger overarching community exists and shares many commonalities as if a fixed network, each performance community asserts its own sovereignty. The theme of reciprocity represents the main bond connecting a network to a particular performance community. The staging of highly patterned, repeatable, ritualized cultural performances constitutes the network's primary means of generating revenue. These networks support a complex economic system.

As relates to sacred music, musicologist Anthony Heilbut stated: "Gospel singers need an audience that shares their feelings and acknowledges their efforts at self-expression." Besides comprising their own chief audience at anniversary programs, Wiregrass gospel singers contribute financially to each other's coffers. Nearly everyone attends not only to hear God's music, but also to bestow monetary gifts. As I have heard it expressed within the offertory frame: "Come on let's do what we're supposed to do. Catch somebody by the hand—boy, girl, woman, man—it doesn't matter. You know what we're here for." Those designated to be on the finance committee even tap those milling about outside for their contributions. The committee immediately counts the proceeds, and it is not uncommon for them to request a specific sum to round the total off: "Somebody give us sixteen more dollars." From there, the request may be lowered a dollar at a time, as financial gifts continue to trickle in. Arguably, reciprocity is the real incentives for the perpetuating and popularity of this musical tradition.

The economic bases of these programs cannot be ignored. Individuals, rather than just the churches and sodalities, are the primary beneficiaries. Some official religious bodies attack local gospel performers due to this more individualized bent. In essence, these networks operate under the assumption of "You wash my hands, and I'll wash yours." Gospel quartets often bear the brunt of some local critic's disdain. Quartet singers are singled out as sometimes not being sincere. For instance, Louise Sapp expressed: "I used to always have quartets come to sing at our programs. But one thing, the quartets got to charging, sixty/forty. They wanted you to pay them sixty cents and the church gets forty cents that's why they stopped using the quartets. Money." Those singers performing at church anniversaries aspire to move from amateur status to becoming semi-professional, at least. As a result, they may perform sacred music in churches, but their actions and often more secular lifestyles fuel suspicion about their motives. No doubt, some seek purely monetary gain, personal glory, or are drug or alcohol dependent. To maintain credibility and their support base, gospel group members disparage those who sully their divinely inspired intent.

Not surprisingly, preachers serve as some of the major critics of these sacred performance communities. On the one hand, they often remark: "If you've come [to church] for the choir, you ought to stay at home. We should come for the word." On the other hand, ministers also deride these gospel performance communities for "swapping money." The stalwart singers charge preachers with being moneygrubbers, too. With enough criticism to go around, Sapp stated: "They selling the gospel so fast. They've got to the place where they set a price on you. And if you don't pay them their price, they don't preach for you. Now where is God?" By eschewing the contemporary gospel sound, some local adherents expect to be exempt from charges of commercialism. Moreover, this level of gospel programming constitutes something of a "chitlin circuit." The few commercially recorded local gospel performers have a longer reach and seek compensation for their time and expenses.

Demonstrating the interdependency of sacred music traditions, "specials" as they were called—solos, duet, trios, quartets, family groups, and piano or organ instrumentals—derived from the dorayme shape-note tradition. Songbook publishers such as Stamps-Baxter, which also sponsored them to boost sales, popularized quartets. Traditionally, among African Americans, the term *quartet* is loosely applied to vocal ensembles including more singers than the implied four. From four to eight singers may compose a quartet, singing in four-part harmony. Urban quartets have recently received a great deal of scholarly attention. This chapter engages the historical role quartets played by recentering the previously conducted research within a rural context. One informant astutely pointed out: "every community and each church had one." Locally, today, they face decline. For some, ironically, *quartet* is now a generic label attributed to all singing ensembles—male and female with and without the characteristic complex harmonizing.

Anniversary programs furnish the main context for gospel musical performances today. Trying not to conflict with already well-established church and community programs, anniversary occasions, then, may not necessarily coincide with a group's actual formation. From an insiders' perspective, one choral singer explained their cultural significance:

Anniversary's a fundraiser for the choirs and for the church. We go back to them and give a donation at each church that came to represent us, showed up as guests or hosts on our programs. . . . Whatever else is left goes additionally to the church. We raise four hundred dollars. We are not going to give it all back to the groups. Sometimes we don't spend two hundred dollars writing out the amounts donated to us. But where we gave extra amounts of money is what we give additionally. And if we like to sell hotdogs or fish sandwiches, that's additional. The meal committee cooks, and we give the rest to the church. We don't like to charge everybody but we found out that it works, and everyone seems pleased with it. The men are handling [the food] now, if no one else is around to do the job.

I also learned that for most anniversary programs are in general "something like a birthday." Probably as an outgrowth of the old Sacred Harp singing tradition, African Americans in Wiregrass Alabama maintain a stringent number of vocalists scattered among them. For singers, anniversary programs are the backbone of this music tradition. Supporters literally can spend every weekend of the year sustaining their networks. As is customary for most sacred performances, anniversary programs also are scheduled frequently for both Friday and Saturday nights and again on Sunday afternoons. Unlike shape-note convention weekends, over the course of a weekend gospel programs may be held in a variety of locales. By so doing, honorees ensure a broad attendance by making their celebration more convenient for those living in outlying areas.

On such weekends, anniversary programs place wheels in motion for considerable, reciprocated travel. It is common for members of a network to attend as many as four anniversaries in one night. It could be said that such programs provide these performers' raison d'être. Travel, undoubtedly, constitutes another custom first set in motion by camp meetings, revivals, and singing conventions. Enthusiasts commonly travel from Friday to Sunday most weekends in support of the various honorees. However, they tend to travel within some self-imposed limitation. Alabama singer Sheryl Melton disclosed: "We go different places in Florida and we go to Georgia. So it's just like a Wiregrass type thing. But we can only go so many miles to the west, to the south and to the east when you think about it." An ingrained sense of reciprocity keeps singers, musicians, and supporters on the road. Once they become part of a network, travel becomes a compulsion. On this level, collective economics also speaks to a culturally bound ethos.

Wiregrass contemporary gospel singers often have a central performance community. They have officers just like those that belong to singing conventions and keep copious financial records. They often maintain an account from which to extract their monetary donation to anniversary programs. Attendees are assessed an enrollment fee of fifteen to twenty dollars to sing. Later, the hosts expect an offering of between five or ten dollars as well. Ritualistically, during the offertory rite or in the midst of singing, paper money is pinned onto the honorees' clothing, forming a streamer of bills. As part of the reciprocity, these donations amount to an investment. As relates to Sacred Harp, folklorist Doris Dyen realized the depth of such networks: "Practically speaking, it is impossible for people to participate physically in all of these activities. An alternative is available, however, in the concept of 'representing' oneself through a token gift of money, which is used as a method of participating by proxy." Today, this practice continues via gospel programs. It is a means of showing appreciation for the year. Unlike professional or semi-professional groups, charging admission to hear gospel is considered ungodly.

Each anniversary program also commonly promotes Bible themes such as "I have opened my mouth unto the Lord, and I cannot go back" (Judges 11:35). Another program theme comes from Proverbs: "It takes faith to step out on nothing and believe that something is there." The themes are often like the music. Explicating the music, folklorist Ray Allen focused on nonprofessional singers who are community-based like Wiregrass singers except they sing in the urban North, with similarities and differences. He indicates: "while gospel lyrics tend to focus on earthly hardship, trouble, and despair, they also offer a positive solution to these problems and the opportunity to transcend worldly burdens through a spiritual commitment. The overall tone of most songs is one of joy, celebration, and optimism." Along with the theme, some printed literature also exhibits a motto: "To see my God Face to Face." Whether based on scripture or dogma, nonetheless, the themes and mottos are intended to be equally uplifting.

Gospel anniversary programs are typically well organized. Due to the popularity of these cultural performances, time becomes a major factor. Customarily, extending from Friday until Sunday, each anniversary program can run more than four hours in length. This amount of commitment epitomizes real devotion. Nonetheless, organizers cannot allow egos to prolong these momentous occasions. Drawing on the already discussed gospel tradition, these programs also limit their singers to A and B selections. Dorothy "Doc" Brown, a singer, gospel promoter, and radio personality, known as the "Queen of Gospel" in Quincy, Florida, delineates the structure: "Especially, if they have a lot of groups there, they will tell you to sing A/B. It's according to how many groups they have on program. Sometimes, it be A/B and C. If you're out at a concert, you have a time limit, ten minutes because of the folks out of town. They come to hear them really, the ones that you bring into town. So they cut down to ten minutes." The acknowledged rule is that, when the emcee calls your name, singers are supposed to be ready. If the enrolled singers do not respond, then they "move on down the line." While sitting around the square indicates participation at shape-note singings, matching and very elegant, radiant attire is the main signifier of intent to sing for these groups. As quartet singer Joseph Johnson expressed it: "Ten percent of gospel singing is appearance."

Unlike singing conventions and some segments of Baptist union meetings, children perform a more integrated role in anniversary programs. They lead songs, give presentations, or even as toddlers just stand with performing parents. "I Didn't Hear Nobody Pray" and "Lily in the Valley" operate as staples among the children who sing in anniversary programs. One often hears comments such as "More children around here than a little bit," spoken with pride. The enduring function, of course, is to pass down heritage and also good discipline. These parents believe in disciplining their young: "I appreciate parents that are chastising their children, bringing them up in the way that they should go wherever they be at. This is God's house. It's supposed to be honored. It's supposed to be respected. And I thank you parents tonight." Anniversaries can be family affairs, with young adults often dominating. Living in a chiefly rural society, gospel music performance grants them an audience and level of recognition not generally awarded to a marginalized age group.

Wiregrass anniversary programs negotiate several time-honored gospel performance strategies. The drive or working section denotes one of the central performance elements in the gospel medium. Drive sections extend a song through vocal improvisation, relying on short repetitions of words and phrases. This stylistic feature creates a powerful effect that augments the emotionality of the songs. Associated with male quartets, each member intuits which parts are expandable. However, in the Wiregrass, many choose to forego this element. Performers sing together at church or as a family and possess personal repertoires. Compared to most of the other cultural performances discussed, anniversary programs are very fluid occasions. One predicable element is that, as a routine concludes, while continuing to sing the singers embrace the anniversary honorees or in some other way acknowledge them. This usually is the moment when performers gift the honorees by pinning money on them, creating a long strand of bills. As a finale, the more grandiose ensembles sometimes exit stylistically with a well-choreographed processional.

Furthermore, emcees are not just a fixture associated with hip-hop culture nor are they mere announcers. Arguably, the ones in greatest demand do not just announce groups but can spontaneously tie together the lyrics to both the A and B musical selections, orchestrating the mood pertaining to each performance. Emcees at anniversary programs play a pronounced role, connecting disparate performances and occasionally sermonizing. This is a position commonly upheld by women, who are called the mistress of ceremony and reveal great verbal dexterity. This role requires an outstanding amount of energy, spoken eloquence, and biblical aplomb. Additionally, emcees must exude excitement and great joy to pick up any lull. Signifying, one emcee exhorted a lackluster audience by exhorting them: "Anybody got any Ben Gay in here?" After a performance, they can arouse the audience by stating, "Come on. You can do better than that!" Then, too, around 9:30 p.m. and with a handful of groups yet to go, they know when to be subdued for the sake of time. Always mindful of the event losing momentum, emcees may only assert themselves at key moments: "I been trying not to talk, but you make me talk anyway." Then, too, when time is waning, emcees must mediate and know when to curtail performances: "I don't want anybody to be angry with me. We have a very lengthy list tonight. We have a very special guest. We want everybody to get a chance to sing. We're going to ask you to do us: one good song. Come on down, amen."

Many honorees distribute written bulletins, representing the ideal order of anniversary activities and for promotional purposes. By and large, however, spontaneity prevails. It is important that gospel anniversaries achieve a life of their own. Sometimes when the announced emcee is late and someone substitutes, as happened at one Gospel Train Special program in Alabama: "I'm just doing this until the main one gets here. I know ya'll about tired of hearing me talk, but I want ya'll to sing. I come all the way from Georgia and I have a group I brought here with me and I'm not ashamed of 'em." With much of the communication about these events coming by way of word of mouth, there are bound to be glitches about dates and places and among personnel. The only rule of thumb is that time be allowed for all singers to perform. No one's reprimanded for arriving late, nor is there censorship, in terms of the quality of the performance each participant displays. Additionally, it is not difficult to limit groups to two selections when most sacred performances communities traditionally advance this structure.

Emcees also may accept appearances at two occasions occurring simultaneously on the same day. Bringing a degree of professionalism, no matter how briefly, adds the desired dynamic to audiences. It is not unusual that an honoree winds up having to emcee his/her groups' own production.

Gospel emcee and singer Ovella Cunningham at the Southeast District Singing Convention Building in Elba, Alabama

Because chapter 7 furnishes greater details about the women, remarks here offer a general segue. For instance, singer Ovella Cunningham lends a certain spirit to any anniversary that she emcees. One year, the second emcee miscalculated appearances and arrived at the tail end of the Cunningham Family's program. The emcee delivered the following gracious explanation for her tardiness: "First, we would like to say: Thank God for His being here, right now. Happy Anniversary, again, to the Cunningham Family! I said to the lady a few minutes ago: 'This must have been a great anniversary because my son was supposed to be on his way home.' We have to keep looking to the hills from which cometh our help. I know tonight that I am not the Lord and I can't be everywhere at the same time but God can; and my mind was here. But I hope that you had a happy anniversary, and I hope Lord let us be here next year. Thank you." The son she mentioned is not only still present, but he played the synthesizer that evening and continued to play softly in the background throughout her address, adding to its effect. By alluding to him, she imparts how only a stellar occasion could have detained him, while acknowledging that by being tardy she missed out. Male quartet singers are more prone to exit programs once they have appeared, often with their musicians in tow, indicative of an overbooked evening.

In addition to the emcee doing so, participants may contextualize their own song selection. For example, a member of the Bible Jubilees begins a selection with this message: "When it seems like the doors of progress are closed in you face, tell the Lord to come on and see about you," commencing a song containing the same lyrics. Other gospel performers, especially those who sing close harmony in the quartet tradition, such as the Henry County Male Chorus, sermonize between songs:

> *Some of you here tonight*
> *   may be going through some things.*
> *And I just want to tell you*
> *   that you don't have to go through them*
> *   all by yourself*
> *'cause there's someone standing*
> *   waiting*
> *   and willing to shonuff aid*
> *   and willing to help you right now.*
> *All you have to do*
> *   is let Him stand*
> *   and wait.*
> *He's walking by your side.*
> *He'll hear you.*
> *He'll be your guide.*
> *And everybody knows*
> *   what the Lord will do (resuming song).*

As with the other African American musical traditions, especially the blues, participants often establish how they were born to sing this music. One of the younger singers, Sheryl Melton, who began to sing in earnest in 1978, asserted: "I was raised in a singing family—my mother's side of the family. There was fourteen of them, two died and that left twelve. My mother always had this high pitched voice. . . . My aunt played piano and they'd sing." Many gospel music performers reject singing secular music in lieu of the sacred forms. As Melton expressed her choice: "I know those people up there and that they be probably be singing along with you, as in a sing-a-long, but to me I just like to do it because I know this way the Lord will bless me; but if I take the gift or what he blessed me with and go over here and sing in the clubs and joints, I just don't think that He will bless me. I just really don't. I don't want to take a gift like that and just go over here. Like I tell anybody, I'm not the best singer but I sure try. I do. I tell you what. I do my part. And as for me, I'm more of a background singer than a leader, but I can sing some lead songs. But I'm with that background because that's what I mostly do." Clearly, as a vocalist, Melton's objective is to perform a viable supporting role. Typically, researchers focus on the lead vocalists, when even the background singers have a testimony and understand the competence they bring to a performance.

Because some of these performers belong to church choirs or musicians play as a band, they do generally rehearse for anniversary appearances. Regardless, they realize that their actual performance will seldom conform strictly to rehearsal. They know that they are given to improvisation and make allowances for spontaneity and the spirit-filled re-creation of lyrics along with vocal changes. Many singers would agree with Melton's assessment: "Well, we do a lot of improvising, when the Holy Spirit comes in. And you ought to bring something with you so you get something out of it. You have always heard that the old folks say so once you get into what's really going on and what matters the most, some things you never thought about will come out. And it can be just as beautiful and the music can be beautiful and the words of the song can be just as beautiful. And then all of a sudden you start putting in these little extra ideas and we found out it works fine. And when the Holy Spirit gets hold of you, you don't want to shut up. That's the thing." In this regard, singing becomes like an addiction, via improvisation: with each performance, one desires to reach an impromptu new height.

Over the past decade, contemporary gospel itself has become even more secular in tone, expression, and sound, especially when it incorporates hip-hop. The changes in storyline and musical phrasing are deemed anathema to what most singers in the region seek spiritually and creatively to achieve. Once again, they prefer songs they adjudge, textually, with a message. Melton provided this appraisal: "When you compare contemporary with gospel, it's not the same. And put that before those people; if they raised anyway like I was trained (when I was coming up), it just won't mix. It is just like water and oil." These singers are not eager to branch out beyond their musical comfort zone. What is most compelling by the established standards found in gospel music is that both the words and the music must tell good stories. When the two diverge, something is lost.

As a folklorist, one of my most fulfilling fieldwork experiences was discovering the Southeast District Singing Convention Building outside of Elba, Alabama. It unfurled another layer of the metaphorical onion. Whenever I thought I was at the saturation point in my fieldwork, another intriguing element unfolded. There is no way to know how many similar autonomous spaces may exist among African Americans. In December 1955, local gospel singers and musicians set upon obtaining a venue for their singing union. This structure antedates the time frame in which most musicologists situate the mainstreaming of gospel music in urban African

American communities. This building even antedates the Seven Shape Singing Convention Center in Greenville. It existed longer and exclusively to support gospel music performances. On Fifth Sundays, the Southeast District Singing Convention Building also hosts its own Baptist union meeting. The first frame parallels structural units happening concurrently at Baptist union meetings throughout Wiregrass Country. The meeting is presided over by an in-house minister, rather than a conglomeration of ministries. Reverend John Lawrence marshals congregants through the key ritual acts common to regular church services. Lawrence bridges both frames by being a minister and gospel musician. He introduced bongos into the musical performances and is a competent electric guitarist.

Whereas in Greenville they adhere strictly to shape-note music on Fifth Sunday, traditional gospel music is the cornerstone of this singing building. The Southeast District Fifth Sunday Union Meeting is formatted like the others. Except when it breaks for lunch, it resumes with an expressive song service. After the break, the second frame consists of a devotional period, a president's address, and finally a full-blown gospel program. It originally featured five umbrella gospel groups: The Seven Stars, Rising Stars, Traveling Stars, Spiritual Five, and Bright Stars. Their groups' names indicate, within the region, the degree to which performers gravitate toward a relatively limited number of proper nouns, often containing the word *star*. At an anniversary program at this same site one January, Morning Star and the Silver Stars were also on the roster. It also is not uncommon for several groups to possess the same name. When there are duplications, possibly only members of the each network know which group will actually appear. Many of the names are certainly duplicated wherever gospel groups flourish. They go by such names as: True Gospel Singers, Friendly Five, Gospel Starlights, Supreme Angels, Traveling Angels, Heavenly Angels, Spiritual Harmonizers, Gospel Interpreters, the Gospel Wheels, and so on. The names containing *angel* often denote male quartets. Ultimately, you sense that the hermeneutics related to group names are of little significance to them, and some are plainly generic such as the Florida Gospel Singers. They are a proverbial means to an end.

Members of the Spiritual Five form the leadership. This ensemble is comprised of three sisters along with one member's spouse. Ollie Henderson is the secretary and her husband, Charles, is a group member and their booking agent. Annie Perlsher coordinates the ushers. Alice Dozier is the assistant director and often emcees the gospel program. The president of the union, A. Z. Stoudmire, does not sing with the Spiritual Five. Ovella Cunningham, who informed me about the existence of this singing building, hosts one of the more elaborate anniversary programs at this sing-ing building. The Cunningham Family's network includes groups through-out the Wiregrass region—Texasville, Enterprise, Montgomery, Webb, Do-than, Ozark, Grady, Lapine, and Defuniak Springs, Florida—and actually reaches as far as Tallahassee.

In between the ritual cycle of Fifth Sunday, both Alabama singing build-ings serve as venues for downhome gospel music anniversary programs. Like singing conventions, gospel programs also customarily exist outside of any official church structure. The close relationship that once existed, even between singing conventions and many small community churches, has become eroded. Gospel singers and musicians, perhaps more than the rest, find it increasingly difficult to negotiate the use of sacred spaces. Accord-ingly, singer Ovella Cunningham testified: "[Gospel singing] got so big, a lot of churches don't want quartets." Due to changing trends, singing buildings exist for the exclusive use for anything "having to do with singing." Gospel music proves to be a relatively lucrative form of artistic expression needing its own space. Also, given their individual and collective purposes, atten-dance numbers do not generally matter. When attendance diminishes, it is not uncommon to hear: "We're not gonna worry about who's here and who's not here. We're here to praise the Lord." Unlike one's personal sense of obligation to attend church worship, it is by more voluntary assent that anniversaries are celebrated. People come, as they will.

Also, it is important to explore the role that remembrance played in the construction of singing buildings. The cultural performances at these sites preserve favorite songs of bygone days. Singing buildings offer space for the production of indigenous sounds and music that serve as devices of archival reclamation. The reclamation of a usable past is a kind of recovery that is part of a communal ideology. The construction of these sites stands as tangible proof of the powerful musical traditions that have withstood the test of time. While not fossils, for outsiders the style of gospel per-formances popularized locally may be tantamount to singing Gregorian chants. The singing building allows for a sacred performance community to stave off disruptive changes that might curtail singing to God's glory without compromising their aesthetic and community values.

These programs generally are not occasions for soloists. Those who do elect to sing tend to perform a cappella and demonstrate skillful vocal dex-terity. One contemporary favorite is "I Won't Complain." However, a soloist seldom stands alone for long, as itinerant backup singers emerge to assist with a faint accompaniment. In the event that only one constituent of a group (due to natural attrition) remains, volunteers again materialize. For instance, Mittie Edwards, a long-term member of the Seven Stars, routinely enrolls and stands alone, but soon a makeshift assemblage of singers will spontaneously appear to accompany her. She responds by saying: "Praise the Lord for those coming up to join me." Because reciprocity is the primary principle and spirituality the foundation of a network, a lone singer may attend programs for years under his or her group's name such as the Stars of Faith: "Ya'll looking for a whole group of people back here behind me, but I've been going for the last three years by myself." There are no regulations to suggest that it should be otherwise.

In smaller towns like Clayton, Alabama, and Greensboro and Marianna, Florida, as in the past, anniversary programs assuage monotony. Instead of singing largely to their musical peers, singers attract a community-wide following. Before singing, group leaders often first address their audience. Sometimes, discourse engages their sense of locality and identity. For instance, the lead singer of the Fantastic Heavenly Angels expressed: "I might live in the city now, but I used to live way backup in here in the sticks—when I was little, when I was just a boy. Country means just as much as the city to me; sometimes, I'd rather be in the country." As with Cottondale's Sunday Morning Band differentials, a sense of locality is not informed by a North–South binary but a city–country one. The Jubilives personify traditional male quartets in Wiregrass Country. Joseph Johnson, president of Sunday Morning Band #363, is the manager of this quartet. He demonstrates the multiplicity of roles assumed by most acclaimed Wiregrass singers. His quartet's genesis dates back to 1965, about the point at which present-day contemporary gospel made its ascent. Unlike other gospel groups, the Jubilives seldom travel without their own musicians, while most anticipate backup. Quartets usually furnish their own musical accompaniment, because they are well rehearsed. As part of the quartet tradition, this style depends on energetic guitar-driven harmonies and harmonizing.

Nonetheless, even the Jubilives' printed anniversary program lists primarily choirs, indicative of the present-day status of quartets in the region. Occurring at Henshaw Chapel AME Church, the site of Sunday Morning Band's Turnout, the roster is transdenominational. Because Jackson County residents support numerous AME enclaves, the Baptist choirs that appear typically hail from surrounding counties. Theirs is a two-day affair, commencing on Saturday at 7:00 p.m. and Sunday at 2:00 p.m. A male emcee is fairly rare as well. Unlike their nearby, relatively more urban counterparts, originally the Jubilives wore sedate attire—identical black suits, matching red paisley ties, and red rosebuds in their lapels. Now, local haberdashery specializing in extravagantly tailored wear grant discounts, making trendy, ornate attire accessible to all.

Also, unique to them the Jubilives' printed lineup is one of the few that completely fills in a full roster of singers from its network. As a result, not to snub anyone, it must issue a qualifier: "All choirs and groups are invited even if your name does not appear on this program." A great deal remains left to spontaneity. For openers, printed programs constitute an ideal projection. Sometimes the unannounced debut group can be quite satisfying, such as the appearance of a local quartet, the Soul Revivers. Out of the gate, this stellar group established the tone with a rousing rendition, singing:

Something on the inside
Working on the outside
It's brought a change in my life.

Quartets are known for their shift in personnel, changing off lead singers to reveal their versatility. Usually youngsters (boys about ten years old) supply a rhythmic drumbeat while background singers perform a cappella with sweet harmony and falsetto notes prevail. Otherwise, the Jubilives' house band softly plays backup, not to overshadow lead singers. A choir typically possesses one strong adult voice to carry any song selection. This sacred performance community's network relies on several churches' youth choirs, too. Although they often possess underdeveloped vocal skills, these programs provide another testing ground for practice and experimentation.

Singers generally prefer songs that approximate a living testimony. For instance, in keeping with an AME choral style, a song such as "So Many Blessings" elicits great approval, although sung with optimal restraint, as those assembled respond: "Oh, Yes!" This display demonstrates again how performance communities are always attuned to the lyrics and not just stylistics. What might be referred to as "dry" elsewhere, soars within this context. Guitarist Spencil Smiley presented an interesting perspective about playing before what he termed a "still" versus "moving" audience. For example, he found it disconcerting to play at tent show revivals before white Christians. Now he has reformulated his view, based foremost on his secular life, and entertains in nightclubs. He came to accept spectators as proof of a solid performance: "I used to didn't want to play before a still audience. I didn't want to play before nobody dead; but over the years come, I learned better. I rather play to a still audience than to a moving audience, under one circumstance: the still audience is receiving it; a moving audience is not. The still audience is enjoying it, but a moving audience is not enjoying it. They are not getting as much out of it as a still audience." Reception is perceived to be greater among the subdued. Those moving may have an ulterior motive such as seeking visibility. His explanation reveals so much about the subdued behavior that typifies rural Wiregrass performance communities. Few are there for show, but to magnify the Lord, praising the same God.

Those sacred performance communities most prone to accept and perform more current contemporary forms of gospel are in closest proximity to the larger capital cities. Quincy, Florida, and Dothan, Alabama, are hotspots for professional gospel revues. Mary Bush Smith is one of Quincy's principal gospel promoters. She also is the founder of her own gospel ensemble, the Shining Stars, and the Tri-State Community Mass Choir (since 1995, its anniversary has been the second weekend in July). On Friday nights, the anniversary program maintains structural units equivocal to a regular church program—relying on solos, poems, with alternating musical selections and including the only pastoral sermon of the weekend. On Saturday night, the gospel program commences in earnest but with a praise service rather than a devotional period. As discussed earlier, praise services or praise teams are a new trend, which grant a greater visibility for women than the traditional devotional period. On Saturday, Smith professed: "We've already did the kickoff, and we're halfway now. So, we going on to the touchdown," meaning Sunday will be even more august.

Communal exuberance is the bedrock of contemporary gospel. Tri-State's inaugural program showcased this tradition. The Saturday format followed a binary structure. Themed "Joy Night," it boasted a Part I and Part II with the ubiquitous offertory rite bridging the two. This locale's anniversaries are never without stellar gospel musicians, who once played secular music professionally. Gospel performances on this level are intended to be Holiness-inspired, and tambourines are much in evidence, leading to the inevitable more vociferous shout. Folklorist Ray Allen spoke to this propensity: "The manner in which the spiritual feeling is passed between participants at a gospel program is a function of the complex interaction between the lead singer, the background singers, and the congregation." Ecstatic forms of spirit possession typify the musical acts of the region's more urbane sacred performance communities.

At this level, anniversary events also showcase the semiprofessionals whom folklorist Allen documented in New York City. They sing more selections and feature more quartet styles of singing. As another cultural boon, there is greater evidence of men who sing pure falsetto. Rarely do their performances replicate sing-a-longs as occurs at Thomasville singing conventions. Instead, throngs thrill to the delightful sound of vocalists who instigate their own unique phrasing and style. The crowd issues acclaim and accord by shouting: "Sang it; sang it!" Additionally, I came to

Mary Bush Smith, a gospel impresario in Quincy, Florida, a hotbed for sacred music

realize that contemporary gospel anniversaries more often occur at the few sanctified churches. The Holiness musical tradition leaves its imprint and supplies a major context for groups to honor one to another. Foremost, the drum is preferred; once unleashed, it adds fervor. Once I even witnessed a youngster playing a washboard, a sight I had viewed only once before, in Philadelphia at a House of Prayer. Nothing is too arcane or too innovative as long as it fits within the desired expression of spirituality, utilizing an iconic aesthetic linked to praise.

As to be expected, with greater opportunity to perform with professional contemporary gospel groups, in Dothan and Quincy current contemporary gospel sounds influence these sacred performance communities the most. For instance, few sing a cappella, even if sung with just a bass line. Additionally, their attire goes beyond the usual fancy aesthetic. It mirrors that of professional gospel singers, with women wearing beaded and sequin dresses and suits while the men wear more garish looking matching attire. On the occasion of their first anniversary, the Tri-State Community Mass Choir's women dressed similarly in shades of purple in satin, silk, and brocade, and the men in equally spangled suits. In keeping with gospel's golden era, these larger anniversaries were always the site for men to appear in red shirts and shoes or in royal blue suits and blue suede shoes. Heilbut attributed the Ward Singers as changing gospel apparel for women: "Tired of the old homespun choir robes, Clara began designing fancy outfits of elaborate and, for gospel, peculiar materials."

In addition, more attention is given to "having their own original sound and style, including innovative song arrangements which are carefully worked out during rehearsals." Knowing the rigors at this performance level, Smith noted that people thought she had disbanded her ensemble once she formed the mass choir: "We still have the Shining Stars. We're gonna shine until all of us die because if one dies another one's gonna carry it on." Her first anniversary's success depended on this already well-established reciprocal network. Organizing the mass choir expands the network with the same communitarian expectations.

A member of Smith's network, Spencil Smiley, born in Panama City, exemplifies the comparatively few accomplished electric guitarists in the region. He acknowledged: "After I started playing music, you know, I never hardly see anyone who play [gospel] guitar." Conforming to recurrent motifs attributed to blues musicians, his father denied him access to his own box guitar, but Smiley would risk punishment by playing it from time to time. His first semblance of a guitar was a broom handle, which he pretended to play beside the road until one day, feeling sorry for him, a stranger bought him a real one from a pawn shop. Both parents were musicians and rhythm-and-blues vocalists, performing at what was called "frolic houses." As a child, he danced with his sister in clubs. Eventually, according to Smiley, he excelled musically until his father requested lessons from him.

From here, his biography diverges from that of most local gospel performers. While studying to become a master electrician at Florida A&M University, he joined a gospel quartet in Tallahassee, the Spiritual Yells. He played bass guitar. Back in Panama City, despite discrimination, he succeeded in his profession, but he also took advantage of living in the resort area locally known as the Redneck Riviera. He began his performance career as a one-man band—combining lead and rhythm guitar along with singing—in nightclubs playing for tips. For years, he made his guitar playing famous in Bay County due to the sheer dearth of performers and his innate skill. He later formed a rock band, going from a three-piece group to sixteen members. However, disco recordings devastated his secular music base. Then Smiley turned to playing lead guitar for a tent revival for ten years, traveling to Mobile, Alabama, all over Mississippi and Georgia, and to Canada. While on the road, he survived by doing electrical jobs wherever he ventured. As he put it, he got "back in gospel."

So, Smiley's musical expertise is bound to stand out within his performance community. His playing style is soulful, a sign of a more consummate musician, well schooled in secular music. When he compares himself with other musicians, the biggest distinction is that they never played rock. His prescription for good musicianship is practice and good listening skills, as a means of learning more styles. Smiley says that he sung so much rock, that he does not even like to sing anymore. Musicians of Smiley's caliber do not customarily host their own anniversaries. The groups he performs with pay him "off the top," without having negotiated a fee because they know his worth and want to show their appreciation. Neither would he think of charging them: "When you're taking the true gospel, there is no charge."

At these more urban gospel anniversaries, usually a full accompaniment of musicians is on hand (including lead and bass guitarists). Although these kinds of sacred performance communities privilege rhythm, a drummer is not present at all times. Perhaps children often learn to drum at an early age to take up the slack. Unmistakably, gospel programs become most energized when there is a full complement of musicians. Utilizing improvised vamps, drive sections are more likely to occur. Some musical numbers may resume spontaneously, after thinking the last chord's been played, reinvigorating the performance. For those groups without their own traveling musicians, the reality is uncertainty, never knowing who might chime in. Sometimes in rural sectors and when dealing with older adults, repertoires can be quite idiosyncratic and even the best instrumentalists cannot pick up the tune. Yet, these circumstances are a built in part of the ebb and flow.

The function of gospel programs, once again, is not to produce the shout or a show. The region offers innumerable venues where those so inclined might shout. These gospel programs proffer a range of possible interpretations. For some, the repetitious words of songs function by furnishing them with desired biblical phrases to reinforce belief. They contain lyrics pertinent to negotiating everyday life. Songs such as "Heaven Is My Goal," "Lord, I Know You Been So Good," "By His Grace, I've Come a Long Way," and "It Feels Good Every Time I Think about Jesus" excite individual hope of holding on and achieving personal salvation. As Heilbut noted, "We're not singing for form or fashion or for outside show of this world . . . but we came to work out our own soul's salvation." This music produces a spirit-filled experience. To their way of thinking, the music is ministry.

One gospel program, however, caused an audience member to exhibit constant, "over the top" ecstatic behavior. Her exuberance leaned toward the gospel stereotype of rapturous movements, which are often lampooned in popular film and on television. At times she was like a whirling dervish—leaping, jooking, and most of all, shouting. She really whooped it up. Finally, she grabbed the mic and spoke of her own volition: "I was told tonight that I'm up here playing; but if any of ya'll think I'm playing, come up here and do it with me. *Hallelujah!* Come up here and see if you have the strength to do it with me. I ain't playing people, Hallelujah! But I was told to my face tonight that I was playing, but I just want ya'll to know tonight that I am real. *I'm real!*" This kind of sacred performance community, then, is not beyond sanctioning its adult members, but it cannot contain those who experience the spirit in alternative ways.

From Marianna, Florida, across the state line on Highway 231 in Madrid, Alabama, the Glory Train Special's anniversaries demonstrate the density of a well-regimented reciprocal network. This anniversary is a three-night event that switches locations to better accommodate its dispersed support network. The Friday and Saturday night gospel rituals occur in Madrid, and Sunday's is in an outlying town northwest of Dothan, Pinkard. This group attracts artistic performances no matter what its location. Lewis is prone to proclaim: "As you always hear me say, this is o-u-r anniversary. The Glory Train Special's signature song is 'If You Can't Help Me, Please Don't Stop Me.'" The song in their repertoire that is a personal favorite is "I Got More Than a Hammer and Nails." Lewis also is prone to preach to any gathering based on metaphor in this selection: "Tonight, if you've got more than a hammer and nails, you can't sit down and just look because we've all got to leave here one day. That's all right, now, God's been good to me, do it for yourself." In 1962, at about the time of the Glory Train Special's formation, the Staple Singers popularized this song.

Membership overlaps within sundry support networks and sacred performance communities. For instance, Doris Lewis is active in the Sacred Harp four-shape tradition as well as gospel music. She admits these networks are so active that she cannot participate in them all: "I used to sing seven-shape quite a bit, but I don't be with them now because, when that time come, I'm gone on with this gospel singing." Stalwart individuals like Lewis denote specialists and need to be singled out. It is through Lewis' reciprocal support network that I met the Cunningham Family, extending my knowledge of this world of musical networks via Elba's singing building. Lewis' network caused me to branch out and attend anniversary programs in more outlying areas, such as the Gospel Starlight's anniversary in Clayton, Alabama. It was the Salemettes of Greensboro, Florida, through whom I first encountered Lewis. Her intricate network truly encompasses the tristate region. For one year, my field notes indicate hers to be one of the

Doris Lewis attired in her Glory Train
Special choir robe

strongest performance communities. Lewis earned my immediate respect due to the willingness of her adherents to assemble even during driving rain. During the summer months severe thunderstorms are standard daily occurrences, but I have witnessed more than a few performances when weather reports diminished attendance.

As an extension of reciprocal support networks, musical benefits are quite profuse, given the sheer economic pressure of living in poor, rural areas. Doc Brown of Quincy, Florida, explained best what motivates them in times of crisis: "It's more than just singing. When someone is in need, you get together and do that as well. People that we know, we give benefit programs. There is no use in going praising the Lord, if we're not going to help someone when they need your help. So, I get together and do benefit programs as well." Brown routinely is the recipient of appreciation programs herself. They are considered love offerings. Along with belief and belonging, the next important predilection is being beloved. Outward communal expressions of appreciation and caring are viewed as assertions of God's constancy and love. The most salient metaphor imposed is "smelling the roses while you're alive." Expressions of love come too late if you wait to deliver them graveside.

In 1995, Doris Lewis suffered a stroke. At the time, it is a miracle that she survived, with only a few visual problems. Within weeks of her health crisis, family, friends, and members of her singing group, the Glory Train Special, hosted on her behalf an appreciation program, "Because We Care."

Held in her hometown of Dothan, Alabama, singers attended from around the tri-state area in full force. Due to her wide-ranging travel to support their cultural performances, about thirty soloists, quartets, and vocal ensembles came through another driving rainstorm, which resulted in a brief power outage. During the electrical blackout, viewing it as a sign, the audience clapped to praise a power bigger than them. They shouted proclamations into the dark void such as: "Yes, suh, thank you, Jesus."

I knew that Lewis was equally active as a layperson in the small AME church, once pastored by her renowned father in the hamlet of Madrid. But I did not know that besides being active in the Alabama–Florida Union Singing Convention and the Glory Train Special, with its own television show, she engaged in so many elected posts among the AME. Just a month prior to her stroke, elected by the women of the Southeast Alabama Conference Women's Missionary Society, she served as its delegate and traveled to Detroit, Michigan. She also is the president of all the laypersons of the Ozark District. At about the same time as the other trip, she was chosen to attend its meeting in Kansas City, Missouri. Furthermore, she is the official assistant secretary of the laity for the entire state. This program allowed for "Encouragement Expressions" to be limited to two minutes. A speaker from Cherry Street AME Church provided this apt testimony: "When she became ill, she became ill working in the vineyard. She's been that way all her life, just worked herself down."

Therefore, it comes as no revelation that Hines Chapel AME Church was the site of her appreciation program. It is the only large Dothan church I know that regularly supports gospel anniversary programs, including their local Citywide Female Gospel Chorus. As a leading AME layperson in the region, Lewis probably was a seminal force bringing gospel anniversaries to this venue. Often, the crowd dissipated as groups performed their selections and exited to attend another program or to get a head start on the dusky two-lane highways home. Many singing groups left after their tribute, having just dropped by to pay respect. A handful of performers, who misjudged their appearance time due to the long wait, left without performing. Significantly, however, as these went others came. The church could not have contained everyone otherwise. The "Because We Care" audience remained standing room only until the last note was sung, everyone had freely given, and the last remarks were made. The following expressions, regarding giving donations to show their love for Lewis, were quite conducive: "If you can't give no m-o-n-e-y, then you can't give nothing. If you can't give all you have, then don't give nothing." By their words and deeds they illustrated: "No program brings more joy than helping somebody." A lifetime of musical and spiritual devotion pays off when networks converge to pay tribute and benefit fellow spiritual activists.

Lewis' tribute embodies an eclectic kind of public display event. This significant outpouring fell outside the fancy aesthetic of most anniversary programs. At the benefit, performers dressed more casually, suggesting a "come as you are to show that you care" attitude. For the most part, they left their colorful, extravagant garments at home. Some of the younger men wore striped polo shirts, rather than the usual garish suits. In addition, a range of performance styles and abilities were on display. Some like The Seven Wonders fit most expectations about gospel music. They sang replete with full musical accompaniment. The lead singer strutted affectively across the floor until many stood clapping to grant them full accolade. Their B selection, "On the Battlefield for My Lord," contained a falsetto thread, which is always appreciated. With an improvised drive section, this group's performance extended to fifteen minutes in length. No one objected. The performance produced near bedlam as the lead singer pulled off all the ornamentation emblematic of semiprofessional gospel music. He stylistically worked the aisles, gained compliance when he asked hands to wave, and caused many in the audience to shout or raise their arms in surrender. A slow, syncopated selection caused the audience to sway, clapping along intermittently in keeping with its tempo. Within the region, singers seldom play to the crowd, asking for specific responses; instead, even in performance, they issue the appropriate call, receiving a spirited, congregational response.

If, unlike other gospel studies, the focus here is not on traditional quartets, it reflects the degree to which there is greater inclusivity. For example, at the "Because We Care" program, the first bona fide quartet, The Golden Bells, did not perform until midway. They were also the only ones who disregarded the two-selection limit. "Prayer Will Fix It Every Time" is one of its staples. Such as they are, the male quartet singers still bring the most polished performances: impeccably harmonizing and always immaculately dressed. I have attended the anniversary programs of numerous groups, and those hosted by male quartets are relatively rare, indicative of the emphasis on family-based ensembles, and this vernacular term is used more loosely. So I do not announce their complete demise.

I had attended the anniversary program of several of the groups present, or I had heard them perform at Lewis' Gospel Train Special anniversary. Although she is actively involved in the Sacred Harp tradition, this performance community was absent—but they are aged and are more likely to populate daytime events. Although singers belong to several distinct sacred performance communities, apparently their networks can be exclusive. People may cross various genres of sacred music but belong to distinct sacred performance communities, which do not always intersect. The various sacred music genres, rooted in the African American sacred musical tradition, may coexist within various contexts but not those who perform them. I assume that others within Lewis' support network may have taken up separate monetary collections.

Additionally, after a stellar performance by the Gospel Caravan, organizers requested that it sing another selection during the offering. This move ensured that contributors would be motivated to give "paper" for this worthy cause, upping the ante financially. The strategy worked, as the collection baskets teemed with bills. No one was stingy about giving because, in the scheme of things, benevolence triumphs and must be reciprocated. It is the only way to receive. Such occasions embody the kind of crisis on which sacred performance community's networks prosper. During the offertory rite, the song selection, "I'm So Glad," spoke volumes about the outlook of these cheerful givers and why they are articulated as love offerings. Love is the mainstay.

I would be remiss not to mention the extent to which food informs these occasions. Usually, it is sold for a relatively nominal price to boost one's revenue. Hosts incur a number of expenses, and some churches impose rental fees. Part of the production is for emcees to enumerate the menu. Besides the expected southern cuisine—chicken, collard greens, potato salad, beans, cornbread, cakes, pies—there might also be goat and plenty of varieties of fish. To offset some of the costs, another feature is to sell badges like the ones at shape-note singing conventions, strips of ribbon, frequently for a dollar. Wearing these badges grant everyone a sense of affiliation whether or not in an ensemble intending to sing. These badges are like name tags at a professional convention, indicating your registration and legitimate support.

For this event, following tradition, some performers entered the network without prior knowledge of Lewis or her family's history. The Oak City Choir from Donaldsonville, Georgia, attended because the event was advertised in their local newspaper. Their presence acknowledges the breadth of the Lewis' reciprocal support network. The promoters advertised the occasion for over a month, signifying Lewis' importance. A young member of the Donaldsonville group issued a disclaimer: "We can't sing like that; but what we do, we sing for the Lord." As a matter of fact, they were the only ones in matching attire, wearing the uniform of choice: white blouses and black skirts, but with large maroon corsages. Their performance was also the first sung with only a piano accompaniment. I want to emphasize again the region's broad canon of taste when it comes to sacred musical expression. It allows for a range of performance styles, musical genres, and gospel singing acumen. The four female members were possibly related, ranging in age from ten to forty. Many of the ensembles feature family units with parents and children, ranging from preschoolers to young adults. If church programs and unions are their training ground, again appearing at gospel anniversaries is their proving ground.

I actually learned of Lewis' stroke days before I was to attend my first Glory Train Special anniversary program, in celebration of then thirty-four years. This anniversary occurred annually the third weekend in June. For me, it would conflict with a Thomas-Grady Counties Singing Convention. When I called to confirm the date, her husband informed me about her health and declared that the program had not been cancelled. As a folklorist, I felt compelled to attend. Putting her ordeal into perspective, one song leader expressed: "I hate to hear about Sister Lewis; but let me tell you, that's that rain in your life. We've got to pray for one another." Others referred to her variously as Sister Glory Train and Mother Lewis, from those who have known her since their childhood. I witnessed that her absence did not diminish attendance but strengthened it. Literally, supporters rally for such occasions to prove the intersubjectivity of their ways. The very next year she was back, administrating both the annual Alabama–Florida Union Sacred Harp Singing Convention and hosting the Glory Train Special anniversary. Her ensemble represents one of the most popular within the region, being one of the few truly tri-state reciprocal support networks.

It was at the regularly scheduled anniversary that I began to recognize the gospel traits that fuel this performance community's contemporary gospel sound. I noted many song titles that are interrogatory. Structurally, unless intended rhetorically, interrogatory statements necessitate an answer. Lead singers may alert listeners: "I am going to ask you a question, and you think about it" before the song "What Will You Be Doing When Jesus Comes?" As part of the antiphonal pattern, another asks, "Can You Feel God Moving?" to which the proper answer by the backup singers and believers alike is an affirmative retort. Then, the improvisational impulse gains greater complexity. The song leader introduces a new synonym, action, or body part for every lyrical word that can be mutated. For instance, the singer switches from feeling Him moving in her soul to her hands, feet, heart, and "all over me." God also transmutes into Jesus, who is touted as the "Son of David," "Leader of Man," "Prince of Peace," and "Mary's Baby." The singer continues feeling him relentlessly—"early in the morning," "late in midnight hour," and "late in the evening." This kind of incremental repetition can sustain such songs for up to ten minutes with just a bass guitar. The applause and praise may go on, even incorporating a common meter tune, as a shortened riff. The revelry is contagious.

Relating to incremental repetition, this sacred performance community brings even greater depth. Acknowledging the stylistics of African American ministers, during their sermonic finale they tend "to string a series of images together." Congregations positively respond to the number of such parallel structures preachers can sustain during their finales, using a piano or organ as an accessory. This moment is when the recognized, repetitive chanting customarily begins. Similarly, gospel performers also utilize similar parallel structural units. For instance, "You Ought to Take the Lord with You Everywhere You Go" clusters the following, with the chorus asserting, "I thank you Lord in the street," "in the crowd," "in the home," "all alone," "on highways," "on byways." As a form of continuity, African American music audiences are receptive to the immediacy of the transmission while engaging such lyrical content. This also is the stuff that the spirituals were made of, depending on communal re-creation. While a mainstay of African American sacred music in general, the contemporary gospel aspect entails greater exuberance due to the fecundity of accomplished musicians.

As part of the stylistic component and perhaps to subvert the two-song imperative, singers perform an introduction on their way to commandeer the mic. For example, Friendship CME Choir would sing: "When you see me coming, I got Jesus on my mind." Another possible ruse, after two songs, is to offer a big surprise: "Our lead musician [guitarist] can sing just like he can play." Those with a full complement of musicians tend to milk the crowd, triggering full-scale cheers usually reserved for concertgoers. For instance, "Heavenly Choir" sparks a spectacular uproar, especially when one singer contributed the clear falsetto vocal riff originally performed by Harvey Watkins Sr. of the Canton Spirituals. The savvier gospel groups tend to achieve immediate audience participation. Along with a few classic quartets and some of the family ensembles, Sheryl Melton's choir is topnotch. It is among those that use an entry piece, entitled "I Want You to Move," to galvanize the crowd. Their repertoire also includes a Soul Stirrers' tune, "Stay with Me, Lord," sung with an incredible female lead singer. She steps out from her group, taking to the aisle in the manner of quartet performers, which excites and incites the audience. Their performance is one of the few by a church choir to generate a truly ecstatic response.

At anniversary programs, typically, singers interject a range of caveats such as "If I make a mistake, don't talk about me. Pray for me." As a matter of fact, one hears the statement, "If we make a mistake, ya'll mistake it as love," so much that it seemingly functions as a talisman. Sometimes the offer is more like an apologia: "We are short of a bass player tonight, but I got one of my old, original bass players here. And we are gonna do a song that I think that you're gonna enjoy. I'm not using my bass player as an excuse. Sometimes, I sing a song 'You Got to Use What You've Got,' and that's what we are going to do tonight. We are going to use what we got." Just as ministers may elicit the approbation of the audience, singers, too, may use the same technique: "Now if ya'll will talk to me, I might sing a little bit more." A more confident quartet leader to arouse the spirit utters: "If you ain't got no fire, you don't need no chimney. Well, I got my fire; I got it in nineteen hundred and fifty-nine! I don't need your fire; but if you put yours with mine, we will make a big blaze in here." After waiting his turn for more than two and a half hours, he desired to rekindle a flagging crowd.

The order of performance is usually predicated on a first-come basis. Once again, communal sharing comes in the form of enrollment fees. As each performer arrives, an enrollment fee is exacted. Typically, the host invites fifty groups, expecting a sixty percent response. Time management is required to ensure that your group opens one program and, perhaps, with time to spare to travel to another program and to close it out. Meanwhile, St. Phillips' AME Church with its old, wooden pews is filled to capacity. It also is without air conditioning, and the heat along with the summer humidity is foreboding. Nonetheless, most stay put, dutifully awaiting their turn or remaining to support their peers. It is sites like this that attest to group solidarity. Nowadays, people do not have to elect to endure such travail. Yet, they return annually like monarch butterflies. Being a greater distance away, I found the church in Pinkard even more rustic. These small Wiregrass Alabama churches represent historic landmarks, monuments to the congregations who won't allow their reduction to a complete state of ruin.

An additional incentive for lending support to these gatherings is to announce one's own upcoming anniversary or church program. On the one hand, a popular group like the Gospel Caravan of Clayton only elects to sing one selection, serving notice that they are en route to yet another concert. On the other, the Gospel Caravan's performance amounts to a public relations promotion. Its members allude to making an immense donation, which also signifies an expectation that their outlay will be reciprocated in kind. The lyrics of choice carry immense appeal: "I Have It Hard Lord / I Know We're Gonna Make It." To some, according to Heilbut, "Gospel lyrics may sound banal, but they talk about the things that matter the most to poor people." Everyone knows that the song is a preliminary treat and they are being enticed to take to the road in full support of a system that keeps on giving.

Perhaps, in Lewis' sacred performance community, one of the most idiosyncratic singers is Billy McBride. He sings solo and garners the kind of encouragement often reserved for the young: "Yes, yes" and "That's alright." He narrated an introduction to his lead song, "I'm Going Away One of These Days," saying: "We all know we're gonna hang on until the last minute." Afterward, the applause was deafening. For his second number, the audience took up a chant with faint, rhythmic handclapping. They treated his performance in the call-and-response mode associated with a chanted sermon. As musicologist Portia Maulsby situated it: "These songs, known as 'church songs,' were manifestations of sermons chanted and sung by Black preachers, whose emotional and repetitive styles motivated spontaneous responses, often in song." I am glad that I encountered this style of musical interaction early within the ethnographic process. It alerted me to this region's iconic musical taste.

Not surprisingly, in general, those who sing refer to each other as brother and sister. One of the few locally featured duets is known as Sister and Brother Jack Daniels. They offer two selections, "Don't Wait Til Tomorrow/Tomorrow May Be Too Late" and "God Will Give the Strength You Need," accompanied by an itinerant guitarist. Ultimately, this husband-and-wife team evince their own performance style, rather than relying on the usual repetition to elevate their performance. Their selections conform to a narrative ballad style, telling vivid stories. The languishing harmonic sound is dependent on the blue notes struck by their musical accompanist. Moreover, the only repetition comes in the bridge between stanzas such as:

> *Don't you wait.*
> *Don't you wait.*
> *Don't you wait.*
> *Don't you wait 'til tomorrow comes,*
> *For tomorrow will be too late.*

The plaintive refrains of the lyrics in each song electrify the audience. The harmonizing and blending of male and female vocal parts along with appropriate gestures, dramatizing the songs, combine for many heartfelt responses. Then, as part of the finale, they make a dramatic procession to their seats, still singing with the husband's arms around his wife's shoulder to a receptive audience's acclaim. In these contexts, I no longer have to inquire about favorite songs. They often blatantly say so, in performance. For the Spiritual Harmonizers, it is "Somebody's Here with Me." For the Cunningham Family, no doubt, it is the beautifully harmonized "Sweet Home." They sing it everywhere. Signature songs function to highlight singing virtuosity while testifying to your spiritual deliverance.

Keeping with the A/B selection frame, it is not unusual for these programs to end around midnight, Eastern Standard Time. It is not just due to the number of participants but their compelling improvisational style. Unlike shape-note singing conventions, there is no established recess for meals. Their fluid arrival and departure signify how, though voluntary, these gospel networks boast a lifetime of spiritual activists. Because Tallahassee is in a different time zone and typically I commuted, documenting these affairs, while physically exhausting, was also spiritually fortifying. The timelessness of the music and its relative novelty invigorated me. No matter which performance community one follows, these gospel anniversary programs delight the soul. To the collective, each performance exudes the promised good times as well as the meaning of *gospel* itself, good news. To African American Wiregrass singers, it does not matter how their sacred music performances might be adjudged. God is at the center of their lives and in charge. To sing his praises all the day long is a sanctified pleasure. To receive a collateral sense of prosperity by the work you do is in keeping with divine order. They gain prosperity and enrichment because they follow in the footsteps of their ancestors—spiritual giants.

CHAPTER 7

"I Feel No Ways Tired"

Sarah's Daughters

Until entering Wiregrass Country, I had seldom met such a strong concentration of emboldened women. As a young girl, I mainly encountered
women who aspired to be "ladies" or, in the least, ladylike. While working
class, they accepted uncritically societal injunctions regarding woman-
hood. They set up a wall of support for domesticity, modesty, piety, and
chastity. Not to say that women in Wiregrass Country do not espouse and
sanction these same ideologies. I just rarely have encountered such a multiplicity of Christian women who contradict and confront these sanctioned
patriarchal tools. During our interviews, I began to understand better how
they came to earn honorific titles such as Ma, Mother, or Aunt or endear-
ing nicknames, like my grandmother, Gip. While growing up in the North,
only a few of my mother's friends stood out because they bore nicknames
such as Red, Draper, and T.G. I consider it gratifying to know a wide range
of self-defining women in a rural context. All of them are very highly esteemed within their sacred performance communities and extensive networks, where (as a rule) women are not relegated to second-class status.
They aspire to be obedient, humble, and loving as dictated by their personal
relationship with God, modifying the usual standpoints as the spirit dictates. They exemplify what it means to be spiritual activists.

Foremost, Wiregrass women are the never-tiring purveyors of God's
work. Through song, they find powerful niches to display their inspirational talent. The amount of godly work that they do, many consider another female social chore. Mother Henderson imparted: "This body gets
tired, but the spirit is willing." I now comprehend better the lyrics: "I am no
ways tired." It means being refreshed and ready with great energy to conduct spiritually enlightened work, and that one's strength and endurance
increases as divine renewal continuously takes hold. This chapter positions
African American women as the bulwark of their various support networks

and performance communities. They are quick to be called matriarchs by those researchers who categorize the stereotypical by overly simplifying the relative strength of some African American women. The women of whom I speak wield no real power in a larger hegemonic sense. Based on their race and gender, the power dynamic faced is far more complex. They derive theirs from a higher vision.

Alas, not all Africana women engender their degree of empowerment. They lack the same competence because they fear being stigmatized. Greater empowerment is theirs to claim by earning true respect outside of the more limiting pose of respectability. The life histories of the women who gain honorific titles such as Aunt Flossie, Ma Henry, and Mother Jefferson indicate how these women repeatedly resurrect a full subjectivity. Additionally, as Mother Henderson indicated: "I'm the Mother of this church here. It is one mother to a [church] family." Clearly, then, every woman who attains a certain age does not gain the proffered certification. The closest parallels to their power-related authority exist in traditional West African contexts. For example, among the Yoruba, certain women are believed to possess female mystical power. To quote anthropologists Henry and Margaret Drewal, this is why "they are called 'our mothers' and are addressed personally with 'my mother' or 'old wise one' in recognition of their positive dimension as protective progenitors, healers, and guardians of morality, social order, and the just apportionment of power, wealth, and prestige." Ironically, many are not biological mothers. They constitute the othermothers within African American culture, who ensure there are no motherless children. Even older adults (their age mates) reference them as such. By staking a claim to agency, certain women do not relegate themselves to object positions with passivity.

Like elsewhere, historically many African American women in Wiregrass Country entered the labor force as washerwomen. Historian Jacqueline Jones positioned them among the "escapees from domestic service." Working out of their homes to avoid the sexual abuse of white men, they tended to be consummate businesswomen. Moreover, wives frequently outlived their husbands. Widows primarily moved to nearby small towns to make a living as wage earners. These women earned a degree of autonomy and independence for themselves by electing to engage in work that could be performed in their homes. The exceptions would be those women who worked in a private laundry or as maids on the hunting plantations. These self-confident women are not opposed to domesticity. Yet they do not dote upon this role as the only source of self-valuation. As a matter of fact, even personal chores enjoy a fairly unique labor history within the Wiregrass.

The domestic arts and the division of labor also necessitate greater consideration as relates to the locale. Historically, men, women, and children engaged in nearly the same workloads or comparable ones. Patriarchy remained strong, but full productivity required that women learn to plow, that men assist in the mass production of certain foods, and that children carry their full weight. Not intended to suggest any role reversals, the intimation suggests that a subsistence existence required a collective response. The labor was the same across the racial divide. Whenever there were onerous tasks to perform, everyone worked as a unit. Living nearly always on a subsistence level, most everyone in the Wiregrass engaged in regular domestic activities. They learned to cut okra, shell peanuts, cook pork, milk cows, grind cane, and so on. Local historian E. W. Carswell wrote, "'If we didn't grow it, we didn't know it,' someone has aptly observed. We didn't grow vegetables as lettuce, asparagus, Brussels sprouts, spinach, rhubarb, artichoke and garlic. We were more familiar with turnips, mustard, cabbage, and collard greens, along with field peas and lima and butter beans." In the same light, domestically, men, women, and children performed a multiplicity of duties.

Domesticity speaks to one's participation in home life, whereas performing domestically connotes one's participation around the homeplace. Being "cash poor" in the Wiregrass, African American women contributed economically to the family's development by raising produce for trade with the local market. Therefore, they lacked a sense of dependency that domesticity alone reified across social class. Instead, they exhibited a brave spirit. In Wiregrass Country, where one's sustenance depended on an arduous work cycle, everyone shared common knowledge about a spectrum of household-related activities. Applying equally to whites, according to Olin Pope, "I can do most anything but cook," elaborating on the statement to include making fruit preserves, syrup making, and curing hogs among his abilities. Women counted sticking tobacco, picking cotton, and stripping cane among theirs. The common objective was "to get all that they could get." Fathers would commonly assist in bringing about this end. Owen Wrice recalled: "Along about February and first of March, then (see back years ago) you didn't have peanut mills like they got now, where you go and buy peanuts all ready shelled and go plant them. And then you go there and buy the whole hundred pounds, or how many you brought; and then you'd bring them home. At night we would sit down and we would shell peanuts. And all them that was cracked, my daddy he'd go in there and make us a large sheet pan of peanut candy." While the family shelled, they sang hymns, attracting any passers-by. Of course, such role reversals probably are not unique to this region. I only mention a few pertinent, notable instances.

Quilting signifies a women-centered artistic expression that holds many meanings. These are everyday, traditional items that require great skill, patience, and creativity. The skill offered those women, often without voice, a cultural and social outlet. Quilts are the multilayered texts on which women traditionally have inscribed their histories. Their quilts tell of wintry nights in the Wiregrass, which could be quite forebodingly cold. These textiles were a necessity for warmth, while also being quite decorative. One rarely finds a Wiregrass woman of a certain age who does not know how to quilt. A very vocal and extroverted woman, Mary Jackson (long married to one of Judge Jackson's sons, John) indicated: "I don't like to quilt. I never have. My mother made me piece one quilt." On the other hand, Dewey Williams' wife, Alice, was an avid, accomplished quilter. Yet her artistry draws no public exhibition or recognition because the focus of ethnographers always centers on her role within the Sacred Harp community. In the same vein, Lela Jackson taught her fa-so-la singing sons how to perform most domestic tasks, including quiltmaking. These gender-bending activities seldom surface about these premier Wiregrass families.

Engaged in a perpetual work cycle, Wiregrass women are the epitome of workaholics. These women also like to "hit the creek," go fishing. It boggles my mind to consider that the same ones who love to sing also manage to fish regularly. As I wrote in *Wiregrass Country*, "Fishing may be an activity that simultaneously satisfies the work ethic while providing recreational pleasure." Often, they would walk six or seven miles to fish. They often raised their own earthworms by throwing dishwater outdoors and adding their own secret ingredients such as cornmeal. In 2004, after a Jackson memorial sing, I watched everyone vacate the parking lot, leaving Eva Mae Greene on her own. So hobbled by age, she moved with a painstakingly slow gait. She arrived at the bumper of my car while the parking lot emptied. I felt beholden to stay with her, although she insisted she did not need any assistance. Obviously, everyone else was used to her feisty willpower. When we reached her car, it was filled with fishing tackle, a cooler, and other paraphernalia appropriate for a seasoned fisherwoman. She explained that her age imposed no limitation on her exuberant spirit or her favorite pastime. She invited me to join her at a nearby creek sometime. Should I take up the offer, I know she will certainly be there.

Women and men are plainly comfortable in the skin they're in and do not all follow specific, hegemonic gender roles. The security of a man's identity does not depend on being the primary wage earner either. As song leader Tommie Gabriel informed me, male unskilled laborers routinely married educated African American women, especially teachers. By so doing, they did not feel emasculated or threatened.

Women also undertook to subvert the male labor force but tended to be thwarted by southern whites. For example, Mary Jackson disclosed how her mother was cheated out of everything when she tried to sharecrop on her own:

> *My mother stopped farming. She was in the middle of her farming at that time [when her father died]. When she finished making the crop, do you know what happened? This man took all my mother's crops because there was ne'er man to talk up. He took all her stuff that she raised and didn't leave her nothing. And my mother was going down the little road like crying. And I didn't know what she was crying about. And . . . but . . . You know what happened? I went to crying too. I was with her, and I broke down and went to crying too because I knew that my mother was hurt about something. And she told me this man had took all of her stuff that she raised (her farming stuff like her corn, her peanuts) and took it away from her. And he wouldn't have took it from my daddy, but he took that. And she didn't get no money out of it.*

Through personal experience narratives and other overt statements, my new mentors taught me their Christian existence was more than what it seemed. Instead, their everyday discourse recognized the sacred and the profane, the saint and the warrior, as well as the iconoclast and humble being. They make the musical world (of their own choosing) go around.

It is within this context of women that the time-honored principles— hospitality, collective economics, and spirituality—triumph. After all, the women supply the bulk of the spiritual leadership. They are in the forefront of the faith. As recorded about the Shouter Baptists of Trinidad, "Women are always great thinkers, scripture scholars, and forceful with wisdom, knowledge, and understanding, who live austere lives of sacrificial work and prayer in the communities they serve." Divine unction defines these women's lives. Among these women, like Mary Lou Henderson, they routinely express: "I've been anointed by God to do His work. I couldn't do it by myself." Their lives, then, are spiritually guided. Henderson further explained: "I'm just a voice crying in the wilderness that's all. I'm just a voice. God give me the voice, and I try to use it to His glory." Thus, these women accept a calling without a pulpit, but they appropriate many platforms. Some feminists may find this juxtaposition to seats of power problematic.

To my amazement, as an ethnographer, I find myself being offered the pulpit from which to thank the home folk plenteously. Although never comfortable when asked to speak from the pulpit, as an implied hierarchical site, I now surmise more about this ritual space. As I venture to reinterpret these ritual spaces, the pulpit area is not necessarily gendered space but can function as an invitational speech zone.

Wiregrass women are the lifeblood of their communities, not only due to their gendered role as caretakers, but by virtue of their ability to attain real authority. As mentioned, Doris Lewis is the daughter of the Methodist preacher H. Webster Woods, one of the few African American composers of Sacred Harp music. Although Lewis holds the office of recording secretary for the Alabama–Florida Union Singing Convention, the male president and vice president represent titular heads. Theirs are positions governed by tradition and seniority but without a simply hierarchical thrust. The women do not garner model subaltern positions. Dyen's attention to social organization bears out my own findings: "Young men may be more looked-up-to than young women, but older men and older women approach equality. Old age is respected regardless of sex and an old woman as well as an old man can be head of a household, or acknowledged head of an extended family." Certain governing roles impose a gender-specific balance, honoring those who came before and those who may be in their dotage.

Their brand of democracy or ceremonial leadership invokes a benevolent monarchy. African American performance communities, both sacred and secular, use an organizational leadership model based on institutions like the Afro-Baptist church. For instance, church politics are often such that Baptist ministers (in particular) reign over their flocks, unencumbered, for years. An efficient leader seldom abdicates; and following the democratic process, an election or vote of confidence is held annually with the same outcome. Only death often disrupts this structural flow. The perpetuation of a performance community only requires the dedication of a single soul, male or female. Most commonly, then, African American women realize access to greater power with age, and the hierarchical structure is often a ruse, subverting the Western model. As sociologist Bennetta Jules-Rosettes stipulated, such patterns indicate a distinction between "rites of power and roles of power." In practice, men may dominate in ceremonial leadership positions, as sanctioned by church affiliates, but women preside over their sacred performance communities, undertaking many key responsibilities for an entire lifetime.

In a blues context, musicologist Jon Michael Spencer introduced "representative oscillation." This phrase applies to those who are the church faithful and whose spiritual teachings sustain less stalwart relatives and friends, outside of a general religious context in a less organized way. In many ways, this construct explains why women's attendance predominates. They are spiritual arbiters wherever they go. One of my most elemental discoveries is the relative autonomy afforded to women church officials. Perhaps because the cultural performances that I document commonly operate outside of the patriarchy associated with organized religion, women are granted more latitude and power. It is this awareness that prompted me to explore the nature of their competence across several genres of sacred music. I came to assess the women as cultivators of culture, which is another form of communicative competence. By competence, I allude to more than singing ability. I mean a cultural fluency related to an awareness of how to implement and manipulate governing societal rules.

Women, operating within the given dynamic of patriarchy, do not eke out a marginalized existence, but experience social agency perhaps unmatched by women cross-culturally. Those who grew up in the Afro-Baptist tradition may never experience a female devotional leader, a tradition performed by deacons. Within many denominations today, women seldom partake of key liturgical roles. Women members of certain sacred performance communities, however, do so without rancor or question, offering an opportunity to examine local cultural/gendered politics.

Consider Mary Lou Henderson again. Born in 1906, Mother Henderson uses the Twentieth of May as a mnemonic device as a reminder of her own conversion when twelve years old, and proclaims never to have strayed. She exemplifies the set of women who, as tireless cultural workers, assume multiple roles: "I been singing every since I was five years old. God give me that talent. I've been singing; and I've been organizing. I been speaking all over Georgia and working in the state convention. I was [on] one of the worship committees there. And I worked in the association. And I went to . . . uh . . . Fitzgerald and I finished there with uh my degree there in Fitzgerald, as a mission worker. (It's out there on the wall.) And I've got many plaques from going around organizing and singing from church to church and what not." She further stated: "My mother's prayers have followed me." She lives next door to Willowhead Missionary Baptist Church, first organized by her mother almost a century ago. Ethnographic research bears out that certain cultural/gendered configurations grant African American women greater agency than generally acknowledged under other patriarchies. They have great mobility and are gifted orators. Consequently, Henderson is the only woman who routinely leads the Devotion at the United Singing Convention of Georgia and Florida.

It is through their roles as song leaders, however, that this esprit de corps of women negotiates respect. They use their vocal virtuosity to secure an eternity of personal honor and esteem. Within these sacred musical contexts, women predominate as singers, often injecting a pronounced blues aesthetic. After all, the blues and spirituals emanate from the same roots, and gospel is another of its branches. The vocal techniques used borrow the same drones, moans, and inflections to express deep feelings. Such abilities place it outside the traditional Western sacred musical aesthetic. Once again, singing conforms to the expressed motto, "You don't have to sing like an angel." According to gospel singer and emcee Ovella Cunningham, "I don't feel that we sing that well, but it's the anointing of the Holy Ghost to get the message over. When the Lord gives it to us, there is a difference." These women use an African American cultural/gendered discourse to stabilize and heighten their subject position.

Many belong to federations of gospel singers, engaging in one of the more dynamic aspects of sacred music. The status that they derive largely from their local reputation as song leader grants the same freedom of expression extended traditionally to blues women. Foremost, their verbal dexterity propels them into the role of emcee or, culturally speaking, mistress of ceremonies. As already discussed in the previous chapter, they use their stylistic speech acts to connect disparate performances and occasionally to present a sermonic text. Ovella Cunningham of Opp, Alabama, embodies this rank of female commentator. She explained the artistry involved: "You have to know *how* to keep a program up, see. And a lot of people bring it down, you know. If you don't know what to say and when to say it (when a group sings), you bring down the program; and the spirit of the Lord leaves out. So the Lord gives me how to keep it up. I don't like a quiet program . . . [laughter]." The astute ability to interpret and direct performances informs another degree of competence. The nurturance of extraordinary cultural performances guarantees the survival of these aesthetic communities. Women emcees are radiant. They scream, they rave, they exhort. Although some would consider such behavior to be outlandishly overblown, one emcee expressed during a program: "I don't like being dignified in the house of the Lord." Their expressive behavior often does not fall within the purview of what others might consider ladylike, nor do they aspire to be. They conform to the dictates of a higher, divine power, which requires exaltation.

The same women function in a variety of church auxiliaries. Deaconess boards, missionary societies, and prayer bands are among the other modalities ascribed to by churchwomen. By doctrine, the Bible supplies the women their role models, whom they emulate. As relates to deaconess, it is Romans 16:1–3 that commends Phoebe as their mentor. As a result, they consider themselves as the businesswomen of the church. They work faithfully in the church as the presidents of the missionary societies and other organizations that help finance the church. They deem this role as distinct from being merely wife to a deacon. In that case, deacons' wives would obtain their honor from their husbands alone. Erroneously, most associate women missionaries with benevolence and as caretakers. Their duties were linked to cleaning up the church, fundraising, and meeting at the house of the infirmed to assist that household. Yet, women missionaries see their real work as to uplifting Jesus Christ and proselytizing in His name. Prayer bands bring women together regularly for communal discussion of a scripture, to pray, to sing, and to testify. They also leave monetary offerings for the evangelists at various church revivals. By accepting these meaningful roles, women routinize ways to interact divinely. I focus on the divine because they indeed live god-centered existences. Therefore, their time, energy, and money are spent in accord with the ideal.

This chapter illustrates that a womanist theology is more than a catchphrase. These women represent the womanists of whom Alice Walker wrote, who are "committed to the survival and wholeness of entire people, male and female." Based on Chikwenye Ogunyemi's analysis, womanism offers a spiritual foundation in which women are more "concerned with the ethics of surviving rather than with the aesthetics of living." This consciousness is engendered through a cultural awareness, which allows transcendence over patriarchal discourse. For the Yoruba, "The problem of constant gendering and gender-stereotyping does not arise." Theirs are voices of persistence and resistance. They often simultaneously belong to women-centered sodalities and modalities, but do not situate themselves discursively and gesturally within a single social sphere. Emilie Townes defined womanist spirituality as "not only a way of living, it is a style of witness and seeks to cross the yawning chasm of hatreds and prejudices and oppressions into a deeper and richer love of God as we experience Jesus in our lives."

While researching African American women and religion, many scholars articulate the longstanding history of sexism in the church. Historically, sexism and institutional oppression has coexisted within most organizational structures. Not to diminish this ubiquitous presence, I posit that a great deal gets oversimplified. An ethnographic reading renders how, in practice, sexism is received as well as resisted. It suggests gray areas that allow for patriarchal aligned contradictions, which privilege senior women over younger men along with other gender role reversals. Certain Wiregrass women embody a womanist theology, which is defined as a "critical reflection upon black women's place in the world that God has created and takes seriously black women's experience as human beings who are made in the image of God." There's no doubt that African American religious institutions support sexist practices; however, the sacred performance communities that I document do not suggest sustainability of such practices. While accessing the same biblical passages, as part of their praxis, women do not stick strictly to auxiliary roles. This orientation by certain Wiregrass women allows them greater self-definition. They provide polycentric examples of African American women's experiences.

For example, Lula Bennett-Mitchell, an anointed choral singer, grew up in the AME church. But upon marrying a Baptist deacon, she joined Macedonia Missionary Baptist Church. She possessed full understanding that the ecumenical services would not cease. She questioned the tendency of couples not to adhere to this principle today: "You're supposed to be together. You're supposed to be one. You're not supposed to be ahead him or behind him, but by his side." She went on to express that sharing a denomination prevented one's children from being confused. The biggest source for confusion was baptism. She had been "sprinkled" (christened) as a child in the AME church, but she "always wanted to be baptized after I got old enough to read the Bible where Christ was accepted to be baptized. I always wanted to follow in Christ's footsteps." In essence, her denominational change enabled her to achieve a personal desire that would not jeopardize her soul. No one is obligated to change.

Bennett-Mitchell reared seven of her husband's children along with being the biological mother of two of her own. She counts among her family twenty-one grandchildren and twenty-two great-grandchildren. Of course, all the stepchildren and in-laws call her mama. She is also known to be a strict disciplinarian, saying their children "will tell you quick: 'Grandmamma will sho' whip you.'" While one granddaughter reportedly disciplines only her daughter's children and not her son's, Bennett-Mitchell does not play favorites. What is perhaps most noteworthy is that she is also prone to discipline her adult children. Rules and discipline do not change whether you are young or old. When her forty-three-year-old grandson who was living with her borrowed her car and stayed out all night, she proclaimed: "I whipped him." She asserts there was nothing else for her to do but to stand her ground when he was inconsiderate. Within her household, she expects total control. She claims a reputation among family members: "I can tell you right now. If mama tells you something the third time, she might say it again but you're gonna be getting a lick too." Rather than being viewed as abusive, family view her measured acts of corporeal punishment as expressions of her God-given authority. She backs up her talk with action in ways that offer correctives, not to be strictly punitive. Consistency is what she offers. Such women are far from demure, even with age. She was most active in The Rural District's Women's Mission Department.

Lizzie "Ma" Henry epitomizes those Christian women whose life intersects with a range of optimal life experiences. As a young woman, she labored briefly in southern Florida on the Muck. In the 1920s, African American migrant laborers worked hard in this fertile region around Lake Okeechobee, picking vegetables by day and carousing by night. Folklorist Zora Neale Hurston immortalized this region with its jook joints, portending violence. Memory sometimes elicits narratives of our past, unlocking events central to our sense of self. Henry recalled one holiday: "Everybody was buying Easter dresses to go to church, and others were buying party dresses to go to dance Monday night." At the time she loved to dance the slow drag. On this occasion, a moment of enlightenment finally came after she injured a female rival by wielding a knife. Such youthful indiscretions prepare these virago women to mature and to assume premier leadership positions in their host community and church. On her wedding day in 1932, she was so glad to be on the usher board that she went back to church to usher the same night but was "set down." Henry ascended to occupying multiple positions at Mt. Zion Missionary Baptist Church, which she joined more than fifty years ago, "following old peoples." Her roles include president of the Mission, captain of Pastor's Aid Club, chaplain of the choir as well as belonging to the Mother Board and Deaconess Board. Each of Henry's personal experience narratives are infused with laughter and blunt language, attesting to her ability to give counsel and advice to a younger generation of women. She imbues them with the spirit to lead and not to accept subjugation.

Alice Stennett represents another spiritually gifted woman. Early in our interviewing process, she identified herself as being special by virtue of her posthumous birth. According to folk belief, being born after the death of one's biological father renders the child with stupendous psychic abilities and the talent to heal at an early age. Her father died from heart complications six months prior to her birth, leaving four children. She subsequently disclosed her ability to cure thrush. Folk belief also grants such individuals of posthumous birth the talent to heal at an early age. In accordance with the belief that having never seen her father gives her second sight, by age five, Stennett began healing infants with sores in their mouth. She was not allowed to talk before working a cure, except to pray. To eradicate thrush, she prayed for the baby and breathed on it seven times.

Mother Lizzie Henry in her Tifton, Georgia, garden

Based on her background, Stennett positioned herself as "loaded with love now." She went on to express: "If somebody is hurting. If you just show them some love and some care and some concern, they'll get better. They might fight it in the beginning because they don't understand and they can't appreciate that somebody would love them who doesn't even know them. If you keep feeding love it's gonna get through." She migrated to New Jersey, where she lived for almost thirty years, returning south in 1981. She is now a fixture, not only in her immediate community, but the larger city of Dothan. It is not uncommon for her phone to ring during the wee hours. She is often singled out as one who can get a prayer through, a powerful avocation. As a matter of fact, the phone rings intermittently throughout our interview, attesting to her true dynamism within her community. In this manner, Wiregrass women deemed as mentors show and gain status.

Baptist union meetings foreground and center the more hegemonic religious institutions. Yet they, too, demonstrate an egalitarian framework in which turn-taking grants women and men the same opportunity to speak to the group. It was their participation in Baptist unions, conventions, and associations as children that allowed women to learn elocutionary, musical, and leadership skills. These special gifts and talents, once nurtured, are valorized throughout various stages of life. Sheryl Melton was thirty-six years of age when we met, and she epitomized this upbringing. Now she is, in turn, her district's youth advisor. She expressed her Christian philosophy:

In the back of your mind, you know that the Lord is real. But until you get to a certain point in life, where you can really feel the spirit and . . . and . . . and enjoy that worshipping part. You know, to me, it makes it even more worthwhile. You know, it's like when you're drinking a soda and it's on a hot day. Only this is better than a soda. Because a soda lasts for a short period of while; but as for this, [the Holy Spirit] lasts for a short while because if it stays on you for so long a lot of people say you couldn't handle it. It's better than drinking a soda on a hot day, you know. But it's just something . . . that most people . . . if you know the Lord and you have been born again . . . and . . . and the Lord has given you the Holy Spirit and the Holy Spirit is within, you will be cautious about how you walk, how you talk, how you socialize with people. Make sure that you watch what you say (you know what I'm saying?) overall. And make sure that whatever you say that you're telling the truth. That's the most important thing.

As relates to women, her philosophy might appear to constrain. Speaking truth to power is now a popular expression; but when applied, it gives voice, direction, and empowerment to generations of African American Christian women. Melton advocates a godly talk and a godly walk, not self-erasure or acquiescence. Moreover, the statement applies equally to Christian men.

These Christian women are the ones you see donning white. When they assemble, whether as a prayer band or at a public service, white is worn uniformly. They also are seldom without hats or some head covering to match. They consider it right to cover your head when going into the house of the Lord. It is different for singing conventions, however. Adherence to tradition does not automatically translate to passivity. They operate as servants to the Lord and not to men. Foremost, it is via the sodalities and modalities to which they belong that they proclaim their authority. They reference biblical women as their role models, but not just the usual suspects. Their speech acts reveal the mechanisms and strategies by which they contest and resist internalizing the triple jeopardy of racism, classism, and sexism. They portray themselves as worldly and pious beings, but with a voice and attitude to be expressive.

The program "Sarah's Daughters" was one of the most unique as well as creative religious services that I have encountered. A Women's Missionary Society program, it took place at Oakey Grove Missionary Baptist Church in Ashford, Alabama. Inside, a large banner declared: "Moving Toward the Future, Forgetting Not the Past." Once again, the order of service conformed to other prototypical church-based programs: devotional, musical selections, welcome, scriptural reading, prayer, etcetera. However, the event was entirely woman-centered with a sense of gender-specific elation rarely engaged (outside of church-sponsored Woman's Day programs). This event featured the Wiregrass Women's Choir, and all the speakers were women. Yet, it is not totally an anomaly for women to preponderate. The audience also comprised a goodly proportion of men, especially the usual complement of ministers sitting near the pulpit area. Church culture draws a line between preaching and speaking. Women speak from the dais on the floor, as is customary for laypersons, regardless of gender. All of the women wore white—not just the ones on the program—and their hats were particularly bodacious.

The first speech act that truly positioned the program as women-centered was Alice Stennett's commentary "Who Are Sarah's Daughters." To introduce her address, she entered the secular realm, beginning with "I will tell you a quick story." She related how a younger man once approached her and praised her for a prayer he heard her deliver at a local hospital for a sick minister. While extolling her, she said, the man "made a sandwich out of my hand." He really was trying to come on to her. Spoken in a humorous tone, the story delighted the audience. Upon spurning him, though, this man actually struck her with his fist. Her response:

> I started smiling,
>   a big smile on my face.
> Never said a bumbling word.
> I didn't go get the law.
> I didn't scandalize him.
> I didn't talk about him.
> I don't know where he live.
> I didn't try to find out where he lived.
> I took it on the chin.
> I wasn't afraid.
> I got something on the inside.
> He didn't even hurt my feelings.
> But we got to learn how to live as Sarah's Daughters.
> This foolishness about who ever works
>   and brings in the biggest salary
>   got to have the most to say.
> That's a lot of nonsense!
> If you can find the place [in the Bible],
>   if ya'll can show it to me,

> *I'll be willing to listen*
>   *and learn.*
> *If a woman brings in the biggest salary*
>   *she's got to boss the house. [sneering]*
> *Sarah was Abraham's wife.*
> *She stood by his side.*
> *We got to learn that.*
> *We've got to get* back *to the* basics
>   *and put down this foolishness.*
> *It ain't about money.*
> *It ain't about clothes.*
> *It ain't about automobiles.*
> *We got to put down this foolishness.*

Needless to say, throughout the presentation the audience issued lively and heartfelt, antiphonic rejoinders. Once again, while on the surface it appears that the speaker's stance upholds patriarchy, in actuality it speaks to economic and social parity. What Stennett and the other women support is that, by leaning on the Lord, they fear no man and none should have dominion over them. In addition, they do not seek personal control. Theirs are not voices of submission but dignified self-assurance.

The very next woman to speak, the Minister of Giving, was equally dynamic, saying as much: "I don't like anything dead! When I was out there in the world, I was loud! So when Jesus saved me, I still was loud!" Stylistically, assertive women rely on sass as a cultural/gendered discursive tool. These women typify those frequently stigmatized as Sapphire, due to their audacity. They fit the adage that I first heard in a church: "Well behaved women rarely make history." Yet their sacred performance communities offer safe spaces where they learn at a young age to be outspoken and eloquent, where they receive adulation for being so, and where they bring this articulation to bear. They are tour de forces to contend with, but their main concern is obedience to the Lord, not men, nor larger societal standards.

The program comprised a transgeneration of ten women explicating an assortment of biblical women (as written in the program brochure): Anna, Abigail, Mary the Mother of Jesus, Pricilla, Esther, Elizabeth, Vashtia, Ruth, Maid of Naaman's Wife, and Deborah. With a few exceptions, most of these figures escape general knowledge. Furthermore, omitted were the Bible's more infamous "fallen women" such as Eve, Jezebel, Delilah, and Bathsheba. However, the omission was overtly expressed: "As for me, I'd rather be called a daughter of Sarah than a daughter of Jezebel." With the exception

Sister Alice Stennett in her
Ashford, Alabama, home

of Mary, the gospel that they bring is primarily from the Old Testament. However, the temptation also is not to glorify these women as biblical objects, marking them fit for emulation as subjects performing God's will. To be a Christian woman means everyday struggle. The main objective is to keep the faith. The words they speak are to bring affirmation to their shared experiences, within a ten-minute time limit.

Each speaker powerfully approached her biblical mentors. This collective presented narratives about barren women such as a "prophetess," Anna, to whom God "gave a wonderful gift," a son named Samuel, whom she compliantly "gave back to God." Mary, the Mother of Jesus, had to get her priorities straight to give birth to Jesus, which removed her from the role of mother, instead offering her motherhood to the family of God. Priscilla stood on God's word, steadfast and unmovable. She is an example of what married women may do in the general service of their churches. One of the older spokeswomen, Addie Buze, a most vociferous speaker, depicted Elizabeth, who conceived a child at an advanced age—John the Baptist. She expressed: "I got something inside of me that won't let me keep my mouth shut. I want you to hear what I have to say. I came here to ask Him to give me something for five minutes because that's hard to do when He starts moving inside." Revealing great wisdom, she continued: "Elizabeth was a strong woman. Ladies, speak up because we are strong." After a litany of godly traits—humble, gentle, kind—and once again the narrative shifted to parity:

She didn't mistreat her husband
   because they did not have.
He didn't mistreat her
   because they did not have.

The name Elizabeth means "God is my hope." Each presenter articulated through words, instead of song, a progressive worldview. They also articulated their actual self-identification with these biblical role models. They relate to these women from the scripture who possessed admirable characteristics and who labored in support of their God and community.

While Esther and Ruth are popularly recognized biblical figures, their presenters exhibited distinct presentation styles. The older of the two spoke extemporaneously and swiftly about Queen Esther in a high-pitched voice. She was obviously a woman of many words, and her audience sped up their antiphonal responses to match her pace. Due to the extent that they actively engaged in her speech act, her conclusion met with raging, loud applause. Maybe two decades younger, although in her forties, the next speaker read her presentation. Such programs offer another training ground for women still reaching a level of verbal maturity. With Ruth, she stressed how God said, "I can use anybody He wants," and "sometimes God wants us to use our head."

Ultimately, these are wives, mothers, and daughters who uphold the status quo, but not blindly. The women give voice to a range of biblical exemplars who may not necessarily illustrate clear signs of agency. For them, God already supplies believers with this ability everyday they use the resurrecting power of Christ. Thus, they express manifestations of success and fulfillment. Like Abigail, they seek to be women "of good understanding." They portray a spiritually based way of knowing God's kingdom while here on Earth, without mincing their words.

Some African Americans eschew Christianity precisely due to its implementation during slavery as a weapon for compliance. But these critics fail to complicate their argument. Once I, too, misinterpreted Christianity, especially as I came to observe it more as a bourgeois tool, not a mere opiate of the people. In the 1970s, I was a cultural nationalist; from this political position, becoming an atheist was the next logical step. Now I refer to my home church, Greater Mt. Pleasant, as my own Africa. For the past twenty years, as part of my ethnographic fieldwork, whether attending the ordination of a woman minister in the daytime or a Haitian Vodou ritual or Santeria Bembe in the night, I personally witnessed an African-based religious fervor infusing each one. As a result, I see how these Christian women can ascribe to being Sarah's daughters without dichotomously and simplistically invoking a submissive text. For instance, I find that many white Christian women read these biblical women solely within a context of subjugation: "Learning to be a daughter of Sarah is learning how to submit." However, African American Christian women privilege Sarah's faith. It is this same faith that supports their survival imperative, making a way out of no way. It steels their will into always considering right action and forever speaking their mind as deemed appropriate.

The youngest grouping of women was thirty-something, like Joann McGriff, who spoke passionately about the Maid of Naaman's Wife. This biblical figure is said to be "a nameless somebody." Obviously, her anonymity is a signifier of her social status as a slave. Among the only twenty words attributed to her, the maid expresses: "I know a Man." As stated, her portrayal appears to substantiate the Bible as being a male-centered text. The selected women, however, do not occupy secondary roles, for even this young enslaved woman turns out to be greater than the king she serves. Naaman is a leper; and she knows a man, Elisha, who, along with faith in God, could cure him. McGriff reinscribed the program's theme, saying: "As one of Sarah's daughters, we have to go to the unseen." Going about their quotidian existences, these women constitute living testimonies by believing and trusting in a higher power. McGriff suggested: "They love to hear the stories of His word." They fortify, they enliven, and they unify. Besides being inspirational, each scriptural interpretation moderates how their belief in God is not infused by patriarchy. They do not internalize gender oppression. As a community of women, they step out on His word and do not evince acceptance of beleaguered roles.

For instance, Deborah's narrative, as told by Gwen Crittenden, is a war story. According to Crittenden, "Women don't like to hear war stories. This is about a woman who was led to battle. Her battle was won." These days, such women are known as prayer warriors. Every day they put on the full armor of God, and like Deborah act as advisors to their people: "What we got here is a common thing, because it is working with us women today." Being dialectical in their thinking, their stances reverberate as not instructing women to be compliant beings but to be supplicants only to God. These women are represented as believers, portraying women as coministers in the early church. Moreover, they demonstrate the cognitive skill to erect their own hermeneutics. Their belief system privileges a divine understanding that posits infinite wisdom as theirs. They cherish the occasion to display their knowledge, while centering community values. Moreover, the program featured a host of local women from whom all could learn much.

Foremost, positioning all of these biblical women under the rubric of being "Sarah's daughters" highlights "the down line": their genealogy. Each speaker embodied different generations of Sarah's son's descendants. As descendants of Abraham, Isaac, and then Jacob, they comprise what is known as the faith line. As inscribed in the Bible, Apostle Paul introduced the language that holds up Sarah and Abraham's female descendants to a kind of conjugal obedience. However, descendants of Ishmael, Abraham's first son whose mother was Hagar, did not figure into the promised seed and were banished. It is generally believed that it is this lineage that African Americans identify with most. Additionally, I remember a sermon by Baptist minister in Philadelphia who preached about Sarah. He accentuated her as spiteful woman and the banishment of her female opponent.

> *Well, as it turns out, when Abraham got even older, The Lord said: "Let me show you what I can do." And so the Lord said to Abraham: "I am going to make you a daddy again, and this time the mother is going to be Sarah." Abraham said, "Lord, you're crazy. We tried that it don't work." And when the angel of the Lord came to Sarah, Sarah laughed and came to the Lord: "You've got to be kidding. As old as I am, I'm going to have a child and as old as he is. . . . You know, it might work with me but as old as he is." And so sure enough one night Abraham and Sarah got together and she conceived and the child was born. And Sarah jumped up and ran around laughing and look what I done and Old Abraham broken down. And here was Hagar with Ishmael. You know what happened now. Hagar and Ishmael had to go.*

While many women used humor, the tone of their address never engaged this degree of vituperation. They eschewed the dominant masculinist interpretations associated with biblical women. While not purely feminist tracts either, instead the focus shifted biblical paradigms to consider how the women, too, advanced Christian doctrine, without promoting controlling negative images of domination.

Just as I thought that I might be reaching the saturation point in relation to women-centered discourse within the region, I witnessed an interesting exchange at the Progressive Baptist District Association of West Florida hosted at Beulah First Baptist Church in Fort Walton, Florida, on June 28, 2003. On Saturday morning of their union meeting, after the devotional service, this modality features what amounts to breakout groups, called classes. Unlike the sacred musical performances of Friday night, this assembly privileged the word. The instruments from the night before were

Order of Service

Devotion -- Sis. Juanita Norris
Sis. Vera Cogman
Sis. Flossie Baker

Selection -- Wiregrass Women Choir
Director Sis. Debbie Smith

Welcome -- Sis. Annie Cochran

Scripture -- Sis. Debra Stokes

Prayer -- Sis. Betty Reese

Who are Sarah's Daughters ----------------------------- Sis. Alice Stennett

Selection -- Wiregrass Women Choir

----Ministry of Giving---
Sis. Annie Tharps - Sis. Helen Dawsey - Sis. Lorine Ward
Sis. Geneva Cull

Solo --- Sis. Rose Taylor

Speakers

Sis. Annie Dawsey ----------------------- Anna
Sis. Naomi Reeves ----------------------- Abigail
Sis. Alice Dawsey -------------- Mary the Mother of Jesus
Sis. Kim Green --------------------------------- Priscilla
Sis. Myrtice Bess ---------------------------------- Esther
Sis. Addie Buze ------------------------------- Elizabeth
Sis. Louvenia Dawkins ---------------------------- Vashtia
Sis. Betty Calloway -------------------------------- Ruth
Sis. Joann McGriff ---------- Maid of Naaman's Wife
Sis. Gwen Crittenden ----------------------- Deborah

SPEAKERS 5 MINUTES

The Order of Service for the "Sarah's Daughters" event hosted by the Rural District's Women's Mission in Ashford, Alabama

silenced in a heap with stacks of hymnals on a nearby rail. There were four class assignments: the Youth Department; Pastors, Ministers, and Deacons; Laymen, Young Men 18–35; and Women. The women's class included senior, intermediate, and junior women. As relates to attendance, this union meeting session had near parity. At the union meeting, the number of men nearly outnumbered that of women. Apparently, most of the men in attendance (above a certain age) no longer qualified as laymen serving in some official capacity at their home churches. Margarettea Kirkman, another example of a vibrant, articulate woman, served as the women's teacher.

The theme of the classes was "The Mission of the Church: How Do We Minister." The women's class focused on the subject "Right Attitudes and Actions," which Kirkman rephrased to mean "Right Mind, Right Attitude." The main thrust was to instill how true believers should exemplify Christian behavior by pursuing paths of peace. With the main text coming from II Timothy 2:14–16 and 19–26, a six-page outline supplied a full lesson plan of accompanying biblical verses. A women-centered approach ensued. The class leader invoked a circularity principle, infusing the sacred text with secular experiences specific to women. For instance, the initial focal point concentrated on teaching humility. However, nothing said pertained to a relationship with their male counterparts. Instead, the discourse asserted: "Don't you know that when you lift your sister up, she can draw someone else?"

Kirkman credited a rebounding church membership to government cuts to welfare recipients and the demise of affirmative action. This view voices a return of many to a harsh economic reality, necessitating a return to organized religion. However, she cautioned: "Ya'll know us—us mission sisters? We been in the way for twenty or thirty years. We know the hymns; we can quote scripture until the cows come home." Indeed, the printed outline seemed redundant because the most prominent accessory of most of the women assembled were well-worn Bibles. Each Bible was stuffed with bulletins, bookmarks, notations, and most were huge. Kirkman queried this body of women about their attitude toward single mothers with multiple children, who "ain't had a chance to believe Christ for a longer dress; she ain't had time to believe Christ for a hat; she ain't had time to believe Christ for correct shoes. So she ain't gonna dress quite like us mission sisters." To further make her point, she drew on humor by addressing their propensity to host women-in-white programs in which the hypothetical young mother "bust up in there in an overall dress." With growing antiphony, the assembly responded, "Accept her." At this rate, with the teacher still being on the first page of the outline after a half hour and with a half hour to go, I sensed that all were having a happy time in the Lord. The first page offered eight preliminary considerations such as berating "a fighting church" and "What kind of church would my church be if every church member were just like me?" One respondent avers: "Thank you, sistah, we're driving folk away."

Over thirty women were present, but their ages were hard to decipher. Calling Kirkman their teacher blurs boundaries because these Bible-toting women already know scripture, verse, and the appropriate interpretation. Kirkman was smartly attired in a gray beaded suit and bodice with short gray stylish hair and silver reading glasses. She's one who is extolled for her energetic promotion of the text, without a microphone. Personal experience narratives offset each preliminary consideration. Moreover, each narrative example acknowledged gender specifics. With lighthearted finesse, Kirkman centered the common experience of leaving the church sanctuary after a good service, "feeling so holy," with your white hat, suit, and shoes on, arriving home "whoops there it is." You find yourself pitted in a kind of altercation suitable for the "Jerry Springer Show." Her audience speedily concurred, identifying with the difficulty "to get it right." Then, Kirkman personalized her examples saying as an undertone, "I know I'm not the only one who ever done that." She jocularly continued: "I'm showing you how pitiful we are, in the name of Jesus."

As part of the instruction, there also was a hint of the African dilemma tale. For example, in Matthew 18:15–17, Jesus provides procedural directions for dealing with fellowship problems. Kirkman introduced a scenario in which a fellow member slanders her before others at church, and adding insult to injury, Kirkman gruffly confronts the slanderer. Upon deeply hurting the feelings of the other, while in character, Kirkman inconsiderately expressed: "It's your tough luck." To add to the hypothetical and to demonstrate the magnitude: "She done described my car; she done described my clothes, done described my house and my husband. So she done told all my stuff." Ideally, the complaint could be easily mediated: "With the right intent, [Kirkman] should be the first to apologize." Then, proactively she would approach the congregation and say: "I've offended my sister." Failing this, Kirkman indicated that ultimately it is appropriate for the church as a body to squelch such malcontent. Being a dues-paying official of the Women's Missionary Society, Kirkman asked how the matter might be correctly handled. Jokingly, to an uproar of laughter, one of the women responded: "Give you a refund." In this fashion, the women good-naturedly explored righteous interaction with one another. The expectation is that the membership would help this pompously Christian leader to grow spiritually because she has a problem. In this fashion, they whiled the time away without centering men in their discourse.

Kirkman also privileged African American vernacular English, without embarrassment or apology. Of course, such language usage pertains least to education attainment or cognitive skills. Within a primary church context, this vernacular is always the parlance of the day, demanded by congregants. As part of being outspoken, Kirkman did not mince her words in any way.

One consideration directed the discussion to tithing: "Is something wrong with your church?" In this framework, the group leader asked: "Have you heard the expression: 'I ain't gonna give those niggahs my money?'" Her esoteric question received invigorating affirmation. She enlivened the discourse further when she followed up with her own reply: "You don't tithe to Negroes. You tithe to God." As a rhetorical practice, she was keeping it real. In recognition of her various ploys, it became obvious how Kirkman came to be a presiding officer. In her case, it is not a matter of seniority but the verbal competence to speak with complexity, while espousing a casual body of knowledge. Foremost, as certified prayer warriors, the term *virago* again comes to mind. These female warriors are women of extraordinary stature, strength, and courage. By their assertive words and aggressive deeds, they operate against the grain, which usually reveres women deemed demure and diplomatic.

Here, I record being in the presence of some exceptional women. They are not power mongers and neither, for the most part, are their men folk. They characterize themselves as simple home folk who sing and pontificate not just because they're happy, but also because they love the Lord. They aspire to implement and live by a covenant passed down as part of a locally ingrained spiritual activism. I will never forget the African American woman I met living in what anyone might call a hovel. I stopped to ask directions at an intersection in Coolidge, Georgia. The frail woman with scabby skin bore many of the classic signs of being malnourished. I only got a glimpse of her skimpy existence; however, I took away a world of spiritual insights. In that brief encounter, her genuine adoration of the Lord and expression of blessings caused me to rethink my atheism. Instead of seeing a zealot, I recognized how her sentiment came from the ages, giving expression to gratitude despite impoverished conditions. I later realized that I mark my own spiritual journey as commencing on this day. It would be years before I would attend a Sunday worship service not connected with my fieldwork. I learned the extent to which these Wiregrass women uphold not just a resistant survival imperative, but a moral authority as well. They seek to live righteously the Gospel Truth, serving the Lord as exemplars of love. They recognize a creative impulse in our word whether sung or orally expressed. Downhome gospel is their medium, through the acceptance of divine order, to vocalize and be renewed.

Epilogue

This sociomusicology related to African American Wiregrass sacred music and spiritual activism more than fulfilled my personal quest. I experienced African American culture in new and unimaginable ways. My research, I suspect, unearthed many southern and regional traditions, in situ, unknown to many. I dare say that the Twentieth of May, Sunday Morning Band, Fifth Sundays, and the sacred music these occasions ritualize fall outside the purview of both the general public and many scholars. Therefore, I hope that my moderately self-reflexive approach raises understanding of the region's cultural diversity. After all, the diverse Wiregrass ecosystem offers some key lessons about multiculturalism. Its fire ecology promoted connectivity between a vast array of plants and animals to withstand a likely conflagration. Botanists now estimate that only one million acres of wiregrass, out of an original ninety-three million acres in the United States, remain. Most people who live in the region have never seen it grow. Wiregrass is practically extinct along with certain species of wildlife, which could not survive within the monoculture that deforestation produced. Yet, many of the region's human social rituals remain vibrant, though strained.

I choose to relay in the epilogue some human and cultural losses. As to be expected, a longitudinal study of this magnitude, with years in the making, would behold many going to glory to sing and shout. Doris Lewis, the backbone of so much within her church community and reciprocal support networks, especially the Glory Train Special, succumbed. The Thomas-Grady Counties Singing Convention mourns their elders who served as my historians: Tommie Gabriel and Willie Johnson. There are so many others whom I might name. Additionally, my own son, Bill, succumbed. I could not have withstood his passing without years of tutelage by these spiritual activists. Over the years, I had not realized how much I had internalized their lyrics and absorbed their prayers. Whether called the Old One Hundred or deemed to be Sunday morning testimony songs, from these I learned to count my blessings. While funeralizing my son, my home church choir performed: "Soon and Very Soon We Are Going to See the King." My intuitive instinct (whether, in this context, appropriate or not) was to adopt Sunday Morning Band's tramping as I marched in on the sanctuary. In retrospect, my participant-observation fortified me as well.

A universalizing theme often fails to consider the complexities of identity formation. This sociomusicology seeks to rectify the tendency, even among African Americans, to depend on very circumscribed notions of race. Instead of race, I identify a cultural domain sharing the same principles. This ethnographic study does not present African American culture as being monolithic, but it does postulate the retention of some core cultural expressions as relates to hospitality, temporality, and a communitarian outlook. Wiregrass spiritual activists privilege a specific worldview. While sharing many commonalities with their white southern counterparts and other regions, I document the quotidian nature of their spirituality. Having a sense of nearness to God gives many the sense of belonging. As a projection of this belonging, their musical view of the universe is expansive. I associate it as downhome gospel to acknowledge the regional aesthetic in all that they sing and do. To perform, one does not have to sing like an angel; rather one strives to possess angelic qualities—an earnest spiritual vibrancy.

I discovered the extent to which local residents love to sing sacred music as a way of life and a way to live. As a part of their African American cultural memory, they claim renditions from spirituals to contemporary gospel. The Twentieth of May is a holiday that celebrates the past via liberation songs of old. While elsewhere Juneteenth functions as Emancipation Day for a growing number of African Americans, Wiregrass celebrants hold onto their own style of celebrating, even if not on the exact date. They tend to infuse the old with the new. Singers break with the traditional spiritual rhythms and prevalent minor chords, changing the melody but not the message and acknowledging their continued struggle for economic and political parity. This holiday will not likely thrive outside of the pockets where families and local civic leaders grant it continuity. Based on the celebrations that I still attend, attendees are reminded of the meaning of freedom to those who endured bondage, ruthless southern apartheid, and now the social changes that integration wrought. They recognize their willingness to never forget as part of a survival imperative, learned from their ancestors. It is worth noting, too, ironically, that sustainability depends on the diligence of a few due to the difficulty of reviving public display events once other activities subsume them.

African American sodalities called burial societies are a case in point. They once thrived in every hamlet and African American enclave. Funerals represent a time-honored life passage rite. African Americans expend great effort to ensure that their loved ones are respectfully interred. Upon emancipation, their ancestors quickly organized secret societies to avoid a pauper's burial. These societies also promote a spiritual component, while maintaining a host of traditional customs. Wiregrass Florida is the site where members of the AME church, foremost, continue such practices. Sunday Morning Band constitutes one of the most ornate and visible organizations. Membership awards assistance not only upon death, but also at times of sickness and misfortune. The annual fall Turnout is the ritual moment when members don their symbolic dress, tote their ceremonial paraphernalia, and "march in" in a procession to raise additional funds and to recruit. These voluntary associations share commonalities with West African secret societies that operate with the same social and economic impetus. Other variations coexist throughout the region, but they, too, are reduced in number.

Paradoxically to me, although my mother's father was a Baptist minister, this information was withheld as my parents elected to reject this "old-fashioned" kind of faith. Among other reasons, I recently learned my parents rejected this denomination due to its ecstatic worship style, protracted meetings, and ample offertory rites. Based on the perspective they passed down, I never could have guessed being so enthralled by Baptist district union meetings. Occurring on every Fifth Sunday (four, maybe five times, a year), I expended many hours enjoying the minutia of their ritual acts. Being bounded by state conventions, in this tri-state region I had a variegated experience. In Wiregrass Alabama, one sacred performance community combines the union meeting with an afternoon gospel extravaganza, held in a building they erected for this purpose. In Wiregrass Florida, district churched built an edifice to host meetings and fellowship in order to unite far-flung Baptist communities. Finally, Wiregrass Georgia retains these basically quarterly meetings with continued fervor and flare. These modalities all offer a local treat for its membership on every Fifth Sunday. In these well-structured contexts, I engaged some of the most primordial forms of African American religious practices. I also witnessed the primary proving ground for Baptist youths.

As part of this update, saddened, I must report the Jackson and Dewey Williams memorial singing conventions, essentially, are no more. As of spring 2009, surviving family members accepted the inevitable. Physically depleted, the fervor began to wane along with dreams of a revival.

At ninety-three, Japheth Jackson discontinued the Jackson Memorial Singing in its seventy-fourth year. Likewise, Bernice Harvey reported: "We just didn't have anybody to sing no more." Requiring singers to perform all four parts, each death signified a lost part. They could not fill the square or start a tune, missing a vocal part. Being unable to travel caused some surviving Wiregrass singers to feel impolite. Due to health issues, unable to attend the integrated National Sacred Harp Convention in Birmingham and the Capital City Singing in Montgomery, the African American Wiregrass contingency acknowledges its demise. As the old cliché goes, "stop the press"; a recent announcement indicates that on April 18, 2010, Judge Jackson's great-grandchildren intend to continue his memorial singing at a different local venue. If the Greenville singing building's existence is any indication the seven-shape conventioneers will assemble there, on Fifth Sundays, without a significant breach.

Thomas and Grady County residents answered the call of the father of gospel music, Thomas Dorsey, early on and regularly attended his National Baptist Convention from practically its inception. Yet, the Thomas-Grady Counties Singing Convention, too, experiences change. Although not crippled by the passage of time and flagging attendance, the convention format is reduced to one Friday night session, which means the demise of the Sunday radio broadcast. The financial business is now conducted before the gospel singing, with the elimination of several offices such as the second vice president and a reporter. While Clifford Williams still officiates as the president, a younger deacon, Kenneth Wright, functions as the vice president. Sam Brown and Mattie Smart offer stability in their roles as finance chairman and recording secretary, respectively. With the loss of seven churches from the enrollment, the convention experienced quite a downturn. Yet, it survives due to some shrewd transformations. More young adults flesh out the choirs that remain along with the introduction of drums and Wright's guitar skills. During the convention's heyday, one church (Rebecca) regularly featured a female duet, and it was gratifying to note the choir loft filled with a choral unit now comprising their offspring in hip-hop gear. The City-Wide Choirs' Union, which meets on Wednesdays, still prospers as well. Spiritual activists seek transcendence, and one form is not being bound by precedent.

The more contemporary form of gospel music booms. With its propensity for three-day weekend performances, often traversing the tri-state region, these reciprocal support networks offer the most fluidity. Being family-oriented by makeup, participation is most rewarding. These sacred performance communities perhaps conform the most to African American

Current vice president, Deacon Kenneth Wright, plays electric guitar at the 477th session of the Thomas-Grady Counties Singing Convention on August 14, 2009

gospel programs elsewhere. Its performers wear extravagant garb and sing replete with drive sections and are backed up by great musicians. As a matter of fact, the singing building in Elba, Alabama, added two new ensembles: the Gospel Wonders and the Soul Gospel Singers. It continues to furnish a popular site, built exclusively to support this musical tradition. When faced with personal crisis, networks host benefits because they care. Therefore, as a lifestyle, these spiritual activists extend a wide berth for interdependent caring and sharing. Their communitarian outlook, literally, goes a long way.

Finally, Wiregrass women who are spiritual activist rule from within every performance community. These women promote a womanist spirituality to ensure the success of their entire network. They function in leadership roles that withstand the test of time. They may also hold similar positions in a number of sacred organizations. As emcees, they also bring much of the glamour and energy to most anniversary programs. Certain ones gain honorific names such as Mother, Ma, or Aunt because they eschew the stereotype of demure, passive Christian women. Instead, they display sass and interpret the Bible in nuanced ways that empower women. They serve as role models and mentor others through the counsel they bring, informally and formally. Programs such as "Sarah's Daughters" allow them a voice to feminize the scripture and promote a realist view of a text often used to suppress women. Because downhome gospel is as likely to occur outside of official religious contexts, women are in the forefront of their performance communities. Most of the sodalities and modalities mentioned in this study have flourished for decades. Their foremothers taught them well.

Once all is said and done, indeed, I was seeking a better understanding of spirituality when I arrived in Wiregrass Country, fresh from conducting fieldwork in Philadelphia. There, being an atheist, I approached my research with a degree of relativism. I achieved more than I bargained for by moving south. I remember, during the intermission for lunch at the South Alabama Seven Shape Singing Convention in Greenville, Alabama, feeling excited about the local high school team's tournament win at the buzzer the night before. I harmlessly remarked: "You must have all really being praying to pull that one off." Everyone at the table stared at me blankly. One of the younger male singers, Bennie McDonald, responded first: "Why would we pray to defeat the other team?" This simple exchange initiated a personal epiphany. I realized that Wiregrass folks, indeed, practice what they preach. I mention this personal experience narrative because, as part of my participant-observation, I began to pay greater heed to every interjection. I comprehended that it no longer was just a matter of me not knowing much about my cultural roots. The onus was placed on me to present my ethnographic findings in a way that gave full voice to these spiritual activists. In the process, I underwent a spiritual awakening to match all that I observed and to do honor to God. I long knew that my synchronous fieldwork experiences answered to some higher power. I hope that this study will enlighten others about an unknown region and its African American spiritual activists.

Notes

PROLOGUE

ix   "But, I went about asking . . . ," Zora Neale Hurston, *Dust Tracks on a Road*, 175.
xii Columbus McGriff's untimely death probably deterred larger acclaim for his folk
     artistry. Nevertheless, Betty-Carol Sellen and Cynthia Johanson (*Self Taught,
     Outsider, and Folk Art*, 223–224) offered some recognition.

INTRODUCTION

xvi   "Greatly misunderstood . . . ," *Daily Times-Enterprise*, "The Fertility of Our Pine
      Land," August 2, 1889, Thomasville, Georgia. The same newspaper, on December
      17, 1889, documented "Cows on the Street," and the new city ordinance to prohibit
      cows "running at large." In terms of the region's sparse population, see Joan Niles
      Sears, *The First One Hundred Years of Town Planning in Georgia*, 1. For a reference
      about being stigmatized as predominantly white and for "cornbread" quotes, see
      Gregor Sebba, *Georgia Studies: Selected Writings of Robert Preston Brooks*, 73 and
      113, respectively.
xvii "Most authors approach . . . ," Ray Allen, *Singing in the Spirit*, 142. Jeff Titon
      (*Powerhouse of God*, 255) contributed the quote "a smooth blend . . ." about the
      aesthetic quality affixed to singing among whites in a particular locale. He also
      indicated a breach between their actual practice and theory (256). Therefore, in
      practice, they tend actually to sing in ways that also eschew established Western
      convention. B. Dexter Allgood's dissertation, "A Study of Selected Gospel Choirs in
      the Metropolitan Area," documented among African Americans the role of formal-
      ized techniques predicated on rehearsal and choir directors. Hurston's quote "each
      singing of the piece . . ." recentered an African American common aesthetic by re-
      jecting a single, correct way to perform a song ("Spirituals and Neo-Spirituals," *The
      Sanctified Church*, 80).
xviii African American musical practices demand a progression beyond dichotomous
      views such as Archie Green's as represented in his quote "the contrast between . . ."
      from "Hear These Beautiful Sacred Selections," 40. Moreover, see Jon Michael
      Spencer's *Blues and Evil* for a study that also pushes the boundaries beyond duali-
      ties. William Lynwood Montell's *Singing the Glory Down*, generally supplied useful
      information pertaining to sacred music traditions among southern whites as well

as the quoted comment "lacking in vocal . . ." (51). However, this comment diverges
significantly from the aesthetic of African Americans in Wiregrass Country today. I
located musicologist Eileen Southern's quotation in Samuel A. Floyd's *The Power of
Black Music* (170). This description better situates local African American singing
style.

xviii "Each song ought to . . . ," Tommie Gabriel interviewed in Thomasville, Georgia, on
August 5, 1994. At an actual performance, a singer also voiced the quote "Too many
of them . . . ," field recording of the Zionette's anniversary program in Greenville,
Alabama, on June 2, 1996. See also Christopher Small, *Music of the Common
Tongue*, from which comes the quote "From the start . . ." (105).

xix Jeff Titon's designation of *downhome* ("a spirit, a sense . . .") is in *Early Downhome
Blues*, xiii. See Harris (*The Rise of Gospel Blues*) for more about Dorsey's construct,
the gospel blues. Moreover, historicizing contemporary gospel, Allen centered one
of its pioneers, Edwin Hawkins, as having "broke ranks with the down-home style
and adopted a more polished approach in their music" (*Singing in the Spirit*, 7).
Like Horace Boyer ("Traditional and Contemporary Gospel Music," 127–167), many
situate contemporary gospel as "a physical and intellectual move from the rural—
or what has come to considered rural—to the urban" (128). However, I would locate the division as being more canonical. Many in urban Black America prefer the
traditional; and I would venture to say, the present-day move is toward something
of a post-contemporary theology, accepting of a pastiche of sacred musical styles
and beliefs.

xx "To study . . . ," Steven Feld, "Sound Structure as Social Structure," 385. To explain
the genesis of my sociomusicology, my methodology seeks to move beyond a generic approach. I choose to be in league with Feld by studying African American
sacred music on its own terms by taking a sociomusicological approach.

xx "Black people share their . . . ," Houston Baker, *Long Black Song*, 61–62. Also, one of
the few studies to consider the topic, *Black Belonging* by Jack Ross and Raymond
Wheeler, provides an overview and a theory about the significance of voluntary
associations in everyday African American life. Also, see Horace Cayton and St.
Clair Drake's *Black Metropolis*. I situate African American belonging as syncretiz-
ing well with West African customs of collectivity. Furthermore, anthropologist
John Gwaltney's *Drylongso* established the foundation for there being a Black core
culture.

xxii "Maybe more things . . . ," Zora Neale Hurston, *Their Eyes Were Watching God*, 76.

CHAPTER 1

4 "'Blacks' or 'Negroes' . . . ," Daniel Littlefield's *Africans and Creeks*, 73. For more on
the American Indian presence, see James W. Covington, *The Seminoles of Florida*,
28–67. A more general study linking the two groups is that by Charles Hudson,
The Southeastern Indians, 457–497. In addition, Larry Rivers' *Slavery in Florida*
(189–209) documents the cooperation between Seminoles and their allies, Black
Seminoles.

4 "In 1816, gunboats attacked . . . ," Jerrilyn McGregory, *Wiregrass Country*, 15.

5 "Africans proved far . . . ," William Katz, *Black Indians*, 5. The earlier Jesup quote
is from Littlefield, *Africans and Creeks*, 275. Congressman Joshua R. Giddings

from Ohio, in concurrence with Jesup, scrutinized the Africana presence further. The historian James Leitch Wright (*Creeks and Seminoles*, 275) documented that Giddings expressed that "the true heroes and freedom fighters were the exiles, including Gopher John, Abraham, and Cudjo, interpreters, military chieftains, and advisors to Indians and whites." The Seminoles were not an identifiable ethnic group until the 1700s. Also, see Robert Cotterhill's *The Southern Indians*, 8–20; Jesse Burt and Robert Ferguson, *Indians of the Southeast*, 173–180; Charles Hudson, *The Southeastern Indians*, 265–267; Ruth Murray Underhill, *Red Man's America*, 36–51; and Walter L. Williams, "Southeastern Indians Before Removal: Prehistory, Contact, Decline," 16–20.

5   "Well into the 1870s . . . ," Mark Wetherington, *The New South Comes to Wiregrass Georgia*, 142. The Appling County statistics appeared in Ruth Barron's *Footprints in Appling County*, 7. The same could be said about African Americans in Pike County, Alabama, as Minnie Clare Boyd asserted in *Alabama in the Fifties*, 16. William Warren Rogers furnished the secession information in "The Way They Were: Thomas Countians in 1860," 131–144. During the Civil War, local history indicates that citizens formed a Home Guard to protect themselves from raids by Confederate deserters and other outlaws, who took refuge in the Wiregrass coastal swamplands. Action like this typified the Civil War years in this vast area. Often ignored by historians, the 1864 Battle of Marianna constitutes the deepest penetration by Union forces into the South. Otherwise, no known battlegrounds exist in the Wiregrass.

6   "The largest farms . . . ," Roland Harper, "Development of Agriculture in Lower Georgia from 1890 to 1920," 335. In terms of African American economic progress, "Freedmen often became . . ." is quoted from Ann Patton Malone, "Piney Woods Farmers of South Georgia, 1850–1900," 69.

6   "Throughout the whole . . . ," Margaret Walker's *Jubilee* (349) also documents the significance of the Wiregrass to African Americans during a period of mass emigration after the Civil War. Her quote attests to the quality of the land of which African Americans managed to achieve ownership.

6   "He was successful . . . ," Mandy Butler interviewed in Cairo, Georgia, on June 22, 1994; "My wife's granddaddy . . . ," Milton Young interviewed in Graceville, Florida, on September 13, 1996; "We moved . . . ," Louise Sapp interviewed in Thomasville, Georgia, on August 25, 1995; "We bought . . . ," Gladys Westbrook interviewed in Cairo, Georgia, on July 16, 1992.

9   "Near Thomasville are . . . ," Hal Steed, *Georgia*, 99. For more related to hunting plantations, see Titus Brown and James Hadley, *African American Life on the Southern Hunting Plantation*. For more about the African American workers and hunting parties, see Charles Elliott, *Ichauway Plantation*.

9   "These so-called northern . . . ," Jerrilyn McGregory, *Wiregrass Country*, 117.

9   "We cooked and . . . ," Alice Stennett interviewed in Gordon, Alabama, on July 19, 1998.

10   "Wrought with allegorical hope . . ." and "By 1919, Juneteenth . . . ," Elizabeth Hayes Turner, *Women, Culture, and Community*, 251. For a more succinct documentation of Juneteenth, from its inception to its inauguration as an official state holiday, see the preeminent folklorist William H. Wiggins Jr.'s "'Juneteenth': Afro-American Customs of the Emancipation." Published by the Texas Folklore Society and edited

by Francis Abernethy, Patrick Mullen, and Alan Govenar, *Juneteenth Texas: Essays in African-American Folklore* features only one article pertaining to the holiday, William H. Wiggins Jr.'s "Juneteenth: A Red Spot Day on the Texas Calendar," 236– 253. In his book *O Freedom! Afro-American Emancipation Celebrations*, Wiggins documented the regional specificity of these freedom celebrations. However, apparently, the May 28 emancipation date in Alabama was the closest Wiggins came to those celebrations indigenous to the Wiregrass. Based on his own travel itinerary, he never entered the Florida Panhandle or Wiregrass Georgia. For many, knowledge of such holidays remains limited to Juneteenth. See Wiggins' "From Galveston to Washington: Charting Juneteenth's Freedom Trail" for greater details about the spread of the Juneteenth holiday. In this publication, Wiggins lists May 22 as the date of significance to Florida.

13 "We wish to thank . . ." appeared on a May 21, 2005, Hill family holiday leaflet.

13 "A lot of the cooking . . . ," Caroline Allen interviewed in Crestview, Florida, on April 25, 2003. "While these performances . . . ," folklorist John Roberts' "Remembering the Spirit of Celebration in a South Carolina Community" documents the importance of May Day in African American southern culture (47). Many locales in the circum-Caribbean basin also traditionalize the maypole, especially Jamaica.

14 "They probably got . . . ," Brown and Hadley, *African American Life on the Southern Hunting Plantation*, 114. In addition, this text provides indication that in Wiregrass Georgia African American elected to celebrate both dates: "They celebrated the 20th of May, and they celebrated the 28th. And the reason they celebrated the 28th, because they said the slaves in Georgia didn't know about it until eight days later. Now that's what was told to me when I was a kid" (108).

15 "The only rituals . . . ," Walter Pitts, *Old Ship of Zion*, 25.

15 "Many observers . . . ," Alan Lomax, *The Land Where the Blues Began*, 81.Moreover, in African American culture, call and response reigns supreme as a tropological characteristic. See Samuel Floyd Jr. in "Ring Shout! Literary Studies, Historical Studies, and Black Music Inquiry," 49–70.

16 "One word, 'freedom,' . . . ," Bernice Johnson Reagon, *If You Don't Go, Don't Hinder Me*, 2.

16 "You ought to be glad . . . ," Deacon Owen Wrice, May 13, 1994, Quitman, Georgia; on the next page, he also verbalized the following messages: "You ought to be glad . . . ," "Your mind go back . . .," and "We, as Black people . . .". Also, see Jon Michael Spenser's *Protest and Praise*, in which he introduced his methodological construct, theomusicology, and stated: "The spirituals lyricized . . ." (14).

17 "These discussions consist . . . ," Charles Briggs, *Competence in Performance*, 60.

18 "The chorus and verses . . . ," Warren, *Ev'ry Time I Feel the Spirit*, 91. Some monographs that emphasized the spirituals' social protest motifs include John Lovell's *Black Song*, Arthur C. Jones' *Wade in the Water*, and V. P. Franklin's *Black Self-Determination*.

18 "We had people . . . ," Wrice also alludes to the lyrics "Down by the Riverside," referencing "Study War No More." This song is associated with Martin Luther King's nonviolent resistance strategy, intoning how foremost spirituals were religious songs of resistance. See James Cone's *The Spirituals and the Blues*. The Lovell quote "started out as . . ." further explicates the song's historical context (*Black Song*, 574).

The Wiggins quote "some having to do . . ." further positions the genre (*O Freedom!*, 87).

19 "The story of situation . . . ," Boyer, "Brewster: The Eloquent Poet," 220. "These stories tell . . . ," Reagon, *If You Don't Go*, 75.

20 "But when I was . . . ," Reverend Simmons, Emancipation Day Celebration, May 17, 1996, Quitman, Georgia.

21 "I can imagine . . ." and "just like Christ . . . ," Deacon Owen Wrice, Emancipation Day Celebration, May 17, 1996, Quitman, Georgia.

22 "They gave us . . . ," Tommie Gabriel quote, appearing in Jerry DeVine and Titus Brown's "The Twentieth of May," 17. For more related to the celebrations on hunting plantations, see Brown and Hadley, *African American Life on the Southern Hunting Plantation*. As quoted by me in *Wiregrass Country* (97), William Rogers further historicizes the day: "If anything blacks . . .".

23 "To have the Twentiethth of May . . . ," Wrice, Emancipation Day Celebration, 1996. "A primary function . . . ," Wiggins, the leading authority on Juneteenth, in *O Freedom!*, 49.

23 "We have come through . . . ," Wrice, Emancipation Day Celebration, 1996.

24 "Don't sing it . . . ," Pastor Jahazel Dawkins, Twentieth of May–Memorial Day Celebration, May 28, 2005, at the Old National Guard Armory in Quincy, Florida.

25 "Singing was not only . . . ," Spencer, *Protest and Praise*, 91.

25 "In church and . . . ," Titon, *Early Downhome Blues*, 23.

CHAPTER 2

26 "Thus, a black community . . . ," Holloway, *Passed On*, 34. Holloway, too, in her otherwise comprehensive text on African American funerary customs, spoke of burial societies in the past tense. Relying extensively on Holloway, Jacqueline Thursby's *Funeral Festivals in America* (52–54) concisely treated African American funerals.

26 "Many cultures had developed . . . ," Edward Ball, *The Sweet Hell Inside*, 45. "More Americans belonged . . ." and "to consider applications . . ." David Beito, *From Mutual Aid to the Welfare State*, 2 and 8, respectively.

27 "To help bury . . . " and later "be of good . . . ," The Constitution and By-Laws and Receipt Book of the Independent Pallbearers Union of South Alabama and Northwest Florida. A booklet; n.d., n.p.

27 "Secret societies have always . . . ," W. E. B. Du Bois' *The World and Africa*, 160. Drawing on Du Bois' research, Betty Kuyk ("The African Derivation of Black Fraternal Orders in the United States," 559–592) traced his contentions among enslaved Africans. Other research has focused on the Poro and Sande secret societies of Liberia. See Stanton Tefft, *The Dialectics of Secret Society Power in States*, 26–47. In Liberia, membership is basically obligatory in that almost all the men and women in a community belong. In Liberia, initiation occurs at puberty and entails a scarification ritual. Moreover, they engage chiefly a political rather than an economic structure. Others have recognized the collective economics involved, equating such secret societies with credit associations. According to Alice Eley Jones, "Within the New World, the American South, and Stagville plantation there arose a system of education for Africans to be initiated into secret societies which addressed their spiritual needs beyond Christianity" ("Sacred Places and Holy Ground," 102).

28 "Societies and lodges . . . ," Roberta Wright and Wilbur Hughes, *Lay Down Body*, 267–268. For further explanation pertaining to bounded communities, see Bayliss Camp and Orit Kent, "'What a Mighty Power We Can Be,'" 439–483.

28 "the underlying reason . . . ," Mary Twining and Keith Baird, *Sea Island Burial Roots*, 91. Anthropologist William Bascom is credited with bringing the Yoruba term *esusu* to the forefront in "The Esusu." For more about these credit associations, see Victor Uchendu, *The Igbo of Southeast Nigeria*, 77–81. Traditional *esusu* is westernized, forming the acronym ROSCAs (rotating savings and credit associations), as fully delineated by Toyin Falola and Akanmu Adebayo, *Culture, Politics and Money Among the Yoruba*. Coined by Clifford Geertz in "The Rotating Credit Association," he voiced pessimism about the future of these alternative economic systems. However, Falola and Adebayo's monograph indicated otherwise. African American burial leagues in Wiregrass Country are no doubt descendants of these systems of collective economics. As Falola and Adebayo position money in Yorubaland, they introduce *ajo*, a system that's virtually escaped scholarly research. Whereas *esusu* means pooling one's resources, *ajo* refers to the creation of savings institutions or banks (127–148).

29 "Then place the left hand . . . ," International Benevolent Society, Inc., Manual, n.d., n.p., 23. Also, Kuyk (578–579) reported the significance of "a sprig of evergreen" in both traditional West African and among the enslaved.

29 "White church was giving up . . . ," Clarence Earl Walker, *A Rock in a Weary Land*, 88.

30 "The AME Church had . . ." and "while the white overseer," Larry Rivers and Canter Brown, *Laborers in the Vineyard of the Lord*, xv and 17, respectively. Essentially, these historians position this evangelical movement more explicitly in Florida in general and Wiregrass Florida in particular. With even greater particularity, they center Marianna, Florida, as the hotbed of such organizational activities. For more about Henry Call, the slave preacher, see Larry Rivers, *Slavery in Florida*. According to theologians C. Eric Lincoln and Lawrence H. Mamiya (*The Black Church in the African American Experience*, 54), by 1989 the AME church boasted an overall membership of 2.2 million, making it the largest within the Methodist denomination.

30 "there any ministers . . . ," expressed during The Independent Pallbearers' Fifth Sunday Program at Mt. Pleasant AME Church, June 29, 2003.

31 "I still kept . . . ," Alex McGlockton interviewed in Tallahassee, Florida, on December 4, 1996. Clarence Earl Walker also mentioned the early impetus to license women clergy (*A Rock in a Weary Land*, 25–26). Jualynne Dodson's *Engendering Church* contributed a major history on the subject. See Campbell, *Songs of Zion*, to fill in a substantial gap about this denomination's quick ascent throughout the South due to Bishop Payne's campaign. Campbell also elaborated on its attitude regarding women preachers (48–49) and women in other leadership roles (93–95).

31 "two months . . . ," Raymond Dickens interviewed in Cottondale, Florida, on December 7, 1996.

32 "Upon seeing them . . . ," Sharoresier White, "The Sunday Morning Band." "Although the main . . . ," Holloway, *Passed On*, 33.

34 "animated by . . . ," Roger Abrahams, *Singing the Master*, 83. Columbia County, Florida, the site of the original Sunday Morning Band, is not far from the Georgia

Sea Islands and McIntosh County, where the ring shout continues as an unbroken tradition and where, "We beat a drum at duh church and we beat a drum on duh way tuh dah grabeyahd tuh bury um" (Rosenbaum, *Shout Because You're Free*, 36). By extension, "tramping" is probably related to this practice. Rosenbaum also quoted Jonathan David, "African worshippers in the Chesapeake region responded by calling this aspect of the shouting service a 'march,' and they generally discouraged crossing feet or lifting feet" (38). I have also quoted "as journeys . . ." from Margaret Drewal, *Yoruba Ritual*, xiii. Regarding journey as a root metaphor, she further dissected to word to mean "travel," positing how "traveling implies a transformation in the process, a progression" (33). This interpretation provides added meaning to the importance of each band's special walk, called tramping.

35   "The Circle is . . . ," Sterling Stuckey, *Slave Culture*, 11. Stuckey also provided details regarding its metaphoric link to the life process (15). See Drewal's discussion of cyclical time in which, philosophically, she located an unending cycle or spiral (*Yoruba Ritual*, 46–47).

35   "signifies the sea . . ." and "By operating under . . . ," Stuckey, *Slave Culture*, 65, 35.

35   "white cloth . . . ," John W. Nunley, *Moving with the Face of the Devil*, 22. See also Elisha P. Renne, *Cloth That Does Not Die*. As a part of funerary customs, other scholars also delineate the role white ritualistically play(ed) within West African societies. Robert Farris Thompson's groundbreaking text, *Flash of the Spirit*, documented the color's symbolism. In addition, John Vlach in *The Afro-American Tradition in Decorative Arts* (143) centered white as the color of graveyard goods in African American cemeteries as an African retention. Also, as pertains to color, see Kuyk, "The African Derivation," 565.

35   "tests of patience . . . ," E. Michael Mendelson, "Primitive Secret Societies," 23. "It is an old . . . ," John Hamilton, *Material Culture of the American Freemasons*, 54. Although relating to Freemasonry, I consider it to be applicable to these secret societies as well.

36   "to preserve the intensity . . . ," Drewal, *Yoruba Ritual*, 66. In *Deep like the River*, historian Thomas Webber provided an ample analysis of the nature of the education of enslaved Africans, which led to them building a solid community life (199–203). J. G. Platvoet (*Comparing Religions*, 24) added the material and immaterial considerations to understanding this form of reciprocity.

36   "Attitudes toward death . . . ," Bennetta Jules-Rosette, "Creative Spirituality from Africa to America," 278.

37   "Deprivation of sight . . . ," Hamilton, *Material Culture of the American Freemasons*, 82. From "Somebody would get out . . . " to "They used to put . . . ," Raymond Dickens interviewed in Cottondale, Florida, on December 7, 1996. "culturally induced suffering . . . ," Barbara Myerhoff, "Rites of Passage," 121.

39   "I have a feeling . . . ," Sunday Morning Band #363 skit.

40   "If you can . . . ," duet, Dorothy Green and Barbara Paramore, Sunday Morning Band #363 in Cottondale, Florida, on September 13, 1996.

43   "Also enact in a powerful . . . ," Martin Stokes, *Ethnicity, Identity, and Music*, 13.

43   "Right after the prayer . . . ," Joseph Johnson singing at Bethlehem AME Church in Cottondale, Florida, on October 10, 1995.

45   "the shuffling around . . . ," Floyd, *The Power of Black Music*, 37. In the only monograph devoted to the ring shout, Rosenbaum (*Shout Because You're Free*, 38) asso-

ciated this ritual with "semi-secret societies functioning apart from official church structures."

46   "Camp Meetings . . . ," Pullen Jackson, *White Spirituals in the Southern Uplands*, 215. The Turner quote regarding "scamp meetings" appeared in Stephen Ward Angell's *Bishop Henry McNeal Turner and African-American Religion in the South*, 203.

47   "Camp meetings provided . . . ," Joyce Cauthen, *Benjamin Lloyd's Hymn Book*, 10.

47   "Further, camp meetings . . . ," Rosenbaum, *Shout Because You're Free*, 38.

48   "sing a song . . . ," recorded on October 25, 2003, at Macedonia Baptist Church in Argyle, Florida.

48   "We sing one song . . . . ," Arthur Jones, *Wade in the Water*, 37.

49   Regarding Scriven, see Warren, *Ev'ry Time I Feel the Spirit*, 265–266.

49   "organized around churches . . . ," St. Clare Drake, "The Social and Economic Status of the Negro in the United States," 779.

50   "Ritual journeys . . . ," Drewal, *Yoruba Ritual*, 46.

CHAPTER 3

51   From "I enjoy every . . ." to "my church . . ." Doris Lewis interviewed in Dothan, Alabama, on August 5, 1994.

52   "The next day was . . . ," Rita Dove, *Fifth Sunday*, 6.

53   "a special wagon . . . ," Fred S. Watson, *Hub of the Wiregrass*, 102.

53   "black Baptists reached . . . ," Mechal Sobel, *Traveling on the Slave Journey to an Afro-Baptist Faith*, 109. Sobel coined the term *Afro-Baptist* to recognize the degree to which, in practice, African Americans ultimately made Christianity their own. As relates to "frontier moral courts," see Dickson Bruce, *And They All Sang Hallelujah*, 48–49.

54   "the church 'excluded' . . . ," E. W. Carswell, *Holmes Valley*, 45–46. Carswell related two instances (on record) of enslaved Africans being excommunicated and was also responsible for the Pedobaptist quote "the church excluded Madison . . ."). For more on this kind of breach by Pedobaptists, see James E. Tull, *High-Church Baptists in the South*.

54   "The exodus of Blacks . . . ," M. P. Farmer, *One Hundred Fifty Years in Pike County, Alabama*, 298. "By the 1890s . . . ," Rogers, *Thomas County, 1865–1900*, 183. More or less, the AME and CME churches became rivals. According to Clarence Walker, "The hierarchy and members of the northern church thought that southern blacks who joined the C.M.E. Church were traitors to their race" (*A Rock in a Weary Land*, 104). CME churches tended to take a more conservative political approach to social equality and social justice.

56   "It was Adeline Adams . . . ," Agnes Windsor interviewed in Slocomb, Alabama, on July 16, 1994. "That church started . . . ," Mary Lou Henderson interviewed in Thomasville, Georgia, on August 4, 1995.

57   "The basic aesthetic . . . ," Ray Funk, "Research Approaches to Black Gospel Quartets," 91–92.

57   "a holy obligation . . . ," Hinson, *Fire in My Bones*, 211.

59   "I get a kind . . . ," Reverend Terrell Hollis interviewed in Quitman, Georgia, on August 24, 1995.

59   "set for the third . . . ," Agnes Windsor interviewed in Slocomb, Alabama, on July 16, 1994.

60   "A typical Baptist church . . . ," Mary Hartsfield, *Tall Betsy and Dunce Baby*, 101.

61   "Church members are given . . . ," Frances Kostarelos, *Feeling the Spirit*, 45.

61   "Baptist tradition . . . ," Wills granted the quote, "explaining the role of associations," 100. "What they did up there . . . ," Louise Sapp interviewed in Thomasville, Georgia, on August 25, 1995.

63   "In the social sense . . . ," Arnold Taylor, *Travail and Triumph*, 155.

63   "to save time . . . ," Elder Jimmy Simmons, South Georgia Local Union Meeting in Beachton, Georgia, on July 28, 1995.

64   "I participate in . . . ," Sheryl Melton interviewed in Gordon, Alabama, on August 10, 1995. "Although each new generation . . ." and "They'll stay alive . . . ," Pitts, *Old Ship of Zion*, 146 and 153, respectively.

64   "in synchrony while out of phrase . . . ," Feld, *Sound and Sentiment*, 120. While their heterophony differs, the phraseology idea seemingly fits.

65   "We gonna sing . . . ," recorded at the Blue Spring Missionary Baptist Union Meeting on November 28, 1997, at St. Paul Missionary Baptist Church in Albany, Georgia.

65   "I reckon they moaned . . . ," Willie Collins, "Moaning and Prayer," 340.

66   "Our Singing Tradition . . . ," Bernice Johnson Reagon, "Pioneering African American Gospel Music Composers" in *We'll Understand It Better By and By*, 18. "moans and groans . . . ," Collins, "Moaning and Prayer," 104.

66   "We are glad that you . . . ," representative speech act, the Progressive District's Quarterly Congress at Beulah First Baptist Church in Fort Walton, Florida, on June 27, 2003.

70   "I learned that you . . . ," Richard Lawyer Jr. interviewed in Thomasville, Georgia, on July 20, 1995.

70   "to promote the . . . ," Wendy Haight, *African American Children at Church*, 6.

70   "Do we have any youth . . . ," The Rural District program at Antioch Baptist Church in Gordon, Alabama, on June 29, 1996.

72   "Come on . . . ," Transcript is from the same Progressive District program in Fort Walton, Florida.

73   "not just a conservator . . . ," Richard Schechner, *The Future of Ritual*, 255.

CHAPTER 4

74   "Creating a network . . . ,"Steven Sabol, "Sacred Harp Singing: History and Tradition." Sabol's Web site (http://www.mcsr.olemiss.edu/~mudws/resource/chap03.html) lists more than fifty regional Web pages. For additional information about the general history of shape-note singing, see John Bealle, *Public Worship, Private Faith*. A singer of Sacred Harp himself, Buell E. Cobb Jr.'s *The Sacred Harp* is a key text explicating the Sacred Harp tradition. Also, see David Stanley, "The Gospel-Singing Convention in South Georgia." A recent publication by Joe Dan Boyd, *Judge Jackson and the Colored Sacred Harp*, significantly augments what is known about the music and its legacy among African Americans. John Work's "Plantation Meistersinger" was written by the first African American scholar to research this musical tradition.

76   "While 'harp' . . . ," Steven Sabol, "Sacred Harp Singing: History and Tradition."

76   "Shape-notes are used . . . ," Montell, *Singing the Glory Down*, 11. "For example, these . . . ," Donald R. Ross, "Black Sacred Harp Singing Remembered in East Texas," 17.

77   "'dispersed harmony' . . . ," Steven Sabol, "Sacred Harp Singing: History and Tradition."

77   "The extent to which . . . ," Montell, *Singing the Glory Down*, 15. "A number is . . . ," Larry Olszewski, "On Singing Old Harp," 2. Also, see "The Pitcher's Role in Sacred Harp Music," *National Sacred Harp Newsletter* January 1986, 3–5.

78   "mirroring the centrality . . . ," Wyatt Tee Walker, *Somebody's Calling My Name*, 118. Adherents to *The Colored Sacred Harp* have become legendary. For more details, see Joe Dan Boyd, "Judge Jackson," 446–551. Also, see "Judge Jackson and *The Colored Sacred Harp*" by Henry Willett in the booklet with an audio recording edited by him, *In the Spirit*, 50–55.

79   "We're going to . . . ," Reverend John Jackson remark on April 18, 1993, at the Fifty-Eighth Annual Memorial Singing Honoring Judge Jackson in Ozark, Alabama.

79   "That was my baby . . . ," John Jackson, April 16, 1995, at the Sixtieth Annual Memorial Singing Honoring Judge Jackson in Ozark, Alabama.

80   "Singers regard Jackson's . . . ," David Warren Steel, "The Colored Sacred Harp," 127. "in southeastern Alabama . . . ," George Pullen White, *White Spirituals in the Southern Uplands*, 106.

80   "a leader . . . ," Doris Lewis interviewed in Dothan, Alabama, on August 5, 1994. David Carlton ("To the Land I Am Bound," 61) pointed out the distinctive use of marcato.

81   "In the center . . . ," Joseph Cumming Jr., "Sacred Singout." Regarding the likelihood of this tradition's survival, "create and then . . . ," Nelson George, *The Death of Rhythm and Blues*, 108.

82   "the dialogical narrative self . . . ," Earl Riggins Jr., *Dark Symbols, Obscure Signs*, 182–185. Providing an endogenous description, "The contrasting sounds . . . ," Wendy Coleman, "A Brief Introduction to 'Vocal Music,'" 3.

82   "When we get to singing . . . ," Japheth Jackson interviewed in Ozark, Alabama, on June 9, 1994. A. M. Cagle, "some were good . . . ," quoted in James Bagwell, A. Marcus Cagle, Paine Denson, S. M. Denson, and T. J. Denson, *The National Sacred Harp Foundation Archives*, 621.

83   "Don't give them . . . ," Japheth Jackson's spoken words during the Sixtieth Annual Memorial Singing Honoring Judge Jackson, April 16, 1995.

83   "shape-note singing . . . ," Ted Olson, "The Sacred Harp Singing Tradition of Calhoun County, Mississippi," 265. "Several of the singers . . . ," E. W. Carswell, *Washington*, 399.

84   "a sense of spiritual . . . ," Bealle, *Public Worship, Private Faith*, 97.

84   "I don't do this . . . ," Japheth Jackson, Sixtieth Annual Memorial Singing Honoring Judge Jackson, April 16, 1995.

85   "the Igbo know . . . ," Uchendu, *The Igbo of Southeast Nigeria*, 75.

85   "Judge Jackson's children . . . ," the bulletin for Sunday, April 16, 1995. Copies of the field recording made by the Alabama Folklife Association are now available in the Library of Congress, Alabama State Department of History Archive, Alabama State Council of the Arts, Alabama Center for Traditional Culture, and Alabama Music Hall of Fame.

86 "Most of our best . . . ," Japheth Jackson, April 16, 1995.

87 "He's the oldest . . . ," Japheth Jackson, April 16, 1995.

87 "He [Dewey Williams] amazes . . . ," Clementine Du Bose interviewed in Gary, Indiana, on July 1, 1995.

87 "They turn [words] loose . . . ," Japheth Jackson interviewed in Ozark, Alabama, on June 9, 1994. "Let's pick it up . . . ," Stanley Smith during the Sixtieth Annual Memorial Singing Honoring Judge Jackson.

87 "Not while . . . ," James Bagwell, A. Marcus Cagle, Paine Denson, S. M. Denson, and T. J. Denson, *The National Sacred Harp Foundation Archives*, n.p.

88 "Black Christians . . . ," Wyatt Tee Walker, *Somebody's Calling My Name*, 111. "This is a song . . . ," Tommy Spurlock at Dewey Williams' memorial, March 7, 2004.

88 "If God didn't . . . ," Dewey Williams on April 16, 1995, at the Sixtieth Annual Jackson Memorial Sing. "elected officers . . . ," John Bealle, *Public Worship, Private Faith*, 183.

90 "By recording singings . . . ," John Bealle, *Public Worship, Private Faith*, 180.

90 "Community leaders and singers . . . ," Chiquita Willis, *The African American Shape Note and Vocal Music Singing Convention Directory*, iii.

91 "They'd have a fire . . . ," Joe Dan Boyd, *Judge Jackson and the Colored Sacred Harp*, 33.

92 "Well, it's a small . . . ," Henry Jackson interviewed in Ozark, Alabama, on June 9, 1994.

92 "We were taught . . . ," Mary Lou Henderson interviewed in Thomasville, Georgia, on August 4, 1995.

92 "reading a musical . . . ," Chiquita Willis, *The African American Shape Note and Vocal Music Singing Convention Directory*, 2. "improve the quality . . . ," Lynwood Montell, *Singing the Glory Down*, 23.

92 "The one thing . . . ," Henry Jackson interviewed in Ozark, Alabama, on June 9, 1994.

93 "Greater importance . . . ," Sabol, "Sacred Harp Singing."

93 "The fifth Sunday . . . ," Wendy Coleman, "A Brief Introduction to 'Vocal Music,'" 3.

94 "traditional ways . . . ," Roger Abrahams, "The Language of Festivals," 167.

94 "They use the seven-shape . . . ," George Pullen Jackson, *White Spirituals in the Southern Uplands*, 405.

98 "I wouldn't walk . . . ," Hugh McGraw's quote appeared in Richard L. DeLong's "Fasola Singing," 5–6.

CHAPTER 5

100 "that this region . . . ," Roland Harper, "Development of Agriculture in Lower Georgia from 1850 to 1880," 116.

102 "Beginning in the 1880s . . ." and "Every morning . . . ," Brown and Hadley, *African American Life on the Southern Hunting Plantation*, 8 and 10, respectively.

102 "The loving spiritual atmosphere . . . ," "A soul is not mature . . . ," "Up the hills to Ochlocknee . . . ," "Many voices . . . ," "Members happiely [sic] and freely . . . ," "They thought deep . . . ," appear in an unpublished brochure, "50th Anniversary of Thomas and Grady Counties Singing Convention," n.p., n.d.

103 "The shaped note singer . . . ," Michael Harris, *The Rise of Gospel Blues*, 21. "Dorayme was . . . ," "everybody thought . . ." and "The young people . . . ," Tommie Gabriel interviewed in Thomasville, Georgia, on August 5, 1994.

105 "This is the tradition . . . ," Bernice Johnson Reagon, *If You Don't Go, Don't Hinder Me*, 47.

106 "During the Depression . . . ," Willie Johnson interviewed along with his wife, Louise, in Thomasville, Georgia, on July 21, 1995.

106 "By March 1933 . . . ," Harris quoting Dorsey, *The Rise of Gospel Blues*, 264.

110 "They had no other . . . ," Tommie Gabriel interviewed in Thomasville, Georgia, on August 5, 1994.

110 "The type of institutions . . . ," Toyin Falola and Akanmu Adebayo, *Culture, Politics, and Money among the Yoruba*, 129.

110 "The same conventions . . . ," Tommie Gabriel interviewed in Thomasville, Georgia, on August 5, 1994. See Joyce Ladner's *A Tomorrow's Tomorrow*, which divulged insights about the role networks play among African Americans in general and women in particular. Carol Stack's *All Our Kin* (90–107) builds on this research.

111 "Singing conventions used . . . ," Mary Lou Henderson interviewed in Thomasville, Georgia, on August 4, 1995.

111 "We needed [funds] . . . ," Willie Johnson interviewed in Thomasville, Georgia, on July 21, 1995.

112 "You were singing . . . ," "This younger crowd . . ." and "Open your mouth . . . ," Mary Lou Henderson interviewed in Thomasville, Georgia, on August 4, 1995.

113 "I grew up . . . ," Louise Sapp interviewed in Thomasville, Georgia, on August 25, 1995. "I always say . . ." and "I pray that you will . . ." Doster Grimes Devotion occurred at the Thomas-Grady Counties Singing Convention on July 14, 1995.

114 "A common saying . . . ," Warren, *Ev'ry Time I Feel the Spirit*, 237.

114 "All in all . . . ," Roberts, *Black Music of Two Worlds*, 168.

115 "They want me . . . ," Louise Sapp interviewed in Thomasville, Georgia, on August 25, 1995.

116 "Then they used . . . ," Louise Sapp interviewed in Thomasville, Georgia, on August 25, 1995.

116 "Once you kick . . . ," Tommie Gabriel interviewed in Thomasville, Georgia, on August 5, 1994.

118 "And gospel song . . . ," Boyer, "Contemporary Gospel," 28.

119 "You're still an individual . . . ," Tommie Gabriel interviewed in Thomasville, Georgia, on August 5, 1994.

119 "Hopefully when . . . ," Doster Grimes at the 392nd Session of the Thomas-Grady Counties Singing Convention in Thomasville, Georgia, on April 14, 1995.

120 "act just like this . . . ," Clifford Williams at the Thomas–Grady Counties Singing Convention in Thomasville, Georgia, on April 14, 1995.

123 "Those are some future . . . ," Grant Revel interviewed in Thomasville, Georgia on August 25, 1995.

124 "I don't want no . . . ," Louise Sapp interviewed in Thomasville, Georgia, on August 25, 1995.

125 "extract[ing] hymn . . . ," John Bealle, *Public Worship, Private Faith*, 77.

CHAPTER 6

126 "In African American communities . . . ," Bernice Johnson Reagon, *African American Congregational Singing Nineteenth-Century Roots*, 87.

126 "patterned interactions . . . ," Melvin Williams, *Community in a Black Pentecostal Church*, 16.

127 "Gospel singers need . . . ," Anthony Heilbut, *The Gospel Sound*, xiii. A recent publication by Robert Darden, *People Get Ready!*, is exhaustive in presenting, analyzing, and historicizing this musical genre.

127 "I used to always . . ." and "They selling the gospel . . . ," Louise Sapp interviewed in Thomasville, Georgia, on August 25, 1995.

128 "Anniversary's a fundraiser . . . ," Sheryl Melton interviewed in Gordon, Alabama, on August 10, 1995.

129 "We go different places . . . ," Sheryl Melton interviewed in Gordon, Alabama, on August 10, 1995. Folklorist Ray Allen (*Singing in the Spirit*, 76–96) gives an in-depth explanation of gospel anniversary programs.

130 "Practically speaking, it is impossible . . . ," Dyen, "The Role of Shape-Note Singing in the Musical Culture of Black Communities in Southeast Alabama," 70.

130 "while gospel lyrics . . . ," Allen, *Singing in the Spirit*, 66. To attribute the various themes, the first derives from the Jubilives' anniversary on August 24–25, 1996, in Marianna, Florida. The next theme, "It takes faith . . . ," derives from the Tri-State Community Mass Choir Anniversary program in Quincy, Florida, on July 8, 2000. The motto, "To see my God," transpired at the Glory Train Special's Thirty-Sixth Anniversary in Madrid, Alabama, on June 15, 1996.

130 "Especially, if they . . . ," Dorothy Brown interviewed in Quincy, Florida, on August 25, 1995. Also, see anthropologist Kip Lornell's *Happy in the Service of the Lord*, which is situated in the urban South speaking to the professionalizing of the sound. As relates to white quartets, see Charles Wolfe, "Gospel Goes Uptown."

131 "Ten percent of gospel . . . ," Joseph Johnson in an informal conversation at the gala honoring his Florida Heritage Award on April 2, 2008, in Tallahassee.

131 "I appreciate parents . . . ," Dorothy Brown interviewed in Quincy, Florida, on August 25, 1995.

132 "Anybody got . . . ," emcee at "Because We Care" benefit, August 19, 1995, in Dothan, Alabama. See folklorist Glenn Hinson's *Fire in My Bones*, in which he delineated required traits of emcees and spoke to the "piggyback[ing]" of appearances," causing the need for "creative juggling" (163–188).

132 "I don't want . . . ," Tri-State Community Mass Choir Anniversary in Quincy, Florida, on July 8, 2000.

132 "I'm just doing this . . . ," Glory Train Special in Madrid, Alabama, on June 15, 1996.

133 "First, we would like . . . ," Cunningham Family Anniversary in Opp, Alabama, on January 19, 1997.

133 "When it seems . . . ," Bible Jubilees, "Because We Care" benefit on August 19, 1995, in Dothan, Alabama.

134 "Some of you here . . . ," "When she became ill . . ." and "If you can't give . . ." at Henry County Male Chorus "Because We Care" benefit on August 19, 1995, in Dothan, Alabama.

134 "I was raised . . ." and "I know those people . . . ," Sheryl Melton interviewed in Gordon, Alabama, on August 10, 1995.

135 "Well, we do . . ." and "When you compare . . . ," Sheryl Melton interviewed in Gordon, Alabama, on August 10, 1995.

137 "[Gospel singing] got so . . . ," Ovella Cunningham interviewed in Opp, Alabama,

on May 20, 1996. "We're not gonna worry . . . ," Ovella Cunningham in Clayton, Alabama, at the Gospel Starlights' Nineteenth Anniversary on August 31, 1996.

138 "Praise the Lord for . . . ," Mittie Edwards and "Ya'll looking for . . . ," Stars of Faith member's commentary at the Southeast District convention building in Elba, Alabama, on July 30, 1995.

138 "I might live in . . . ," Fantastic Heavenly Angels spokesman at the Gospel Starlights Anniversary in Clayton, Alabama, on August 31, 1996.

139 "All choirs and groups . . . ," unpublished program of the Jubilives' Thirty-First Anniversary at Henshaw Chapel AME in Cottondale, Florida, on August 24, 1996.

139 "I used to didn't . . . ," Spencil Smiley interviewed outside Bainbridge, Georgia, on August 4, 1995.

140 "We've already did . . . ," Mary Bush Smith at Tri-State Community Mass Choir First Anniversary Jamboree "95" on July 7, 1995, in Quincy, Florida.

140 "The manner in which . . . ," Allen, "Singing in the Spirit," 139.

141 Heilbut, *The Gospel Sound*, 109.

141 "We still have . . . ," Mary Bush Smith at the Tri-State Community Mass Choir First Anniversary Jamboree "95" on July 8, 1995.

142 "After I started . . . ," Spencil Smiley interviewed outside Bainbridge, Georgia, on August 4, 1995.

143 "When you're taking . . . ," Spencil Smiley interviewed outside Bainbridge, Georgia, on August 4, 1995.

143 "We're not singing . . . ," Heilbut, *The Gospel Sound*, xv.

144 "I was told tonight . . . ," unknown speaker at the Gospel Starlights' Anniversary in Clayton, Alabama, on August 31, 1996.

144 "As you always . . ." and "Tonight, if you've . . . ," Doris Lewis, Gospel Train Special Anniversary on June 15, 1996.

144 "I used to sing . . . ," Doris Lewis interviewed in Dothan, Alabama, on August 5, 1994.

145 "It's more than . . . ," Dorothy Brown interviewed in Quincy, Florida, on August 25, 1995.

146 "When she became . . . ," supporter at the Doris Lewis "Because We Care" benefit on August 19, 1995, in Dothan, Alabama.

146   "If you can't give . . . ," Doris Lewis "Because We Care" benefit on August 19, 1995, in Dothan, Alabama.

148 "We can't sing . . . ," Donaldson group at "Because We Care" benefit on August 19, 1995, in Dothan, Alabama.

149 "I hate to hear . . . ," Glory Train Special anniversary on June 17–19, 1995, in Madrid, Alabama.

150 "to string a series . . . ," Gerald Davis, *I Got the Word in Me and I Can Sing It, You Know*, 112.

151 "Gospel lyrics may sound . . . ," Heilbut, *The Gospel Sound*, xi.

152 "These songs, known . . . ," Portia Maultsby, "West African Influences in U.S. Black Music," 39.

CHAPTER 7

154 "This body gets tired . . . ," Mary Lou Henderson interviewed in Thomasville, Georgia, on August 4, 1995.

155 "I'm the Mother . . . ," Mary Lou Henderson interviewed in Thomasville, Georgia, on August 4, 1995. "they are called . . . ," Henry John Drewal and Margaret Drewal, *Gelede*, 9.

155 "escapees from domestic service . . . ," Jacqueline Jones, *Labor of Love, Labor of Sorrow*, 148.

156 "If we didn't . . . ," E. W. Carswell, *Remembering "Old Rhoady,"* 14.

156 "I can do . . . ," Olin Pope interviewed in Barwick, Georgia, on May 26, 1994. "Along about February . . . ," Owen Wrice interviewed in Quitman, Georgia, on May 13, 1994.

157 "I don't like . . . ," Mary Jackson interviewed in Dothan, Alabama, on November 27, 1992. Roland Freeman (*A Communion of the Spirit*, 199) documented several male quilters, including a younger man, Alfred Sams. In "We Got Our Way of Cooking Thinking," sociologist Josie Beoku Betts documented the same set of values related to gender role divisions in Gullah communities.

157 "Fishing may be . . . ," Jerrilyn McGregory, *Wiregrass Country*, 126.

158 "My mother stopped . . . ," Mary Jackson interviewed in Dothan, Alabama, on November 27, 1992.

158 "Women are always . . . ," Eudora Thomas, *A History of the Shouter Baptists in Trinidad and Tobago*, 58. "I've been anointed . . ." and "I'm just a voice . . . ," Mary Lou Henderson interviewed in Thomasville, Georgia, on August 4, 1995.

159 "Young men may . . . ," Doris Dyen, "The Role of Shape-Note Singing in the Musical Culture of Black Communities in Southeast Alabama," 62. Sociologist Bennetta Jules-Rosette distinguished between rites of power and roles of power. In one article, "Creative Spirituality from Africa," she defined ceremonial leadership as "the possibilities for women to exercise virtual power in ritual interactions" (202). Furthermore, in practice, African American churchwomen adhere more closely to Jules-Rossette's documentation of Maranke Apostolic women who, through song, "exercise a form of ceremonial leadership and are able to voice their opinions on moral and biblical themes" (105). Also, see Jules-Rosette's "Privilege without Power." For research that investigates seniority within Yoruba society, see, Oyeronke Oyewumi, *The Invention of Women*.

159 "representative oscillation . . . ," Jon Michael Spencer, *Blues and Evil*, xxii. I also appropriate Dell Hymes' sociolinguistics in formulating definitions for the following terms: *competence, performance,* and *cultural fluency*. See Hymes, *On Communicating Competence*.

160 "I been singing . . ." and "My mother's prayers . . . ," Mary Lou Henderson interviewed in Thomasville, Georgia, on August 4, 1995. Folklorist Elaine Lawless has thoroughly researched the church roles of Pentecostal white women as relates to gender. See Lawless' "Shouting for the Lord," "Making a Joyful Noise," and "Brothers and Sisters." In her chapter, "Access to the Pulpit," Lawless distinguishes the conservative role fulfilled by Pentecostal women pastors, centering their mothering capacities. Yet African American women can inject a more particularistic cultural dimension that does not uphold strict patriarchal lines.

161 "I don't feel . . ." and "You have to know . . . ," Ovella Cunningham interviewed in Opp, Alabama, on May 20, 1996.

162 "committed to the survival . . . ," Alice Walker, *In Search of Our Mother's Garden*, xi–xii. "concerned with the . . . ," Chikwenye Ogunyemi, "Womanism," xi. "not only a way . . . ," Emilie Townes, *In a Blaze of Glory*, 11.

162 "critical reflection . . . ,"   Linda Thomas, "Womanist Theology, Epistemology, and a
     New Anthropological Paradigm." Also, see Jacquelyn Grant, *White Women's Christ
     and Black Women's Jesus.*

163 "You're supposed . . . ," "always wanted to be . . . ," "will tell you quick . . ." and "I can
     tell . . . ," Lula Bennett-Mitchell interviewed in Ashford, Alabama, on May 20 1996.

164 "Everybody was buying . . . ," Lizzie Henry interviewed in Tifton, Georgia, on
     September, 26, 1992.

165 "loaded with love . . ." and "If somebody is hurting . . . ," Alice Stennett interviewed
     in Gordon, Alabama, on June 24, 1998.

166 "In the back of your . . . ," Sheryl Melton interviewed in Gordon, Alabama, on
     August 10, 1995.

167 "I will tell you . . . ," Alice Stennett at the "Sarah's Daughters" program on May 24,
     1998, in Ashford, Alabama.

167 "I started smiling . . . ," Alice Stennett at the "Sarah's Daughters" program.

168 "I don't like anything . . . ," The Minister of Giving at the "Sarah's Daughters" pro-
     gram.

169 "I got something inside . . ." and "She didn't mistreat her . . . ," Addie Buze at the
     "Sarah's Daughters" program.

171 "Learning to be . . . ," now defunct Web site: http://fernshomestead.com/sarahs-
     daughter.html, accessed in 2005. However, one can locate countless Web sites that
     reject a feminist reading of Sarah on biblical grounds. The anthology *Praise Her
     Works* edited by Penina Adelman engages a Jewish perspective related to Sarah's
     lineage. Christian women are not the only ones to evoke theology related to Sarah's
     daughters. Such discourse is common within Judaism as well. Isaac, the son of
     Abraham and Sarah, is considered the patriarch of Jews. In 2005, *U.S. News and
     World Report* published a special collector's edition entitled *Women of the Bible:
     Provocative New Insights*; in "Dueling Mothers: Why Scholars Just Can't Stop
     Talking about Sarah and Hagar," by Julia M. Klein, besides citing Jewish beliefs, she
     delineated the traditional association of Muslims and Arabs tracing their lineage
     to Hagar and Ishmael. Likewise, due to the theme of enslavement, Klein stated:
     "African Americans have appropriated Hagar," too (18). Womanist theologian
     Jacqueline Grant (*White Women's Christ and Black Women's Jesus*, 207) also docu-
     mented a Black perspective that indicates Sarah to be an "inadequate model for
     Black women."

171 "a nameless somebody . . ." and "As one of Sarah's . . . ," Joann McGriff, speaker at
     the "Sarah's Daughters" program.

171 "Women don't like . . ." and "What we got here . . . ," Gwen Crittenden, speaker at
     the "Sarah's Daughters" program.

172 "Well, as it turns . . . ," Jerrilyn McGregory, "'There Are Other Ways to Get Happy,'"
     178–179. All remaining quotes by Margarettea Kirkman, teacher, Third Quarterly
     Session of the Congress of the Progressive District Baptist Association of West
     Florida, recorded June 28, 2003.

Bibliography

Abbington, James. 2001. *Let Mt. Zion Rejoice!: Music in the African American Church.* Valley Forge, Pa.: Judson.

Abernethy, Francis, Patrick Mullen, and Alan Govenar, eds. 1996. *Juneteenth Texas: Essays in African-American Folklore.* Denton: University of North Texas Press.

Abrahams, Roger D. 1982. "The Language of Festivals: Celebrating the Economy." In *Celebration*, edited by Victor Turner. Washington, D.C.: Smithsonian Institution Press, 161–177.

Abrahams, Roger D. 1992. *Singing the Master: The Emergence of African American Culture in the Plantation South.* New York: Pantheon Books.

Adelman, Penina, ed. 2005. *Praise Her Works: Conversations with Biblical Women.* Philadelphia, Pa.: Jewish Publication Society.

Allen, Ray. 1987. "Singing in the Spirit: An Ethnography of Gospel Performance in New York City's African-American Church Community." Ph.D. dissertation, University of Pennsylvania.

Allen, Ray. 1991. *Singing in the Spirit: African-American Sacred Quartets in New York City.* Philadelphia: University of Pennsylvania Press.

Allgood, B. Dexter. 1983. "A Study of Selected Gospel Choirs in the Metropolitan Area." Ph.D. dissertation, New York University.

Angell, Stephen Ward. 1992. *Bishop Henry McNeal Turner and African-American Religion in the South.* Knoxville: University of Tennessee Press.

Bagwell, James Daniel, A. Marcus Cagle, Paine Denson, S. M. Denson, and T. J. Denson. 1991. *The National Sacred Harp Foundation Archives: Transcriptions of Unpublished Manuscripts and Documents.* Thesis (M.M.), Florida State University.

Baker, Houston. 1972. *Long Black Song.* Charlottesville: University Press of Virginia.

Ball, Edward. 2001. *The Sweet Hell Inside: A Family History.* New York: HarperCollins.

Barron, Ruth. 1981. *Footprints in Appling County, 1818–1976.* Baxley, Ga.: Appling County Board of Commissioners.

Bascom, William. 1952. "The Esusu: A Credit Institution of the Yoruba." *The Journal of the Royal Anthropological Institute of Great Britain and Ireland* 82(1), 63–69.

Bealle, John. 1997. *Public Worship, Private Faith: Sacred Harp and American Folksong.* Athens: University of Georgia Press.

Bealle, John. 1999. "Introduction." In *Benjamin Lloyd's Hymn Book: A Primitive Baptist Song Tradition*, edited by Joyce Cauthen. Montgomery: Alabama Folklife Association, 1–5.

Beito, David. 2000. *From Mutual Aid to the Welfare State: Fraternal Societies and Social Services, 1890–1967*. Chapel Hill: University of North Carolina Press.

Bell, Catherine. 1992. *Ritual Theory, Ritual Practice*. New York: Oxford University Press.

Bell, Catherine. 1997. *Ritual: Perspectives and Dimensions*. New York, Oxford University Press.

Betts, Josie Beoku. 1995. "We Got Our Way of Cooking Thinking: Women, Food, and Preservation of Cultural Identity among the Gullah." *Gender and Society* 9(Oct.), 535–555.

Boyd, Joe Dan. 1970. "Judge Jackson: Black Giant of White Spirituals." *Journal of American Folklore* 83(Oct.), 446–551.

Boyd, Joe Dan. 2002. *Judge Jackson and the Colored Sacred Harp*. Montgomery: Alabama Folklife Association.

Boyd, Minnie Clare. 1931. *Alabama in the Fifties: A Social Study*. New York: Columbia University Press.

Boyer, Horace. 1971. "Contemporary Gospel." *The Black Perspective in Music* 7, 5–59.

Boyer, Horace. 1985. "Traditional and Contemporary Gospel Music." In *More Than Dancing: Essays on Afro-American Music and Musicians*. Westport, Conn.: Greenwood, 127–146.

Boyer, Horace. 1992. "Brewster: The Eloquent Poet." In *We'll Understand It Better By and By*, edited by Bernice Johnson Reagon. Washington, D.C.: Smithsonian Institution Press, 211–231.

Briggs, Charles. 1988. *Competence in Performance: The Creativity of Tradition in Mexicano Verbal Art*. Philadelphia: University of Pennsylvania Press.

Brooks, Robert Preston, and Gregor Sebba. 1969. *Georgia Studies: Selected Writings of Robert Preston Brooks*. Freeport, N.Y.: Books for Libraries Press.

Brown, Titus, and James Hadley. 2000. *African American Life on the Southern Hunting Plantation*. Charleston, S.C.: Arcadia.

Bruce, Dickson. 1974. *And They All Sang Hallelujah: Plain-Folk Camp-Meeting Religion, 1800–1845*. Knoxville: University of Tennessee Press.

Burt, Jesse, and Robert Ferguson. 1973. *Indians of the Southeast: Then and Now*. Nashville, Tenn.: Abingdon.

Camp, Bayliss, and Orit Kent. 2004. "'What a Mighty Power We Can Be': Individual and Collective Identity in African American and White Fraternal Initiation Rituals." *Social Science History* 28(Fall), 439–483.

Campbell, James. 1959. *Songs of Zion: The African American Episcopal Church in the United States and South Africa*. New York: Oxford University Press.

Carlton, David. 2003. "To the Land I Am Bound: A Journey into Sacred Harp." *Southern Cultures* 9, 50–63.

Carswell, E. W. 1983. *Holmes Valley*. Chipley, Fla.: E. W. Carswell.

Carswell, E. W. 1991. *Washington: Florida's Twelfth County*. Tallahassee, Fla.: Rose.

Carswell, E. W. 1993. *Remembering "Old Rhoady."* Chipley, Fla.: E. W. Carswell.

Cauthen, Joyce, ed. 1999. *Benjamin Lloyd's Hymn Book: A Primitive Baptist Song Tradition*. Montgomery: Alabama Folklife Association.

Cayton, Horace, and St. Clair Drake. 1945. *Black Metropolis*. New York: Harcourt, Brace.

Chernoff, John Miller. 1979. *African Rhythm and African Sensibility: Aesthetics and Social Action in African Musical Idioms*. Chicago: University of Chicago Press.

Cobb, Buell E., Jr. 1978. *The Sacred Harp: A Tradition and Its Music*. Athens: University of Georgia Press.

Coleman, Wendy. 1995. "A Brief Introduction to 'Vocal Music': A History of the North Wayne County (MS) Singing Convention." Unpublished student paper.

Collins, Willie. 1988. "Moaning and Prayer: A Musical and Contextual Analysis of Chants to Accompany Prayer in Two Afro-American Baptist Churches in Southeast Alabama." Ph.D. dissertation, University of California–Los Angeles.

Cone, James. 1992. *The Spirituals and the Blues: An Interpretation.* Maryknoll, N.Y.: Orbis.

Cotterhill, Robert. 1954. *The Southern Indians.* Norman: University of Oklahoma Press.

Covington, James W. 1993. *The Seminoles of Florida.* Gainesville: University Press of Florida.

Crowley, John. 1999. *Primitive Baptist in the Wiregrass South.* Gainesville: University Press of Florida.

Cruz, John. 1999. *Culture on the Margins: The Black Spiritual and the Rise of American Cultural Interpretation.* Princeton, N.J.: Princeton University Press.

Cummings, Joe, Jr. 1978. "Sacred Singout." *Newsweek* (Nov. 20), 108–109.

Darden, Robert. 2006. *People Get Ready!: A New History of Black Gospel Music.* New York: Continuum.

Davis, Gerald L. 1985. *I Got the Word in Me and I Can Sing It, You Know: A Study of the Performed African-American Sermon.* Philadelphia: University of Pennsylvania Press.

DeLong, Richard. 1985. "Fasola Singing: Its History and Traditions." *National Sacred Harp Newsletter* July.

DeVine, Jerry, and Titus Brown. 1993. "The Twentieth of May: Celebrating African American Freedom in Southwest Georgia." *The Journal of Southwest Georgia History* 7(Fall), 12–28.

Dixon, Christa. 1976. *Negro Spirituals: From Bible to Folk Song.* Philadelphia, Pa.: Fortress.

Dixon, Robert M. W., John Godrich, and Howard Rye. 1997. *Blues and Gospel Records, 1890–1943.* Oxford, U.K.: Clarendon Press.

Dobie, James Frank, ed. 1932. *Tone the Bell Easy.* Publication no. 10. Austin: Texas Folk-Lore Society.

Dodson, Jualynne. 2002. *Engendering Church: Women, Power, and the AME Church.* Lanham, Md.: Rowman & Littlefield.

Dove, Rita. 1985. *Fifth Sunday.* Lexington: University of Kentucky Press.

Drake, St. Clare. 1965. "The Social and Economic Status of the Negro in the United States." *Daedalus* 94(4), 771–814.

Drewal, Henry John, and Margaret Thompson Drewal. 1983. *Gelede: Art and Female Power among the Yoruba.* Traditional Arts of Africa. Bloomington: Indiana University Press.

Drewal, Margaret. 1992. *Yoruba Ritual: Performers, Play, Agency.* Bloomington: Indiana University Press.

Du Bois, W. E. B. 1981. *The World and Africa.* New York: International.

Dyen, Doris. 1966. "The Role of Shape-Note Singing in the Musical Culture of Black Communities in Southeast Alabama." Ph.D. dissertation, University of Illinois–Urbana.

Elliott, Charles. 1974. *Ichauway Plantation.* n.p.

Falola, Toyin, and Akanmu Adebayo. 2000. *Culture, Politics, and Money among the Yoruba.* New Brunswick, N.J.: Transaction.

Farmer, M. P. 1973. *One Hundred Fifty Years in Pike County, Alabama, 1821–1971.* Anniston, Ala.: Higginbotham.

Feld, Steven. 1984. "Sound Structure as Social Structure." *Ethnomusicology* 28, 383–409.

Feld, Steven. 1990. *Sound and Sentiment: Birds, Weeping, Poetics, and Song in Kaluli Expression.* Philadelphia: University of Pennsylvania Press.

Floyd, Samuel, Jr. 1991. "Ring Shout! Literary Studies, Historical Studies, and Black Music Inquiry." *Black Music Research Journal* 11, 49–70.

Floyd, Samuel, Jr. 1995. *The Power of Black Music: Interpreting Its History from Africa to the United States.* New York: Oxford University Press.

Franklin, V. P. 1984. *Black Self-Determination: A Cultural History of the Faith of the Fathers.* Westport, Conn.: Lawrence.

Freeman, Roland. 1996. *A Communion of the Spirit: African American Quilters, Preservers, and Their Stories.* Nashville, Tenn.: Rutledge Hill.

Funk, Ray. 1991. "Research Approaches to Black Gospel Quartets." In *Sounds of the South*, edited by Daniel Patterson. Durham, N.C.: Duke University Press, 90–109.

Geertz, Clifford. 1962. "The Rotating Credit Association: A 'Middle Rung' in the Development." *Economic Development and Cultural Change* 10, 241–263.

George, Nelson. 1988. *The Death of Rhythm and Blues.* New York: Pantheon Books.

Grant, Jacquelyn. 1989. *White Women's Christ and Black Women's Jesus: Feminist Christology and Womanist Response.* Atlanta: Scholars.

Green, Archie. 1970. "Hear These Beautiful Sacred Selections." *Yearbook of the International Folk Music Council* 2, 28–50.

Gwaltney, John Langston. 1980. *Drylongso: A Self-Portrait of Black America.* New York: Random House.

Haight, Wendy L. 2002. *African-American Children at Church: A Sociocultural Perspective.* Cambridge, U.K.: Cambridge University Press.

Hamilton, John. 1994. *Material Culture of the American Freemasons.* Lexington, Mass.: Museum of Our National Heritage.

Hampton, Barbara. 1993. "Notes." *The Colored Sacred Harp.* Wiregrass Sacred Harp Singers. Recorded Anthology of American Music. New York: New World Records, NW 80433-2.

Harper, Roland. 1922. "Development of Agriculture in Lower Georgia from 1850 to 1880." *Georgia Historical Quarterly* 6 (June), 112–121.

Harper, Roland. 1922. "Development of Agriculture in Lower Georgia from 1890 to 1920." *Georgia Historical Quarterly* 6 (Dec.), 326–343.

Harris, Michael. 1992. *The Rise of Gospel Blues: The Music of Thomas Andrew Dorsey in the Urban Church.* New York: Oxford University Press.

Hartsfield, Mary. 1987. *Tall Betsy and Dunce Baby: South Georgia Folktales.* Athens: University of Georgia Press.

Heilbut, Anthony. 1971. *The Gospel Sound: Good News and Bad Times.* New York: Simon and Schuster.

Hinson, Glenn. 2000. *Fire in My Bones: Transcendence and the Holy Spirit in African American Gospel.* Philadelphia: University of Pennsylvania Press.

Holloway, Karla. 2002. *Passed On: African American Mourning Stories.* Durham, N.C.: Duke University Press.

Hudson, Charles. 1976. *The Southeastern Indians.* Knoxville: University of Tennessee Press.

Hurston, Zora Neale. 1978. *Their Eyes Were Watching God: A Novel.* Urbana: University of Illinois Press.

Hurston, Zora Neale. 1981. *The Sanctified Church.* Berkeley, Calif.: Turtle Island.

Hurston, Zora Neale. 1984. *Dust Tracks on a Road: An Autobiography.* Urbana: University of Illinois Press.

Hymes, Dell. 1971. *On Communicating Competence.* Philadelphia: University of Pennsylvania Press.

Jackson, George Pullen. 1933. *White Spirituals in the Southern Uplands.* Chapel Hill: University of North Carolina Press.

Jones, Arthur C. 1993. *Wade in the Water The Wisdom of the Spirituals.* Maryknoll, N.Y.: Orbis.

Jones, Alice Eley. 1998. "Sacred Places and Holy Ground: West African Spiritualism at Stagville Plantation." In *Keep Your Head to the Sky: Interpreting African American Home Ground*, edited by Grey Gundaker. Charlottesville: University Press of Virginia, 93–108.

Jones, Jacqueline. 1985. *Labor of Love, Labor of Sorrow: Black Women, Work and the Family, from Slavery to the Present.* New York: Vintage.

Jules-Rosette, Bennetta. 1980. "Creative Spirituality from Africa to America: Cross-Cultural Influences in Contemporary Religious Forms." *Western Journal of Black Studies* 4, 273–285.

Jules-Rosette, Bennetta. 1987. "Privilege without Power." In *Women in African and the African Diaspora*, edited by Rosalyn Terborg-Penn, Sharon Harley, and Andrea Benton Rushing. Washington, D.C.: Howard University Press, 99–119.

Katz, William. 1986. *Black Indians.* New York: Antheneum.

Keil, Charles, and Steven Feld. 1994. *Music Grooves: Essays and Dialogues.* Chicago: University of Chicago Press.

Kostarelos, Frances. 1995. *Feeling the Spirit: Faith and Hope in an Evangelical Black Storefront Church.* Columbia: University of South Carolina Press.

Kuyk, Betty. 1983. "The African Derivation of Black Fraternal Orders in the United States." *Society for Comparative Study of Society and History* 25, 559–594.

Ladner, Joyce A. 1971. *Tomorrow's Tomorrow: The Black Woman.* Garden City, N.Y.: Doubleday.

Lawless, Elaine J. 1980. "Making a Joyful Noise." *Southern Folklore Quarterly* 44, 1–21.

Lawless, Elaine J. 1983. "Shouting for the Lord." *Journal of American Folklore* 96, 434–485.

Lawless, Elaine J. 1986. "Brothers and Sisters." In *Folklore Groups and Folklore Genres*, edited by Elliott Oring. Logan: Utah State University Press, 99–113.

Lawless, Elaine J. 1988a. *God's Peculiar People: Women's Voices and Folk Tradition in a Pentecostal Church.* Lexington: University Press of Kentucky.

Lawless, Elaine J. 1988b. *Handmaidens of the Lord: Pentecostal Women Preachers and Traditional Religion.* Publications of the American Folklore Society vol. 9. Philadelphia: University of Pennsylvania Press.

Lawless, Elaine J. 1993. "Access to the Pulpit: Reproductive Images and Maternal Strategies of the Pentecostal Female Pastor." In *Feminist Theory and the Study of Folklore*, edited by Susan Hollis, Linda Pershing, and M. Jane Young. Urbana: University of Illinois Press, 258–273.

Lincoln, C. Eric, and Lawrence H. Mamiya. 1990. *The Black Church in the African American Experience.* Durham, N.C.: Duke University Press.

Lipsitz, George. 1990. "Mardi Gras Indians: Carnival and Counter-Narrative in Black
    New Orleans." In *Time Passages: Collective Memory and American Popular
    Culture*. Minneapolis: University of Minnesota Press, 233–256.
Littlefield, Daniel F. 1979. *Africans and Creeks: From the Colonial Period to the Civil
    War*. Contributions in Afro-American and African Studies no. 47. Westport, Conn:
    Greenwood Press.
Lomax, Alan. 1993. *The Land Where the Blues Began*. New York: Delta.
Lornell, Kip. 1988. *Happy in the Service of the Lord: Afro-American Gospel Quartets in
    Memphis*. Music in American Life. Urbana: University of Illinois Press.
Lovell, John. 1972. *Black Song: The Forge and the Flame—The Story of How the Afro-
    American Spiritual Was Hammered Out*. New York: Macmillan.
MacKenzie, Norman Ian. 1968. *Secret Societies*. New York: Holt, Rinehart and Winston.
Malone, Ann Patton. 1986. "Piney Woods Farmers of South Georgia, 1850–1900:
    Jeffersonian Yeomen in an Age of Expanding Commercialism." *Agricultural History*
    60, 51–61.
Maring, Norman, and Winthrop Hudson. 1991. *A Baptist Manual of Polity and Practice*.
    Valley Forge, Pa.: Judson Press.
Maultsby, Portia. 1985. "West African Influences in U.S. Black Music." In *More Than
    Dancing: Essays on Afro-American Music and Musicians*, edited by Irene Jackson.
    Westport, Conn.: Greenwood, 25–58.
McGregory, Jerrilyn. 1991. "'May the Work I've Done Speak for Me': The Migration Text
    of the Lucky Ten Social Club." *Sage* Summer, 10–14.
McGregory, Jerrilyn. 1992. "'There Are Other Ways to Get Happy': African American
    Urban Folklore." Ph.D. dissertation, University of Pennsylvania.
McGregory, Jerrilyn. 1997. *Wiregrass Country*. Jackson: University Press of Mississippi.
McGregory, Jerrilyn. 2002. "'Because We Care': Competence in Performance by African-
    American Women in Wiregrass, Alabama." *Tributaries* 2, 72–80.
Mendelson, E. Michael. 1967. "Primitive Secret Societies." In *Secret Societies*, edited by
    Norman Mackenzie. New York: Holt, Rinehart and Winston, 20–37.
Montell, William Lynwood. 1991. *Singing the Glory Down: Amateur Gospel Music in
    South Central Kentucky, 1900–1990*. Lexington: University Press of Kentucky.
Myerhoff, Barbara. 1982. "Rites of Passage." In *Celebration: Studies in Festivity and
    Ritual*, edited by Victor Turner. Washington D.C.: Smithsonian Institution Press,
    109–135.
Nunley, John W. 1987. *Moving with the Face of the Devil: Art and Politics in Urban West
    Africa*. Urbana: University of Illinois Press.
Ogunyemi, Chikwenye. 1985. "Womanism: The Dynamics of the Contemporary Black
    Female Novel in English." *Signs* 11, 63–80.
Olson, Ted. 1999. "The Sacred Harp Singing Tradition of Calhoun County, Mississippi."
    Prospects: An Annual of American Cultural Studies 24, 261–283.
Olszewski, Larry. 1988. "On Singing Old Harp." *National Sacred Harp Newsletter* May, 2.
Oyewumi, Oyeronke. 1997. *The Invention of Women: Making an African Sense of
    Western Gender Discourses*. Minneapolis: University of Minnesota Press.
Patterson, Beverly Bush. 1995. *The Sound of the Dove: Singing in Appalachian Primitive
    Baptist Churches*. Urbana: University of Illinois Press.
Payne, Daniel Alexander. 1969. *Recollections of Seventy Years: The American Negro, His
    History and Literature*. New York: Arno Press.

Pitts, Walter. 1993. *Old Ship of Zion: The Afro-Baptist Ritual in the African Diaspora.* New York: Oxford University Press.

Platvoet, J. G. 1982. *Comparing Religions, a Limitative Approach: An Analysis of Akan, Para-Creole, and IFO-Sananda Rites and Prayers.* Religion and Reason no. 24. The Hague: Mouton Publishers.

Reagon, Bernice Johnson. 1992. *We'll Understand It Better By and By: Pioneering African American Gospel Music Composers.* Washington, D.C.: Smithsonian Institution Press.

Reagon, Bernice Johnson. 1994. *African American Congregational Singing Nineteenth-Century Roots.* Vol. 2, *Wade in the Water.* Washington, D.C.: Smithsonian/ Folkways.

Reagon, Bernice Johnson. 2001. *If You Don't Go, Don't Hinder Me: The African American Sacred Song Tradition.* Lincoln: University of Nebraska Press.

Reed, Theresa. 2003. *The Holy Profane: Religion in Black Popular Music.* Lexington: University of Kentucky Press.

Renne, Elisha P. 1995. *Cloth That Does Not Die: The Meaning of Cloth in Bùnú Social Life.* Seattle: University of Washington Press.

Riggins, Earl, Jr. 1993. *Dark Symbols, Obscure Signs: God, Self, and Community in the Slave Mind.* Maryknoll, N.Y.: Orbis.

Rivers, Larry. 2000. *Slavery in Florida: Territorial Days to Emancipation.* Gainesville: University Press of Florida.

Rivers, Larry, and Canter Brown. 2001. *Laborers in the Vineyard of the Lord: The Beginnings of the AME Church in Florida, 1865–1885.* Gainesville: University Press of Florida.

Roberts, John. 1993. "Remembering the Spirit of Celebration in a South Carolina Community." In *Jubilation! African American Celebrations in the Southeast,* edited by William H. Wiggins Jr. and Douglas DeNatale. Columbia, S.C.: McKissick Museum, 43–49.

Roberts, John Storm. 1972. *Black Music of Two Worlds.* Tivoli, N.Y.: Original Music.

Rogers, William Warren. 1973. *Thomas County, 1865–1900.* Tallahassee: Florida State University Press.

Rogers, William Warren. 1976. "The Way They Were: Thomas Countians in 1860." *Georgia Historical Quarterly* 60, 131–144.

Rosenbaum, Art. 1998. *Shout Because You're Free: The African American Ring Shout Traditional in Coastal Georgia.* Athens: University of Georgia Press.

Ross, Donald R. 1996. "Black Sacred Harp Singing Remembered in East Texas." In *Juneteenth Texas: Essays in African-American Folklore,* edited by Francis Abernethy, Patrick Mullen, and Alan Govenar. Denton: University of North Texas Press, 15–19.

Ross, Jack C., and Raymond H. Wheeler. 1971. *Black Belonging: A Study of the Social Correlates of Work Relations among Negroes.* Westport, Conn: Greenwood.

Sabol, Steven. 2005. "Sacred Harp Singing: History and Tradition." http://www.his .com/~sabol/SHhistory.html.

Sabol, Steven. 2008. "Newsletters and Singing Schedules." http://www.mcsr.olemiss .edu/~mudws/resource/chap03.html.

Schechner, Richard. 1993. *The Future of Ritual: Writings on Culture and Performance.* New York: Routledge.

Scottish Rite Masonic Museum of Our National Heritage and John D. Hamilton. 1994. *Material Culture of the American Freemasons.* Lexington, Mass.: Museum of Our National Heritage.

Sears, Joan Niles. 1979. *The First One Hundred Years of Town Planning in Georgia.* Atlanta, Ga.: Cherokee.

Sebba, Gregor, ed. 1952. *Georgia Studies: Selected Writings of Robert Preston Brooks.* Athens: University of Georgia Press.

Small, Christopher. 1998. *Music of the Common Tongue Survival and Celebration in African American Music.* Hanover, N.H.: University Press of New England.

Sobel, Mechal. 1979. *Traveling on the Slave Journey to an Afro-Baptist Faith.* Westport, Conn.: Greenwood.

Spencer, Jon Michael. 1990. *Protest and Praise: Sacred Music of Black Religion.* Minneapolis, Minn.: Fortress.

Spencer, Jon Michael. 1993. *Blues and Evil.* Knoxville: University of Tennessee Press.

Stack, Carol. 1974. *All Our Kin: Strategies for Survival in a Black Community.* New York: Harper Colophon.

Stanley, David. 1982. "The Gospel-Singing Convention in South Georgia." *Journal of American Folklore* 95, 1–32.

Steed, Hal. 1942. *Georgia: Unfinished State.* Philadelphia, Pa.: Knopf.

Steel, David Warren. 1996. "The Colored Sacred Harp." *American Music* 14 (Spring), 127–128.

Stokes, Martin. 1994. *Ethnicity, Identity, and Music: The Musical Construction of Place.* Berg Ethnic Identities Series. Oxford, U.K.: Berg.

Stuckey, Sterling. 1987. *Slave Culture: Nationalist Theory and the Foundations of Black America.* New York: Oxford University Press.

Taylor, Arnold. 1976. *Travail and Triumph.* Westport, Conn.: Greenwood.

Tefft, Stanton. 1992. *The Dialectics of Secret Society Power in States.* Atlantic Highlands, N.J.: Humanities Press.

Thomas, Eudora. 1987. *A History of the Shouter Baptists in Trinidad and Tobago.* Wellesley, Mass.: Callaloux.

Thomas, Linda. 1998. "Womanist Theology, Epistemology, and a New Anthropological Paradigm." *Crosscurrents* 48(4). http://www.aril.org/thomas.htm.

Thompson, Robert Farris. 1984. *Flash of the Spirit: African and Afro-American Art and Philosophy.* New York: Vintage Books.

Thursby, Jacqueline. 2006. *Funeral Festivals in America: Rituals for Living.* Lexington: University Press of Kentucky.

Titon, Jeff. 1979. *Early Downhome Blues: A Musical and Cultural Analysis.* Urbana: University of Illinois Press.

Titon, Jeff. 1988. *Powerhouse of God: Speech, Chant, and Song in an Appalachian Baptist Church.* Austin: University of Texas Press.

Townes, Emilie. 1995. *In a Blaze of Glory: Womanist Spirituality as Social Witness.* Nashville, Tenn.: Abingdon.

Tull, James E. 2000. *High-Church Baptists in the South: The Origin, Nature, and Influence of Landmarkism.* Macon, Ga.: Mercer.

Turner, Elizabeth Hayes. 1997. *Women, Culture, and Community: Religion and Reform in Galveston, 1880–1920.* New York: Oxford University Press.

Turner, Victor Witter. 1982. *Celebration: Studies in Festivity and Ritual.* Washington, D.C.: Smithsonian Institution Press.

Twining, Mary, and Keith Baird, eds. 1991. *Sea Island Burial Roots*. Trenton, N.J.: Africa World.

Uchendu, Victor. 1965. *The Igbo of Southeast Nigeria*. New York: Holt, Rinehart and Winston.

Underhill, Ruth Murray. 1953. *Red Man's America*. Chicago: University of Chicago Press.

Vlach, John Michael. 1978. *The Afro-American Tradition in Decorative Arts*. Cleveland, Ohio: Cleveland Museum of Art.

Walker, Alice. 1984. *In Search of Our Mother's Garden: Womanist Prose*. New York: Harcourt.

Walker, Clarence Earl. 1982. *A Rock in a Weary Land: The African Methodist Episcopal Church during the Civil War and Reconstruction*. Baton Rouge: Louisiana State University Press.

Walker, Margaret. 1966. *Jubilee*. Boston, Mass.: Bantam.

Walker, Wyatt T. 1979. *Somebody's Calling My Name: Black Sacred Music and Social Change*. Valley Forge, Pa.: Judson.

Warren, Gwendolin Sims. 1997. *Ev'ry Time I Feel the Spirit*. New York: Holt.

Watson, Fred. 1972. *Hub of the Wiregrass: A History of Houston County, Alabama, 1903–1972*. Anniston, Ala.: Higginbotham.

Webber, Thomas. 1978. *Deep like the River: Education in the Slave Community*. New York: Norton.

Wetherington, Mark. 1994. *The New South Comes to Wiregrass Georgia, 1860–1910*. Knoxville: University of Tennessee Press.

White, George Pullen. 1933. *White Spirituals in the Southern Uplands*. Chapel Hill: University of North Carolina Press.

White, Sharoresier. 1994. "The Sunday Morning Band." Unpublished student paper, Florida State University.

Wiggins, William, Jr. 1987. *O Freedom! Afro-American Emancipation Celebrations*. Knoxville: University of Tennessee Press.

Wiggins, William, Jr. 1989. "'Juneteenth': Afro-American Customs of the Emancipation." In *The Old Traditional Way of Life*, edited by Robert Walls and George Schoemaker. Bloomington, Ind.: Trickster, 146–158.

Wiggins, William, Jr. 1993. "From Galveston to Washington: Charting Juneteenth's Freedom Trail." In *Jubilation: African American Celebrations in the Southeast*. Columbia, S.C.: McKissick Museum, 61–67.

Wiggins, William, Jr. 1996. "Juneteenth: A Red Spot Day on the Texas Calendar." In *Juneteenth Texas: Essays in African-American Folklore*, edited by Francis Abernethy, Patrick Mullen, and Alan Govenar. Denton: University of North Texas Press, 236–253.

Willett, Henry, ed. 1982. *Wiregrass Notes: Black Sacred Harp Sing from Southeast Alabama*. Recording. Montgomery: Alabama State Council on the Arts and Humanities.

Willett, Henry, ed. 1995. "Introduction" and "Judge Jackson and the Colored Sacred Harp." In *The Spirit: Alabama's Sacred Music Traditions*. Montgomery, Ala.: Black Belt Press, 11–16 and 50–55.

Williams, Melvin D. 1984. *Community in a Black Pentecostal Church: An Anthropological Study*. Prospect Heights, Ill.: Waveland Press.

Williams, Walter L., ed. 1979. "Southeastern Indians before Removal: Prehistory, Contact, Decline." *Southeastern Indians since the Removal Era*. Athens: University of Georgia Press, 16–20.

Williams-Jones, Pearl. 1975. "Afro-American Gospel Music: A Crystallization of the Black Aesthetic." *Ethnomusicology* 19(3), 373–385.

Willis, Chiquita. 1994. *The African American Shape Note and Vocal Music Singing Convention Directory.* A Special Publication of Mississippi Folklife no. 27. Center for the Study of Southern Culture, University of Mississippi.

Wills, Gregory A. 1997. *Democratic Religion: Freedom, Authority, and Church Discipline in the Baptist South, 1785–1900.* New York: Oxford University Press.

Wolfe, Charles. 1982. "Gospel Goes Uptown: White Gospel Music, 1945–1955." In *Folk Music and Modern Sound,* edited by William Ferris and Mary Hart. Jackson: University Press of Mississippi, 80–100.

Work, John. 1941. "Plantation Meistersinger." *Musical Quarterly* 27, 97–106.

Wright, James Leitch. 1986. *Creeks and Seminoles.* Lincoln: University of Nebraska Press.

Wright, Roberta, and Wilbur Hughes. 1996. *Lay Down Body: Living History in African American Cemeteries.* Detroit, Mich.: Visible Ink.

Acknowledgments

Spiritually, over the course of my fieldwork, I have come full circle. I want to thank the Holy Spirit for increasing my cultural and spiritual awareness. My parents, Jerry and Henrietta McGregory, moved to Florida in the midst of this project without knowing the depth of my research and personal quest. Thankfully, they both are alive to witness the fruit of my labor. I lament, however, that a week after his thirty-sixth birthday, on March 18, 2006, my eldest son, William, "moved on." Since our move to Tallahassee, he had engaged in a number of significant rites of passage. To my everlasting envy, he even experienced a southern-style river baptism. From the time of Bill's transition, I developed an unconquerable attitude of gratitude. My Wiregrass teachers' spiritual activism so enlightened me.

Over the span of this project, my middle son, Keith, entered and graduated medical school and completed a post-doc in pulmonary critical care at the University of California–San Diego. He now practices medicine and lives in Florida with his beautiful wife, Kandice. They married in Las Vegas on March 21, 2006. I owe my youngest son, Julian, special thanks. Growing up, he accepted the lifestyle I imposed as I scoured field sites, visited archives, and delivered numerous presentations at national and international conferences. He is now married to Lia and a father himself. I want also to acknowledge my grandchildren, to whom I dedicate this book: Syrus Isaiah, Kalli Dora, and Elijah William.

I sit at the feet of the men and women whom other folklorists call their key informants, but I—like one of my folklore professors, Henry Glassie— call my teachers. From them, I have received spiritual nourishment and knowledge at every juncture. Foremost, to name a few of my Wiregrass teachers, special thanks to some who are now deceased: Caroline Allen, Lee Mae Gissendanner, Reverend Richard Hewitt, Doris Lewis, Japheth Jackson, Bernice Harvey (along with her father and mother, the late Mr. and Mrs. Dewey Williams), Tommie Gabriel, Willie and Louise Johnson, Owen and Bertha Wrice, Raymond Dickins, Mary Lou Henderson, Gladys

Westbrook, Alex McGlocken, Ovella Cunningham, Joseph and Catherine Johnson, Grant Revels, and Sharoresier White Salisbury. While certainly omitting many, I'd like to thank the members of their various networks: including Sunday Morning Bands #363 and #369, the Independent Bands, the various Baptist district unions, the South Alabama Seven Shape Singing Convention, the Alabama–Florida Sacred Harp County Convention, the Thomas-Grady Counties Singing Convention, and the Southeast District Singing Convention. The list could go on.

The fieldwork on which this research is based was conducted between 1993 and 2009, throughout Wiregrass Georgia, Alabama, and Florida. This research was funded by a number of university awards: three Florida State University Black Faculty Grants, three Florida State University COFRS, a sabbatical, and several years of support by the English Department's Research and Creative Activities Fund. I also thank two summer interns along the way: Nakeesha Brown from the McNair Program at the University of Wisconsin–Whitewater and Michelle Commander, at the time a Florida State University Humanities graduate student. I am also endeared to my support group of university women, my bosom buddies, who know the hours we expend not only critiquing but bonding: Carol Batker, Anita Gonzalez, Donna Marie Nudd, Delia Poey, Carrie Sandahl, and Stacy Wolfe. I also wish to thank a dynamic friend, William Rollins, for listening to my meanderings throughout the process and sharing his six-generation Tallahassee legacy.

Also, crucial to my work, I thank Hedgebrook, a retreat for women writers on Whidbey Island in Washington State. Hedgebrook devotes itself to the creation of a space where women can find solitude and conquer their imagination. Being in residence at this site enabled me to restore a human voice comparable to the singers whom I've long pursued. I cannot thank Hedgebrook's staff enough for their genuine warmth and unconditional care, especially Denise Lee and Anne Huggins. My fellow residents included Susan, Ann, Sasha, Vickie, and Rhea. I will never forget the experience of meeting this diverse community of women. My stay at Hedgebrook was both humbling and inspiring. In addition, my in-laws, Jesse and Beverly Scott, offered me terrific respite and hospitality in their new Seattle home, a product of their big hearts and hard work.

I owe a debt of gratitude to certain folklorists knowledgeable about this region: Joey Brackner, Jan Rosenberg, and Henry Willett. As always I thank my deans of fieldwork, Roland Freeman and Worth Long, who earlier in my career taught me how to endure the road and the load. In memoriam, I acknowledge the role the late Gerald Davis played in offering unwavering support to each leg of my academic journey. I would be remiss not to mention Susan W. Fair, a deceased colleague who encouraged my folklife study and interest in pastoral places and lives. I am also indebted to editor-in-chief, Craig Gill, for his patience.

Index

African Americans, ix, xii, xvi, 8; and American Indians, xxii, 3–5; and burial societies, xxii, 26–50; and Fifth Sundays, xxii; and gospel music, xix, 23, 24, 82, 103–25, 126–54, 180; on hunting plantations, 9, 14; and landowners, 6–7; and lining hymns, 15; and Negro spirituals, 19–25; and Sacred Harp, xxiii; and sacred music, xvi–xvii, xix–xxi; and southern violence, 7–8; and Twentieth of May, xxii, 9–25, 54, 59, 160, 177, 178

African Methodist Episcopal Church, xxii, 29–31, 42–43, 67, 122, 138, 146, 163, 179

Alabama-Florida Union Singing Convention, 89, 146, 149, 159

Allen, Caroline, 113

American Indians, xxii, 3–5, 7, 100

Appling County (Georgia), 5

Aristida stricta, xiv, xv

Baptist, xxii, 51–73, 179; and union meeting, 62–63, 72, 136, 172–73, 179; and women, 159–60, 165, 172

Bedgood Family, 93–94

Bennett-Mitchell, Lula, 163

Bethlehem AME Church (Florida), 30, 31, 42–45

Brooks County (Georgia), 14

Brown, Dorothy (Doc), 130, 145

Butler, Mandy, 6

Call, Henry W., 30, 42

Children, 12–13, 21, 23, 43, 44, 69–72, 90, 91, 131, 143, 149, 156, 165

Christian Methodist Episcopal Church, 51, 54, 122

City-Wide Choirs' Union, 108, 112, 123–24, 125, 180

Colored Sacred Harp, 74, 76, 78–79, 80, 84, 89, 91

Cunningham, Ovella, 133, 136–37, 144, 153, 161

Devotion, 15, 48, 65–66, 69, 72, 79, 119–20, 123, 124, 125, 160

Dickens, Raymond, 31, 47

Dorayme, 76, 103

Dorsey, Thomas, xix, xxiii, 48, 103, 106, 115, 180

Dothan, Alabama, 74, 80, 95, 98, 137, 140, 141, 144, 146, 165

Du Bose, Clementine, 87, 91

Easter, 14, 38, 102, 106, 119–20, 164

Edwards, Mittie, 138

Fifth Sunday, 46, 51–52, 60, 62, 64, 65, 67–68, 72, 93, 95, 97, 105, 108, 119, 124, 136–37, 179

Florida Panhandle, xv, 7, 46, 62, 67

Freeman, Roland, 63

Gabriel, Tommie, 22, 55, 103, 105–6, 110, 115, 119, 121, 123, 158, 177

Gospel, xix–xx, 26, 92–93, 94, 96; contemporary, xvii–xviii, xxiii–xxiv, 24, 38, 40, 71, 72, 82, 89, 126–53; traditional, xxiii, 15–16, 49, 63–64, 92, 100–25

Gospel Train Special, 132, 147
Griggs, Pauline Jackson, 79, 86
Grimes, Doster, 113, 119

Hadley, Jack, 102
Harvey, Bernie, 86, 88, 180
Henderson, Mary Lou, 56, 92, 111, 112, 113, 114, 118, 124, 125, 154, 155, 158, 160
Henry, Lizzie, 155, 164–65
Henshaw Chapel, 31, 38, 42, 44, 138
Hill Family, 11–13
Hollis, Terrell, 59
Hurston, Zora Neale, ix, xi, xviii, xxii, 164
Hutchinson, Willie, 48, 49

Independent Bands, 26, 45, 46
Independent Pallbearers Union, 27, 46–49

Jackson, Japheth, 76, 78, 79, 82, 83, 84, 85, 86, 91, 92, 180; and Lela, 84, 157
Jackson, John, 78, 79, 98–99, 157
Jackson, Judge, 74, 76, 78, 79–80, 84, 85, 87, 91
Jackson, Mary, 157, 158
Johnson, Joseph, 37–38, 42, 43, 131, 138
Johnson, Louise, 112
Johnson, Willie, 100, 105, 111, 177
Jubilives, 138–39
Juneteenth, 9–11, 13, 23, 178

Kirkman, Margarettea, 174–76

Lawyer, Richard, Jr., 70
Lewis, Doris, 51, 80, 89, 144–49, 152, 159, 177

McDonald, Bennie, 96, 182
McGlockton, Alex, 30–31
McGriff, Columbus, xi–xiii
Melton, Sheryl, 64, 70, 129, 134–35, 150, 165–66
Moaning, xviii, 65–66

Old One Hundred, 64, 72, 92, 93, 177

Progressive Baptist District Association, 72–73, 172

Quincy, Florida, 13, 24, 130, 140–41, 145
Quitman, Georgia, 13–14, 17, 23, 53, 59

Revels, Grant, 122, 123
Riley, Craig, 42

Sacred Harp, xvii, xxiii, 74–93, 98, 114, 125, 129, 130, 144, 147, 149, 157, 159, 180
Sacred music, xii–xiii, xvi–xxii, 3, 9, 14, 15, 38, 41, 48, 73, 76, 88, 92, 93, 98, 99, 100, 106–7, 117, 124, 125, 127–28, 148–49, 150, 153, 160–61, 172, 177–78
Salisbury, Sharoresier White, 32, 33, 37
Sapp, Louise, 7, 62, 108–9, 113, 115, 118, 127, 128
Sarah's Daughters, 166–73
Second West Florida MB Union, 52, 67–69
Seven Shape Singing Convention Center, 93–97, 136
Smiley, Spencil, 63, 139, 142–43
Smith, Mary Bush, 140–41
Snell, Ed, 81
Southeast District Singing Convention Building, 133, 135–38
Spiritual activism, 17, 27, 53, 70, 73, 93, 109, 125, 126, 176, 177
Stennett, Alice, 9, 164–65, 167–69
Sunday Morning Band, xxii, 26–27, 29, 31–38, 47, 50, 110, 138, 177–78, 179; SMB #339, 42–46; SMB #363, 38–42, 44, 138

Thomas-Grady Counties Singing Convention, xxiii, 100–19, 122, 125, 149, 177, 180–81
Thomasville, Georgia, 5, 54–55, 102
Twentieth of May, xxii, 9–25, 54, 59, 160, 177, 178

United Singing Convention of Georgia and Florida, 108, 124, 125, 160

White, Inez, 43, 50
Williams, Clifford, 120–21, 180
Williams, Dewey, 76, 85–88, 98, 119, 157, 179
Willing Workers, 122, 123, 125

Windsor, Agnes, 56, 59
Wiregrass Country, ix–xi, xiii–xiv, xv–
    xvii, xix–xxii, 3–9, 22, 25, 27, 30, 39, 51,
    54, 60, 62, 68, 75, 76, 90, 101, 126, 136,
    138, 154, 156–57, 182
Womanist theology, 162, 181
Wrice, Owen, 14, 15, 16, 17, 23, 156; and
    Bertha, 13

Young, Milton, 6

CPSIA information can be obtained at www.ICGtesting.com

260339BV00002B/3/P